Comparative ethnic and race relations

Ethnic communities in business

Comparative ethnic and race relations

Published for the ESRC Research Unit on Ethnic Relations at the University of Aston in Birmingham
Edited by
Professor John Rex *Director*
Dr Robin Ward *Deputy Director*
Mr Malcolm Cross *Deputy Director*

This series has been formed to publish works of original theory and empirical research on the problems of racially mixed societies. It is based on the work of the ESRC Research Unit for Ethnic Relations at Aston University – the main centre for the study of race relations in Britain.

The first book in the series is a textbook on *Racial and Ethnic Competition* by Professor Michael Banton – a leading British sociologist of race relations and the former Director of the Unit. Future titles will be on such issues as the forms of contact between majority and minority groups, housing, the problems faced by young people, employment, ethnic identity and ethnicity, and will concentrate on race and employment, race and the inner city, and ethnicity and education.

The books will appeal to an international readership of scholars, students and professionals concerned with racial issues, across a wide range of disciplines (such as sociology, anthropology, social policy, politics, economics, education and law), as well as among professional social administrators, teachers, government officials, health service workers and others.

Ethnic communities in business

Strategies for economic survival

Edited by

ROBIN WARD

and

RICHARD JENKINS

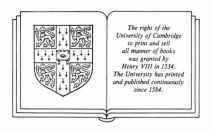

The right of the
University of Cambridge
to print and sell
all manner of books
was granted by
Henry VIII in 1534.
The University has printed
and published continuously
since 1584.

CAMBRIDGE UNIVERSITY PRESS

Cambridge
London   New York   New Rochelle
Melbourne   Sydney

Published by the Press Syndicate of the University of Cambridge
The Pitt Building, Trumpington Street, Cambridge CB2 1RP
32 East 57th Street, New York, NY 10022, USA
296 Beaconsfield Parade, Middle Park, Melbourne 3206, Australia

© Cambridge University Press 1984

First published 1984

Printed in Great Britain at the University Press, Cambridge

Library of Congress catalogue card number: 83–26242

British Library Cataloguing in Publication Data

Ethnic communities in business. – (Comparative ethnic
and race relations)
1. Minority business enterprises. – Great Britain
I. Ward, Robin II. Jenkins, Richard
III. Series
338.0941   HF5349.G7

ISBN 0 521 26327 1

1447887

WD

Contents

Contributors   *page* vii
Preface   xi

Part one The context of ethnic business
1 Ethnic business development in Britain: opportunities
   and resources   1
   GERALD MARS *and* ROBIN WARD

2 Small entrepreneurs in contemporary Europe   20
   JEREMY BOISSEVAIN

3 Small business vulnerability, ethnic enclaves and
   ethnic enterprise   39
   ELLEN AUSTER *and* HOWARD ALDRICH

Part two Diversity in ethnic business
4 Ethnicity and the rise of capitalism in Ulster   57
   RICHARD JENKINS

5 The development of Jewish business in the United
   Kingdom   73
   HAROLD POLLINS

6 The rise of the Britalian culture entrepreneur   89
   ROBIN PALMER

7 Choice, chance or no alternative? Turkish Cypriots
   in business in London   105
   SARAH LADBURY

8 West Indian business in Britain   125
   FRANK REEVES *and* ROBIN WARD

v

Part three The Asian experience

9   Snakes and ladders: Asian business in Britain   149
     SUSAN NOWIKOWSKI

10   Business on trust: Pakistani entrepreneurship in the
     Manchester garment trade   166
     PNINA WERBNER

11   Ethnic advantage and minority business development   189
     HOWARD ALDRICH, TREVOR P. JONES, DAVID McEVOY

12   Acquiring premises: a case study of Asians in Bradford   211
     JOHN CATER

Part four Overview

13   Ethnic minorities in business: a research agenda   231
     RICHARD JENKINS

     Notes   239
     References   247
     Index   264

Contributors

RICHARD JENKINS is Lecturer in Sociology, University College, Swansea. A social anthropologist, he undertook postgraduate research at the University of Cambridge, before moving to the ESRC Research Unit on Ethnic Relations in 1980 to do research on racism and equal opportunity in the labour market. In 1983 he was appointed 'new blood' lecturer in the Department of Sociology and Anthropology at Swansea. As a somewhat deviant anthropologist, his main areas of interest are the demand side of the labour market, young people and the transition from school to work (or, these days, unemployment), urban sociology and social theory, in particular, theories of social practice. Richard Jenkins has published two other books: *Hightown Rules: Growing up in a Belfast Housing Estate* (National Youth Bureau, 1982), and *Lads, Citizens and Ordinary Kids: Working-Class Youth Life-Styles in Belfast* (Routledge and Kegan Paul, 1983). He is commencing research into the impact of unemployment on social life in South Wales.

ROBIN WARD is Deputy Director of the ESRC Research Unit on Ethnic Relations and Senior Research Fellow in Ethnic Business in the Faculty of Management and Policy Sciences at the University of Aston. He has directed a multi-disciplinary research programme on Race and Housing which has given rise to numerous publications including an edited volume, *Race and Residence in Britain: Approaches to Differential Treatment in Housing* (ESRC, RUER, 1984), and a forthcoming book on race and housing in Birmingham (with Peter Ratcliffe and Valerie Karn). He is developing a research programme on ethnic business which includes an examination of Afro-Caribbean retailing and service activity and Asian involvement in the clothing industry, as well as international comparisons in minority business development. He has edited an issue of the journal *New Community* on the theme of ethnic business (vol. 11, nos. 1 and 2,

1983). Before joining the Research Unit in 1972, Robin Ward taught for seven years in the Department of Sociology at Manchester University and was a joint author and editor of the Penguin introductory sociology texts.

HOWARD ALDRICH is Professor of Sociology in the Department of Sociology at the University of North Carolina, Chapel Hill. He has been Associate Editor of the *Administrative Science Quarterly* since 1974, and taught at Cornell University for thirteen years. He is currently doing research on organisations from the population perspective. With his collaborators, he has been conducting research on small shops and their local environments. He has published numerous articles in organisational sociology, ethnic relations and network analysis.

ELLEN AUSTER is an Assistant Professor in the Management of Organisations Division at the Graduate School of Business, Columbia University. She is a sociologist whose main interests include organisations, stratification and race and ethnicity. Her current research focusses on comparing differences and similarities between black and white urban small business owners and the relative impact of individual, organisational and neighbourhood characteristics on business survival.

JEREMY BOISSEVAIN is Professor of Social Anthropology at the University of Amsterdam. He was Chief of Mission for the Cooperative for American Relief to Everywhere (CARE) in the Philippines, Japan, India and Malta. He has taught at the Universities of Montreal, Sussex and Malta and carried out research on power relations, immigrant adjustment and the impact of tourism. His publications include *Saints and Fireworks* (Holt, Rinehart and Winston, 1965), *Hal-Farruq* (Athlone Press, 1969), *The Italians of Montreal* (Royal Commission on Bilingualism and Biculturalism, Ottawa, 1970), *Friends of Friends* (Basil Blackwell, 1974) and, as co-editor, *Network Analysis* (Mouton, The Hague, 1973) and *Beyond the Community* (Ministry of Education and Science, The Hague, 1975). He is editing a book on European ethnic minorities and carrying out research on small Surinamese enterpreneurs in Amsterdam.

JOHN CATER lectures in Geography and in Urban Policy and Race Relations at Edge Hill College of Higher Education, Ormskirk, Lancs. He was previously employed as Research Fellow on an SSRC-funded study of 'Retail and Service Business and the Immigrant Community' at Liverpool Polytechnic. He is currently completing doctoral research on Asian segregation and business development in Bradford, West Yorks.

TREVOR P. JONES is a Senior Lecturer in Geography and Race Relations in the Department of Social Studies, Liverpool Polytechnic. His research and publications are in the fields of rural depopulation in South Devon, ethnic residential segregation of Asians (especially in Huddersfield and Bradford), the role of ethnic minorities in retailing and the problems of peripheral local authority housing. He is currently writing a book on European regional issues.

SARAH LADBURY works in the North London Industrial Language Training Unit. Her present work involves devising and teaching courses that aim to improve communications within the workplace and combat discriminatory attitudes and systems. She has a PhD from London University, having worked with the Turkish Cypriot community in London between 1975 and 1979. She continues to have close personal, but non-academic, links with Turkish Cypriots in London and Cyprus.

DAVID McEVOY is Principal Lecturer in Geography in the Department of Social Studies, Liverpool Polytechnic. His research and publications are in the fields of the retail geography of Greater Manchester, distribution in North East England, the geographical origins of students, the teaching of political geography, ethnic residential segregation of Asians and the role of ethnic minorities in retailing. He is currently investigating the role and potential abolition of the metropolitan counties.

GERALD MARS, a social anthropologist, was trained at Cambridge (BA) and the LSE (PhD). He is currently Reader and Head of the Centre for Occupational and Community Research at Middlesex Polytechnic. He is author or co-author of several books, the latest being: *Cheats at Work: An Anthropology of Workplace Crime* (Allen and Unwin, 1982), and (with M. Nichoal) *The Secret World of Waiters* (Allen and Unwin, forthcoming). He is presently researching the Soviet Union's Black Economy.

SUSAN NOWIKOWSKI is a Lecturer in Sociology at the University of Stirling. Her main interests include developments in post-colonial countries, racism and women's position and organisation. Her doctoral research is a study of migration and settlement focussing on the Indian subcontinent and Asians living in Manchester. Her recent research activities include action research in Glasgow and fieldwork in Kenya and Tanzania.

ROBIN PALMER is the Senior Lecturer in Anthropology at Rhodes University. His doctoral research whilst attached to the University of Sussex concerned Italian migration to Britain, and involved fieldwork in both London and Central Italy between 1972 and 1974. He is currently engaged in research among the Xhosa of Ciskei and Transkei with the aim of determining 'consumer' responses to the extensions of conventional and plasmapheresis blood donor services in the area.

HAROLD POLLINS is a Senior Tutor at Ruskin College, Oxford, and has done research in economic history and sociology. His work on West Indians in London was published in Ruth Glass, assisted by Harold Pollins, *Newcomers: The West Indians in London* (Centre for Urban Studies and Allen and Unwin, 1960). He also wrote 'Coloured People in Post-War Fiction', *Race*, vol. 1, May 1960. He has written extensively in the field of Anglo-Jewish history and sociology and recently published *Economic History of the Jews in England* (Associated University Presses, London and Toronto, 1982).

FRANK REEVES is a Senior Lecturer in Multi-Cultural Education at the Polytechnic, Wolverhampton, and an Honorary Visiting Research Fellow of the ESRC Research Unit on Ethnic Relations. He is the author of *British Racial Discourse* (Cambridge University Press, 1983) and has published a number of articles on race and education. His current research is in race relations and borough politics.

PNINA WERBNER is an urban anthropologist with a special interest in symbolic behaviour in towns. Her doctoral research focussed on ritual and social networks amongst Pakistani migrants in Manchester. She has published several articles on process and change in immigrant communities. She has been Coordinator of the Minority Arts Advisory Service, North West, and has undertaken fieldwork with her husband in rural Botswana. She is currently writing a book on ritual and exchange amongst Pakistani labour migrants.

Preface

The origin of this volume was a realisation by the editors, in the light of the Unit's submission of a memorandum to the Home Affairs Sub-Committee on Race Relations and Immigration (Ward and Reeves 1980), that the academic study of ethnic business in Britain was proceeding along several complementary but largely unrelated lines. It was agreed that it would be valuable to bring together those who were studying aspects of business development among minorities in Britain, along with scholars with experience of parallel developments in the United States and continental Europe. From the outset it was seen as an exercise drawing on the whole range of the social sciences. As a result a two day workshop was held at the ESRC Research Unit on Ethnic Relations at Aston University in March 1981 at which most of the contributors to this volume gave papers on their research or summarised the way in which they thought their work could fit into a review of the development of ethnic business in Britain. Following the workshop, papers were written and rewritten and submitted to a second meeting of the contributors. This allowed a clearer insight into how, from a wide variety of disparate research projects, undertaken from the viewpoint of different disciplines within the social sciences and to achieve different objectives, a single volume could emerge which presented a broad overview of what is agreed to be an important feature of the social life of minority communities throughout the industrialised world. The final volume embodies further revisions made in the light of this increased understanding of how anthropologists, geographers, historians and sociologists could each throw light on key aspects of the organisation of business activities among ethnic minorities.

While the bulk of the chapters report on developments within Britain, they are set in the context of an interpretation of the contribution ethnic businesses are making to capitalist economies in industrialised societies as a whole. Particular attention is paid to parallel trends in Britain, the United States and Western Europe. Given the scanty state of current knowledge concerning the factors underlying the sharply contrasting patterns of business activity among ethnic minorities in Britain, it seemed premature to be making prescriptions as to how government policy should address this area. American scholars have pointed to the lack of such an understanding in accounting for the limited effectiveness of policy on minority business in the United States. We hope that the present volume points the way towards research which can address questions of policy interventions much more securely.

We should like to thank those members of the Unit's staff who helped to ensure the smooth running of the workshop and who have wrestled with assorted manuscripts. We are particularly grateful to Christine Dunn and Rose Goodwin for bearing the brunt of this. Finally, we should acknowledge an enormous debt to the individual contributors whose enthusiasm and constructive criticism ensured the success of the enterprise, making the end product a fully collaborative venture.

PART ONE

The context of ethnic business

1

Ethnic business development in Britain: opportunities and resources

GERALD MARS and ROBIN WARD

The basic aim of this book is to give an account of ethnic business in Britain which avoids popular stereotypes that are unsupported by evidence, but draws out the different patterns of business development among ethnic minorities and the factors underlying each pattern. The prevailing view of ethnic business in Britain is probably that it is small. But this simple view conceals varying perceptions and expectations of the involvement of different minorities in the world of business. For example, the Jews are widely seen as the archetypal example of successful ethnic business development, success being judged by the growth from small to large scale enterprises (such as Tesco and Marks and Spencers) and by the important role played by Jews in the financial institutions underpinning the British economy. Yet most Jewish businesses are still by any standards small in scale. Other minorities, such as the Chinese and Italians, are recognised as heavily involved in particular types of enterprise (restaurants, fish and chip shops, ice cream vans, snack bars and trattorias) and it is often assumed that their continued presence in such areas is a sign of commercial success. Asians, however, are more likely to be seen as shopkeepers, a view which overlooks both the highly diverse origins of Indian, Pakistani and Bangladeshi immigrant communities in Britain and their concentration in manual work in industry rather than business. Finally, it seems to be widely assumed that West Indians in Britain on the whole are not involved in business but perhaps ought to be; Lord Scarman has argued, for instance, that a greater involvement in business would produce more community stability and allow ethnic minorities to feel that they possessed a greater stake in society (Scarman 1982: 167–8).

There are thus good reasons for assessing the extent and vitality of ethnic business and for attempting to assess the nature of its differences

1

and similarities. For instance, at a time of deep recession the notion that some minorities have an inherent flair for business and can play a major part in regenerating the economy in inner areas of British cities has obvious attractions. But how realistic is this? Many thousands of Asians and West Indians who were drawn to Britain in the 1950s and 1960s by the need for labour to keep up the pace of economic expansion have found themselves precisely in those sectors of the economy (foundries, textile mills etc.) most threatened by new technology and changes in industrial competitiveness. How realistic is it for self-employment to be seen as a way of responding to such structural changes in the economy? Indeed, for many of those members of racial minorities most alienated from the white British way of life, employment within a firm (or a cooperative) run by others from the same community may be the only way of getting a job. Finally, at a time when larger numbers of school-leavers are becoming unemployed, particularly among the black population, does the demand for goods and services within the ethnic communities provide some opportunities for employment which are less accessible to those from the majority society?

Definitive answers to such questions cannot be given at this stage, since there has so far been little systematic research into ethnic business development in Britain. But there is a growing body of evidence. Some statistics are available and there have been enquiries into the business activities of particular minorities in particular places, mostly local case studies or surveys of Asian shopkeepers. In this volume we have sought to bring together the best of what research has been undertaken, so that at least a provisional assessment can be given of the variety, current state and future potential of ethnic business in Britain.

The structure of the book

The contributions in the book are divided into four categories. In the first, there is a description of the changing context in which business activity takes place. In chapter 2 recent changes in the part played by small business in the economies of Western Europe are examined and suggestions put forward as to what factors are responsible for giving economies a new lease of life. In chapter 3 this is broadened to cover business trends in the United States. It is argued that Britain, along with the United States, has a capitalist economy which has advanced to a degree of maturity where separate niches for small business are much harder to establish than in most countries of continental Europe. But while small firms in general may find it difficult to hold their own in the British economy, the demand created by culturally distinct minorities for particular types of goods and services offers some limited openings for ethnic enterprise that are unavailable to outsiders.

However, it would be wrong to give the impression that ethnicity provides business opportunities only for those communities whose recent arrival and low level of economic resources put them in a fragile, marginal position in the economy. Indeed, chapter 4 on the development of the economy in Northern Ireland shows that the protestant majority have consistently used ethnicity as a basis for acquiring and holding on to economic dominance. This chapter and the remainder of the book consists of a series of reviews of the business activity of particular ethnic communities in Britain, followed by a brief conclusion which brings together the main findings from earlier chapters and sketches out some possible directions for future research. Part Two also covers Jewish, Italian, Turkish Cypriot and West Indian business in Britain and shows the diverse paths that minority entrepreneurs may take. An examination of the Jewish case in chapter 5 is of particular importance since they are the longest established surviving ethnic community in Britain and the long term consequences of their involvement in business are most easily seen. However, this does not mean that the entrepreneurial activities of all ethnic groups in Britain will follow a similar pattern. Indeed, the following chapter (chapter 6) on Italian enterprise shows a quite different process. In this case community members have to a large extent concentrated on making a living by selling items which represent aspects of Italian culture – hence the label 'culture entrepreneurs' which is applied to them. While there are many examples of business success in this community, there is little sign of a regular progression from small scale to large scale through to a form of business so closely integrated into the wider society that it could hardly be called 'ethnic' at all.

This chapter also serves as a reminder of two other points. First, running a business based on the ethnic identity of particular cultural products (pizza, pasta, espresso coffee etc.) need not depend on custom from within the community; this may be 'exported' with profit to the wider society – ethnic products may, of course, be reshaped in the process so that they bear little resemblance to the original objects (as the classic case of chop suey illustrates). Secondly, the future of ethnic enterprise in Britain may depend not only, or mainly, on business opportunities in Britain, but equally on conditions in the country of origin, or elsewhere in Europe or indeed further afield. If wages improve in the Italian restaurant industry, there is less incentive to migrate to Britain and set up in business. Hong Kong Chinese have in recent years found conditions in

continental Europe more attractive than in Britain (Watson 1977: 183–4).
West Indians and Indians alike may feel that trading prospects are better
the other side of the Atlantic (Foner 1979).

Part Two also examines the business performance of two New Commonwealth minorities, Turkish Cypriots and West Indians, who arrived
in Britain in large part in the early sixties. As chapter 7 shows, much
Turkish Cypriot business centres on the rag trade and the restaurant
industry. In both, the resources of the ethnic community are of great
value in making business viable, though more in the provision of labour
than as a market for products. The 'captive' labour supply provided by
immigrant wives, whose way of life keeps them largely separate from the
wider society, is vital to the success of the enterprise, as is the interest of
potential entrepreneurs in accepting low wages for their work in return
for gaining the experience which will equip them to set up on their own in
due course. West Indian business, by contrast, is largely concentrated in
quite different sectors of the economy, notably construction and a variety
of service activities, and seems to rely much less on community resources.
Any tendency to think of West Indians as somehow inherently lacking the
qualities or resources needed for success in business has to take into
account the comparative success of Caribbean immigrants in the United
States in this sphere. Self-employment among West Indians in Britain is
a recent development and, while there are grounds for concern, it is far
from clear what path it will take and how far it will be held back by discrimination, particularly in access to the resources (funds, premises,
supplies etc.) on which commercial success depends.

Part Three is concerned with business among Indian and Pakistani
immigrants in Britain. That Asian business in Britain is also in various
ways a product of racial disadvantage (at a global level, not just within the
British economy) is made clear in chapter 9 which traces the origins of different components of Asian business in Britain to the dominant role exercised by the British in the historical development of the Indian economy.
But despite their constrained circumstances, Asian immigrants may have
the chance to succeed in business where they can find a niche which suits
the resources to which they have access. Chapter 10 on Asians in the rag
trade in Manchester shows that the transition from market stall to
Mercedes is not available to all, but remains a realistic target for those
who make the most of their limited opportunities.

Chapters 11 and 12 are concerned with Asians in the retail sector.
Again, this is presented as a response largely conditioned by the lack of
other opportunities to make a living. Asian shopkeeping is most prominent in trades which have become less attractive to white British shopkeepers, either because of the changing composition of residential areas

or the long and frequently unsocial hours involved in some types of retailing. The final chapter in Part Three examines the acquisition of premises by Asian retailers and the role of estate agents in this crucial aspect of the move to self-employment. The terms on which they buy shops can be seen as a product both of discrimination in access to resources and of the withdrawal by whites from those areas where Asians have come to dominate.

Finally, Part Four consists of a brief research agenda for guiding future research in the area of minority business.

The material presented in each chapter inevitably reflects the style of the research on which it is based. In some cases there is a general overview of the pattern of business among an ethnic minority; other chapters report the results of intensive research in a particular locality and reveal more about the processes underlying such business development than its overall extent and range. All contributors have, however, endeavoured to analyse the economic context within which businesses have been shaped and to describe the resources (often highly constrained) to which members of each minority have typically had access in setting up on their own. In the remainder of this chapter we set out a rather more systematic schema within which ethnic business development can be analysed and to which the results in particular chapters can be related.

We start by examining the role of small business in general within the economy. What are the implications of economic and social trends and of changing political interests in the area of small business for would-be entrepreneurs, whatever their ethnic background? This is followed by a consideration of ethnic business in particular. The prospect of an ethnic business sector showing growth and vitality is particularly attractive because it offers numerous benefits without constituting a visible threat to any other section of society. But how far is business an avenue to social mobility and how far a precarious attempt to make a living on the margins of the economy when access to more productive areas is blocked? There is no easy answer: some ethnic entrepreneurs are notably successful whilst others do well to remain viable. Many, however, go out of business but because their demise is largely overlooked, this contributes to a myth of successful ethnic business comparable to the widely held view that small business in general shows a stability which is belied by the facts (see p. 40).

So in this book we attempt to account for the *variable* success of ethnic enterprise in Britain. This is seen as a product of two sets of factors: the structure of opportunities to go into business and the resources to which minorities have access in attempting to set up on their own. In looking at the latter we make a distinction between the cultural predispositions likely to facilitate success in business which minority group members may bring with them and the structural circumstances that propelled them to Britain from their previous milieu. A similar distinction is made in considering business opportunities in Britain. Objective characteristics of the economy are important, but so may be the attitudes and values of suppliers, competitors, financiers and those constituting the market for goods and services.

The role of small business in the economy

An important starting point in examining the role of small business in the economy is to note the end to the long decline in the contribution of small firms to the economy. There are problems in measuring such trends, since there is a dearth of accurate statistics on the numbers and performance of small businesses. This is complicated by the fact that for those operating on a small scale the hidden economy may provide an attractive alternative to 'legitimate' business (Mars 1982: 218–19). However, if we rely on official sources, it appears that there may have been a turning point in the late 1970s in the proportion of small firms in the economy both in Britain and in much of Western Europe (see chapter 2). The Bolton Committee, which produced a definitive account of small business in Britain in 1971, concluded that the process of long term decline in the small firm sector 'appeared to have gone further in the United Kingdom than elsewhere' (Bolton 1971: 342). But by 1980 there was a net increase in small manufacturing establishments in Britain (p. 26). Further, while 'births' of new firms in Britain in 1980 were 2,000 less than in 1979, in 1981 there was an increase over the 1980 figure of 14,800 (Ganguly 1982). It remains true, however, that the small firm sector in Britain is proportionately smaller than anywhere else in the EEC and, with the exception of Sweden, anywhere in Western Europe (p. 22). Boissevain suggests that this may indicate some 'empty space' in the British economy to which minority entrepreneurs may be able to lay claim. However, it may be an indication of the stronger and more competitive position of large firms, given the way the economy has developed in Britain.

Auster and Aldrich conclude in chapter 3 that this is in fact the case. They argue that it is the result of factors operating at the level of the global capitalist system, reinforced by the effects of government policy on the economy, which, compared to some other European countries, shows a lack of political support for small business. Large firms are thus able to dominate in many sectors and the prospects for petty entrepreneurs are correspondingly reduced. Supporting this interpretation is the view of the Bolton Committee that there has been an unduly low birth rate among small businesses in Britain, a conclusion endorsed more recently by the

Economists Advisory Group (1978: 10). Indeed, business starts have been low in Britain even in comparison to the United States, another country with a highly centralised industrial economy where the small firms sector is at a greater disadvantage than in most of Europe (see chapter 3).

But there are some factors which encourage the maintenance, and indeed the growth, of small business in Britain as well as elsewhere. These can be divided into economic factors, trends in life styles and political considerations.

(i) Economic factors

The Bolton Committee noted various functions of small business (see pp. 24–5), most of which were held to be 'self-rewarding', i.e. to operate spontaneously as long as market conditions were reasonably free. For example, small firms provide an important source of innovation. So, at a time when innovation is important in the restructuring of the economy, small firms are likely to have something of an advantage in this respect. Boissevain argues in the next chapter that some of the factors the Bolton Committee identify and others too underlie recent growth in the small firms sector. Thus, large enterprises may use decentralisation to reduce the bargaining power of large units in the work force. Smaller firms may avoid such problems of size by subcontracting production or marketing, for instance. Boissevain also holds that one result of large scale immigration into Western Europe over the postwar period has been to accumulate a pool of foreign workers who, because of discrimination at the workplace, have an incentive to set up on their own account. This point can be generalised to cover all those rendered redundant through the effects of recession. But the availability of redundancy payments together with a desire for self-employment does not in itself create business opportunities, and the firms which do get started are highly vulnerable. Auster and Aldrich note that over half of all new small firms in the United States fail within two years and 90 per cent within ten years (p. 40). In Britain, too, a high proportion of small firms collapse within the first few years (Ward and Reeves 1980: 5).

A further factor which serves to increase the number of supporting niches in the economy derives from what Gershuny (1978) calls 'the self service society'. His argument is that as manufacturing becomes more capital intensive two things follow. First, the wages it can afford to pay its reduced number of employees will be higher than in the rest of the economy – particularly so in relation to labour intensive personal services which will find it increasingly difficult to pay these higher labour rates. Secondly, this will encourage a demand for and a supply of 'do it yourself' goods and materials such as electric hand tools and easily applied paints which will themselves be produced by capital intensive manufacturing.

But when people do it for themselves they can also do it for others. As Mars (1982: 214) points out, much of this personalised economic activity is unregistered and difficult to know about but the evidence is that the hidden economy to which it contributes is increasing throughout the industrialised West. Once this process gets under way, it is not readily reversed, since unregistered hidden business tends to drive out formalised business which necessarily bears extra costs.

It is not argued that ethnic communities are more prone than are members of the majority society to hidden economic activity, but that insofar as small business is concerned, whether ethnic or not, they are more likely to operate in the hidden economy than has hitherto been the case. The hidden economy of course provides a more sheltered niche than is available for formal registered enterprises.

(ii) Life style trends

A further stimulus to small business is provided by features of changing life styles. The demand for a wider range of services, especially personal services, has contributed to a major expansion in the service sector of the economy. Further, the desire for independence and the value placed on 'natural' products (food, medication, clothing, ornaments etc.) have stimulated interest in entrepreneurship and a demand for such products in niches in the economy where small size may be an advantage (see pp. 36–8). Finally, the cultural attributes of ethnic minorities have created a further element of demand to which immigrants with a predisposition for business are well placed to respond. The growing realisation among many that settlement in Britain is for life has had the effect of broadening the range of cultural products for which there is now a market (p. 34).

(iii) Political considerations

Finally, Boissevain points to the influence of government policy, especially on taxation and social security, in discouraging large scale enterprise within the formal economy. This has in some countries been matched by a desire positively to encourage the small firms sector. Governments of the right have a natural bias towards protecting the petty bourgeoisie, who represent the values of autonomy and personal competitive striving as well as implicitly supporting the economic model of perfect competition on which theories of capitalism are based. Governments of the left may show an equivalent bias towards cooperatives and self-help organisations in which the socialist values of solidarity and mutual support are visibly encouraged; almost all such enterprises will remain within the small sector of the economy. Indeed, the large scale transformation of the economy currently under way has given those in power, both nationally and locally, every reason to support job creation, whatever form it takes. Nowhere in Britain is the changing attitude towards encouragement of new business more clear than among local authorities in traditional industrial centres, of whatever political complexion. For the collapse of local industry sharply reduces both the income from the rates which is needed to pay for local services, and overall demand in the locality, thus threatening other sectors which rely on personal spending to remain viable.

What then are the implications of this general analysis of the small firms sector for ethnic business in particular? First, ethnic firms tend to be small firms and it is clear that small business in Britain is in a weak position compared to almost all of Western Europe. However, the forces which have reversed the long term decline among small firms seem to be operating in the United Kingdom as well as continental Europe. There is some suggestion that economic factors underlie this trend. But changes in demand which reflect changing life styles (and ethnic demand is an important component of this) have clearly had a major influence, particularly on opportunities in the service sector. Government policy has been broadly unhelpful to big business, but it has not, at least in Britain, done a great deal to encourage small firms either.

Thus, secondly, overall economic trends seem to have done much more to discourage small businesses, including those run by members of minority groups, than government policies have done to encourage them. This point is made by Auster and Aldrich (p. 53) with reference to recent economic trends in the United States, where a Small Business Administration has been in existence for some years to coordinate policies to promote this sector. Nor is there much evidence that efforts to promote minority business enterprise in America have so far been particularly successful, though this does not allow us to conclude that they have been ineffective.

Thirdly, the highly centralised nature of the economy in Britain, which has made the small business sector less competitive because there are fewer protected niches where small firms can flourish, may thereby give something of a competitive advantage to minority entrepreneurs who can benefit from the specialised ethnic market. The circumstances in which this has proved possible and the ways in which resources have been used to seize opportunities is the substance of the rest of the book. But first it is useful to consider a framework for analysing these resources and their distribution among ethnic communities in Britain.

Ethnic business: resources and opportunities

We have seen that there is no single path to success in business trodden by ethnic minorities in Britain. On the contrary, there are major variations in the proportion of different groups involved in business, in the profitability of their concerns, the sectors in which they have sought to operate and their entrepreneurial style. Not enough is known about ethnic business in Britain to enable us to give a full and systematic account of the factors underlying the business profile of different communities. However, the framework set out below shows that they are not random variations; rather they reflect the relationship between the resources different groups possess and the business opportunities they encounter.

The range of variation in involvement in business is seen in chapter 8: Table 8/1 (p. 126) shows, for example, that in 1971 22 per cent of immigrant men from Cyprus and Malta were self-employed or employers, compared to just over 2 per cent of those from the Caribbean (the comparable figure for the whole population is 9 per cent). From Table 8/4 (p. 129) we can see that there are enormous variations too in the type of business: virtually three quarters of business people from Pakistan and Bangladesh are engaged in the distributive trades, compared to 2 per cent of West Indians; almost half of the West Indians are in construction but there is no sign of Pakistanis in this sector.

To find that some ethnic groups are much more actively involved in business than others suggests that the key to business success lies in the resources needed to operate profitably – some minorities have come to Britain, for instance, from a background of trading and so have an obvious advantage. But this is only part of the explanation. For it is typical to find that members of the same ethnic community are extensively involved in business in one area while in others they are almost all employed as manual workers. In Birmingham and Wolverhampton, for example, only 6 per cent of Pakistani household heads are engaged in any form of self-employment, as against over 35 per cent in Manchester and Leicester (Ward and Reeves 1980: 42). Figures for Indians show similar contrasts. In many urban areas in Britain, indeed, there are few Asian settlers at all, either at work or in business. Major variations between localities imply that opportunities to go into business are far from uniformly distributed and that this is the main determinant of the pattern of ethnic business, rather than whether members of particular groups have a flair for (or experience of) business. Perhaps predictably, we suggest below that it is the interaction of resources and opportunities that is important.

(i) Business resources

It is commonly assumed that the main quality needed for commercial success is 'a sound business sense' in the proprietor, with some minorities being considered 'good at business' and others ill-suited. The value of the 'human capital' stored in the business owner should not be underestimated and it is beyond question that some minorities are much better equipped to set up on their own when they come to Britain. Irishmen in England, for example, are identified with work on building sites rather than self-employment, whereas for some South Asian communities business is not just a way of making a living but a way of life. Tambs-Lyche (1980) shows how a 'merchant ideology' permeates all aspects of social life among Gujerati settlers in North London, and in this volume Werbner analyses a not dissimilar pattern among Pakistanis in Manchester (chapter 10). Gujerati and Pakistani communities in the Black Country, however, have until recently had little involvement in business of any kind.

But an aptitude for business, whatever its origin, and however loosely defined, is only one of the resources needed for commercial success. It may be more useful, then, to divide up the resources contained within the owner into (i) *previous experience in business*, (ii) *skills relevant to running a business* (including both the professional and manual skills that can be applied within an enterprise and the knowledge of how to run a business efficiently) and (iii) those less specific *characteristics and qualities which will facilitate success in business*. Bonacich (1973) has argued, for example, that immigrant groups who see their stay as a strictly temporary period in which to achieve some specific goal before returning home are more likely to be engaged in business than permanent settlers. Resources coming within this third category are less easily identified, and so it is worth pausing to consider in what ways features of the culture of minorities and their structural position in the sending society may affect their commercial prospects in Britain.

Several *cultural attributes* are crucial in affecting commercial success: (i) literacy (not necessarily in the host country language), (ii) concepts of time and resource allocation that encourage deferred gratification, (iii) a cultural experience of the possibility of achieved roles and the legitimacy of competitive achievement, (iv) experience of the use of money, of the manipulation of credit and of capital accumulation (clearly this factor merges into the other categories listed above, i.e. business experience and skills relevant to business, but it covers a much wider field of experience which is *indirectly* relevant), (v) family structure: the interplay of individualism and wider family controls appears crucial – too great an obligation to family dissipates capital, but too little precludes support when needed; similarly, flexible roles in family authority structures are important which allow authority to be achieved on merit, (vi) a cultural experience of marginality with a variety of callings to select from and build on and (vii) a trading ethic, especially where this is linked to variable market conditions which extend widely in space and time.

It is worth noting too that some of these cultural attributes may not only be absent but that opposing attributes may be present that actively inhibit commercial prospects. Thus some cultures, for instance, positively value equalitarianism at the expense of individualistic achievement and this would be likely to encourage the dissipation of capital rather than its accumulation (Douglas and Isherwood 1978; Mars 1983).

The *structural position* of immigrants in the society of origin and the circumstances of migration will be directly relevant to running a business. However, we are here concerned with those features of their situation that were of less direct relevance. Central among these are the circumstances which led them to migrate in the first place. For instance, as Dahya (1974) shows, small peasant farmers in Pakistan with insufficient land to farm profitably came to Britain to accumulate wealth to enable them to buy extra land, to acquire capital equipment which would allow them to farm more efficiently and to build a more durable and higher quality residence than is commonly found. So they have a strong incentive in Britain to accumulate capital as quickly as possible, so as to achieve the objectives of their migration without delay. In due course the prospect of return home may become more of a myth than a reality (Anwar 1979), but the fact remains that attitudes to involvement in the economy are heavily conditioned by a structural interest in the rapid accumulation of capital to invest back home. Where there is a choice between taking a job or setting up a business, therefore, we may expect financial considerations to weigh heavily. Thus, many Asian immigrants have been attracted to the foundry industry in Britain, where high wages are paid to those prepared to undertake hard and unpleasant work. In districts where employment in the foundries has been available few Asian settlers are engaged in any form of business. By contrast, work in the textile mills, which has also drawn in many thousands of Asian operatives, is less well paid. Significantly, where Indians and Pakistanis have settled in mill towns, far more of them are running small businesses (Ward 1983a).

But while cultural and structural features are separate abstractions from reality, it is important to stress that they are far from independent of each other. Thus the values and cultural attributes of immigrants are derived from the positions they held in their homeland: literacy, concepts of time, attitudes towards competitive achievement and the other cultural attributes we listed are all aspects of the social system of the country of origin, along with economic and political institutions. The predispositions they derive from their homeland may or may not be helpful in getting a job or setting up in business in the country of settlement. But the absence among some immigrant groups of particular attributes which facilitate commercial success and the presence of others that inhibit it does not mean that they have no 'natural' aptitude for business. It means that any such disadvantages have to be overcome by positive learning and training until the experience of successful participation in business generates its own reinforcing culture.

The second important business resource, in addition to the human capital possessed by the owner, is access to an adequate supply of *labour* with appropriate skills and employable on favourable terms. Indeed in many types of business whatever skill is needed can be learnt on the job. What matters most, particularly in the labour intensive service sector, is to keep labour costs lower than those of competitors. For ethnic entrepreneurs the chance to employ relatives and other community members, both as managers and as operatives, at reduced rates may be the key to remaining viable or the basis of enhanced competitiveness (see chapters 7 and 10).

The third essential business resource is *finance*. Again the structure of the ethnic community is of great significance. Where there is a preparedness to transfer capital quickly and perhaps at less than market interest rates between members of a family or within a wider unit in the community, and where mechanisms exist to achieve this, entrepreneurs are at a great advantage. This is especially so in those types of small business where uncertain prospects make entry easier for ethnic entrepreneurs (because of reduced competition or opportunities to buy a going concern which has failed) but where banks are particularly cautious in making business loans. Long established minorities such as the Jews have had a chance to build up their capital and their reputation with financiers (some of whom will themselves be Jewish). Others have come to Britain with an established reputation for commercial acumen (Asians from East Africa, for example). But those who have arrived most recently and are seen as employees rather than businessmen will have the greatest difficulties in obtaining finance (see chapter 8 on West Indian enterprise in Britain).

The main immigrant communities in Britain rank quite differently according to these three types of business resources. It might be supposed that those who are most anglicised, and can therefore adapt most easily to the fabric of economic life in Britain, would have the advantage in striving for commercial success. But this is at best a half-truth. Those who come from societies whose way of life is close to that in Britain (from the Irish Republic, for instance) may be able to present themselves more effectively when looking for loans, premises, licenses or other business facilities. But there are other considerations. Entrepreneurs from communities whose separateness from British society is marked by differences in language, religion and most other aspects of culture may paradoxically experience this very separateness as an asset. For apart from providing them with a protected market (considered below), it may also offer a pliable, not to say exploitable, pool of labour. Further, such businesses may be financed from within the ethnic community, with a minimum of bureaucratised constraints and at more flexibly set interest rates rather than at high rates of interest and with the many externally set constraints that would accompany a loan from the bank. A high degree of cultural separateness need not therefore disqualify ethnic entrepreneurs from making money in the 'open' market, as the success of Indian restaurants shows, while the practice of 'ordering by numbers' in Chinese restaurants makes this point even more clearly. Where ethnic business people have both a personal familiarity with the world of commerce and remain in touch with members of an encapsulated ethnic community, they may be the best equipped of all to take advantage of commercial possibilities.

(ii) Business opportunities

What we are concerned with in this book is teasing out *processes* of business development, seeing this in terms of the dynamics of cultural attributes set within constrained structural opportunities and congruent structural support. So far we have looked at some of the indigenous sources of cultural traits that are transported to the new milieu, along with a briefer consideration of some of the structural features that propelled migrants from the original setting. We have now to consider the new structure in which they find themselves after migration, to which they must adapt (and which they may in some respects alter). An important aspect here is the cultural environment in the new surroundings which, as we saw in our brief examination of life style trends in recent years, may be of great importance in identifying business opportunities.

(a) The ethnic market

The first main area of opportunity is the market provided by an ethnic group's own consumption patterns. This assumes, of course, that there are sufficient openings in the labour market (or in business in the wider market) to create a large enough demand for the provision of ethnic products and services for this to be a viable form of business. This point is of particular importance in the service sector where provision is largely locally based. It may matter less with manufacturing, since products can be made in one location to sell elsewhere – even here, though, other factors, such as the use of ethnic labour, are likely to confine most business to those areas where there is already an ethnic community with the status of employees. A clearly defined ethnic submarket is most likely where a minority is culturally most separate from the host society. There are more business opportunities, therefore, among Indian and Pakistani communities than among those from the Caribbean whose life style is less divergent from that found in Britain.

But the existence of such a market is no guarantee of profitability among businesses set up to serve it, as the case of Asian shopkeepers well illustrates (chapter 11). Where well paid jobs in the employed sector are hard to obtain, there may be far too many shopkeepers chasing too little trade. Again, some ethnic products may be inherently expensive to provide in Britain – tropical foodstuffs, for example, where in addition to low overall demand there are high transport costs and high wastage rates to take into account. Other groups, too, may wish to take advantage of specialised ethnic markets. The tendency has been noted for West Indian business to be somewhat less well developed in those areas in England where there is a strong Indian community which includes many businesses in the distributive sector (Ward and Reeves 1980). This is, indeed, only a continuation of the pattern typical in the Caribbean where Chinese, Armenians, Indians and other Asian minorities have for many years dominated the retail sector of the economy.

Other factors to be taken into account by entrepreneurs wishing to take advantage of the ethnic submarket include the *size of the market*, its *compactness*, which enhances prospects for business among those South Asian communities that are more residentially concentrated than those from the Caribbean (Ward and Reeves 1980) and prospects for using it as a *platform from which to expand* into the wider market. Indeed, whether the demand for a product or service is strictly confined to the ethnic community or potentially attractive to outsiders may spell the difference between survival and prosperity in business. Cosmetics designed for a black complexion and saris and shalwars are less likely to appeal to a wider market than the type of hair care provided in Afro-Caribbean salons, though in many cases techniques and products can be adapted to cater for the majority market.

Where the ethnic market is small, and expansion into the wider market difficult, then other possibilities might be considered. First, it may be profitable to diversify into other areas still using existing premises: from retailing, for instance, to insurance, travel agent services, dry cleaning or taxiing. The most suitable areas to move into would be those where there was a protected market for which labour with appropriate skills was available, but this may not be possible. Entrepreneurs may, in fact, be relying on getting custom from the ethnic community not because the services or products supplied are ethnically distinctive but because they may not be so freely available on the same terms when provided outside the ethnic context. This seems to be a path frequently taken by Afro-Caribbean business people.

Secondly, horizontal extension into other premises in the same line of business may be advantageous. Since most small ethnic businesses are labour rather than capital intensive, the economies of scale to be achieved through expansion at a single site may be fairly small, and not necessarily greater than economies deriving from extension into further units. This may be true with retailing, for instance: another corner shop can be added on, giving similar advantages, in terms of the purchase of supplies, to upgrading the shop into a small supermarket. The latter may carry other benefits, such as reduced administrative costs or overheads, but where the ethnic market is restricted, demand may be too small to allow for expansion on existing premises. Both these forms of expansion apply most of all within the service sector.

Thirdly, where expansion into the wider market is particularly difficult, there may be some possibilities for vertical integration. Thus a move may be possible from retailing clothes in the ethnic sector into wholesaling, and from thence into manufacturing or import/export, relying on the demand for ethnic products at each stage. This may present the chance to compete more effectively on the open market through a new but related area of enterprise. For example, it may be easier to win the business of white retailers by setting up in wholesaling than to attract white customers to a retail store. Chapter 10 presents a fascinating account of the relationship between ethnic and non-ethnic sectors involved in the clothing trade.

(b) The open market

Many of the points noted in the previous section apply equally to minority businesses operating outside the ethnic sector. Thus some of the circumstances which determine whether vertical or horizontal integration is profitable in a particular instance apply regardless of who is running the business and who are the customers. The main difference to be expected in operations in the open market is that, since there is less protection against competitors, it may be even more important to use ethnic resources to gain a competitive edge. But the experience of the Chinese in Britain (Watson 1977) and in the United States (Light 1972) shows that profits can be made in ethnic businesses which rely almost entirely on the wider market. So what sort of opportunities are available to ethnic entrepreneurs, given the kinds of resources discussed earlier?

First, some types of business depend on the practice of a professional or manual *skill*. In many small enterprises where the owner works on a self-employed basis, having the appropriate skill (often marked by possession of a particular qualification) is essential to set up in business. Clearly, it is an advantage, too, for the skill to be fairly scarce: running a taxi or mini-cab requires a driving licence which is widely possessed, but a skill (and particularly a qualification) in hairdressing may be much less common. In other businesses the owner needs to be skilled in at least one trade and have the ability to manage employees working in others; so a small builder, for instance, depends on the quality of his own and his employees' work but general management considerations assume more importance. Finally, there are businesses where the owner has identified an opportunity to make money and needs the ability to recruit and manage other staff with particular skills and in general to run the business profitably.

It is not surprising, then, that many of the sectors in which minority enterprises are most common are those which require skills (driving, sewing, shoe repairing, carpentry, cooking etc.) possessed by community members before arriving in Britain. Finally, the system for teaching skills in the home countries of immigrant communities in Britain may be a source of both disadvantage and advantage. While some qualifications acquired abroad are, rightly or wrongly, not accepted for entry to skilled positions in Britain, the process of learning a trade in India or Jamaica, for example, may involve a much wider experience of using technical knowledge to improvise solutions to problems which crop up in practice. This helps to explain particular strands of success, such as that of West Indian carpenters running businesses in which woodworking skills are applied in non-standard situations such as shopfitting, exhibition contracting and studio sets (Ward and Reeves 1980).

But possessing a useful skill is not usually sufficient to run a successful business, especially where it is widely practised and there is no particular advantage for ethnic practitioners. A second resource of potentially great importance is the *preparedness to work long and unsocial hours*. In many cases minority group members are acting as replacement entrepreneurs in trades where working long hours is either normal practice (e.g. newsagents, restaurants) or a strategy to ensure continued viability (e.g. corner shop grocers). Working hours extend to, or may even be based on, those periods (evenings, weekends) which are normally kept clear for private life – a requirement laid upon entrepreneur and staff alike. Where there is a strong tradition of petty entrepreneurship in an ethnic community, and social life is largely an extension of business life, this may not be a limiting factor. But where an individual, whatever his ethnic origins, works long hours getting a business going and is still expected to keep up his social life and family obligations as if he were in a normal job, private and business life may be quite incompatible.

Of course, none of this is peculiar to ethnic minorities (Scase and Goffee 1980). But as a consequence of changing attitudes towards working long hours, those who are unaffected by such cultural evaluations (and this may be more likely among those who are ethnically distinct) may find some extra opportunities for business opening up.

Thirdly, access may be easier to those businesses where *conditions* as well as working hours are unattractive. Many Pakistanis have gained a toehold in the rag trade by taking an open air stall in a windswept market in one of the northern towns (chapter 10). As with hours of work, access to such openings reflects changes in host society attitudes to what is satisfactory at work. What is acceptable depends in part on what alternatives are available. Since discrimination frequently excludes members of racial minorities from the more attractive jobs in the labour market, as well as from favoured areas of business, they may be driven to accept what is least acceptable to others. Hence, concentration in such areas of the labour market as asbestos spinning, reclaimed rubber and foundry work is paralleled by a strong presence in those areas of small business not generally favoured. Where women are highly segregated from the economic life of the host society by cultural taboo, work with sewing machines under unfavourable conditions may be all that is available.

Our first three points concerned the skills, experience and values of the business owner. The fourth deals with the *margins* available in running a business. We suggest that minority entrepreneurs will have an advantage where they can use their resources to increase margins by (i) reducing labour costs or (ii) acquiring finance on particularly favourable terms. Labour costs can be kept down, as noted above, where the time of family members is available to assist with the business and where, either through racism, economic factors or cultural prescriptions, there is little alternative to working in a firm run by a community member. A community where immigration is largely by males, or at least not in complete family units, as with the Irish, is therefore at a disadvantage in this respect. Since most ethnic business is labour intensive, access to family or community members as employees at low rates is a key advantage for many entrepreneurs, who may be able to offer fringe benefits to help compensate for low wages (see chapter 7).

Finally, there will be openings for minority entrepreneurs where substantial finance is required to set up or expand a business in a sector where access to bank loans and other formal sources of finance on reasonable terms is heavily constrained. Many of the types of business where minority firms abound have high casualty rates (many of the casualties being in the ethnic sector) and so some caution is understandable on the part of financiers. Chapter 8 suggests, however, that they are being unnecessarily cautious and acting in a discriminatory fashion in the process. So where owners have access to funds through family or community connections and can avoid the problem of starting a business with the strait-jacket of a high level of fixed interest repayment on a large bank loan, their competitive position is undoubtedly stronger. That there has been a measure of success as well as many failures in such areas as clothing manufacture, retailing and landlording is in part due to the acquisition of funds within the ethnic community.

Conclusion

The contributors to this volume carried out the research on which the chapters are based with differing aims and from various theoretical perspectives. Each chapter makes its own contribution towards an understanding of the present state and likely future of ethnic business in Britain, and by implication in other Western societies with capitalist economies. At the same time, we have thought fit to set out a general framework within which the results of specific pieces of work can be viewed. We have stressed the interaction of resources and opportunities in explaining the pattern of minority business and pointed to the relation between the cultural and structural dimensions of social life in the sending and receiving societies in accounting for the processes of development observed. Further reflection and the results of the next round of research may lead to this approach being confirmed, modified or rejected. A research agenda based on the results of this volume is contained in the final chapter. Detailed examination of the pattern of ethnic business in Britain and elsewhere will, it is to be hoped, yield a clearer understanding of the positive role that it can play in the development of the national economy and in providing social mobility for members of minority groups. At the same time a better appreciation of the ways in which policy can circumscribe the effects of racism and create more opportunities for minorities to participate in all areas of the economy on equal terms, as employees as well as entrepreneurs, is urgently required. We hope that this book will at least assist in fulfilling these aims.

2

Small entrepreneurs in contemporary Europe[1]

JEREMY BOISSEVAIN

This chapter takes a wide look at small non-agricultural entrepreneurs in the light of recent developments in Europe.[2] This discussion is relevant to the purpose of this book for two reasons. Firstly, it helps to place the material on the United Kingdom into a broader perspective. Britain is, after all, part of Europe. Secondly, it highlights more general long term developments that provide an important part of the context of self-employment. The growing activity of ethnic entrepreneurs in Britain is part of a wider groundswell among small businessmen throughout Europe.

The long term decline in the number of entrepreneurs and small enterprises appears to have halted. In 1978, for the first time since the Second World War, Common Market countries registered a net increase in the number of entrepreneurs and family workers. In concrete terms, in countries where unemployment is soaring, jobs are being created in this obscure sector. 'Obscure', for little is known about the problems and lives of small entrepreneurs in post industrial society. For more than a century the development of Western civilization has been firmly linked to the notion that progress is achieved through more technology and bigger and, therefore, better industry. Unilever, Shell and Volkswagen captured the imagination of both scholars and the public. The corner grocer, the small machine shop owner and the little builder were ignored. Many were concerned with the lot of the vanishing peasant (Franklin 1969; Mendras 1970), but the plight of the petit bourgeois evoked little interest, and even less sympathy. The Common Market spends billions on protecting its small peasants, but until recently all but ignored its little businessmen. Yet even in Britain, which has the smallest proportion of entrepreneurs and small firms in the Common Market, nearly 10 per cent of the population run their own enterprises and just under half work in units employing less than 100 people (Eurostat 1979: 85–8; and CBI 1980: 12). Small

20

non-agricultural entrepreneurs and their enterprises form a significant section of West European society and their relative importance is growing.

The decline of the small business

The proportion of employers, self-employed and family workers of the non-agricultural working population in Common Market countries from 1961 to 1979 declined from 13.81 per cent to 11.73 per cent. Not surprisingly, these aggregate figures mask a range of variations. While the decline in West Germany and the Netherlands, for example, paralleled the general trend, the reduction in France, Belgium and Luxembourg was more rapid. Self-employment in Britain may actually have increased (see Table 1).

The share of small firms in the economy also declined. In 1971 the Bolton Report (1971: 68) noted the almost continuous decline since the mid 1920s of the share of small firms in employment and output in Great Britain. It also observed that the process of concentration had progressed further in Britain than elsewhere. This is still the case (see Table 2). From 1935 to 1963 the number of manufacturing enterprises in Britain employing fewer than 200 persons declined from 136,000 to 60,000 and their proportion of total employment fell from 38 per cent to 20 per cent (Bolton 1971, Table 6.3). The greatest decline was in the number of small shops and with it the number of self-employed shopkeepers (RCDIW 1979: 42). For example, in 1921 there were some 512,000 shopkeepers. By 1975 those employed in the 'distributive trades' (a somewhat wider classification) had declined to 425,000 (*ibid.*). Large shops slowly but steadily edged small shops out of business. Corner grocers were particularly hard hit.

This long term decline also occurred in other countries. In the Netherlands, for example, between 1950 and 1977 the market share of retail enterprises employing less than 50 persons declined from 78 per cent to 74 per cent. During the same period the number of retail outlets decreased by almost 60,000 (from 196,156 to 137,838) and the share of large firms (employing over 50) in the grocery business almost doubled (13 per cent) (Dieten 1980: 141).

It is clear that during the past three decades there has been a steady decline in the number of people working on their own account, either as self-employed or as employers, and in the number of small firms. What are the factors behind this long term decline?

The Bolton Report, the most exhaustive analysis of the position of small firms to date, attributed the general decline to one main factor: the

Table 1. *Employers, self-employed and family workers as per cent of non-agricultural working population 1961–79*

	1961	1972	1973	1974	1975	1976	1977	1978	1979
W. Germany	12.69	10.17	10.11	10.20	10.26	10.08	10.00	9.82	9.72
France	16.52	6.40	6.28	6.00	5.92	5.93	5.79	5.82	10.97
Italy	25.46	24.21	23.17	23.00	22.66	22.60	22.39	22.79	22.39
Netherlands	11.98	11.66	11.48	11.28	11.07	10.79	10.40	10.25	10.11
Belgium	19.41	14.44	14.16	13.85	14.04	14.35	14.21	14.33	14.30
Luxembourg	17.04	10.56	10.14	9.69	9.59	9.65	9.60	9.63	7.19
United Kingdom	5.79*	6.94	6.97	6.90	6.77	6.81	6.78	6.76	6.72
Ireland	12.33*	10.47	10.29	9.99	10.31	10.31	10.67	10.32	10.13
Denmark	Na	11.91	12.05	11.84	12.26	11.80	11.75	11.23	10.85
Total EEC %	13.81	12.20	12.04	11.99	11.97	11.91	11.83	11.85	11.73
N = ('000)	83551	91471	93042	93582	92692	92676	93377	93935	95301
Spain	Na	21.10	21.04	20.83	18.75	19.05	19.22	19.20	19.99
Portugal	Na	Na	Na	12.75	14.05	13.60	14.70	14.69	14.45

*Not including family workers.
Sources: Based on Eurostat 1973: Table 6 11/4; Eurostat 1979: Table 11/4, Table VII/7.

Table 2. *The contribution to employment
in manufacturing of small enterprises (under
200) in the Common Market*

	Per cent
Denmark* (1973)**	52.1
Ireland* (1968)**	49.8
Italy (1971)**	47.3
Netherlands* (1973)	47.8
Belgium (1970)	43.4
Germany (1970)	37.0
France (1976)	34.2
Luxembourg (1973)	28.2
UK (1976)	22.6

*Includes energy and water industries.
**Figures for these countries exclude employment
in very small enterprises and therefore under-
state the contribution of small enterprises.
Sources: CBI 1980: 16 (Small and Medium-sized
Enterprises and the Artisanat, Commission of the
European Communities January 1980, 1976
Report on the Census of Production).

economies of scale achieved by larger firms. The report pinpointed seven
areas where this was evident (*ibid.*: 75–82): (1) 'technological creep'
increased the optimum plant size; (2) research and development could be
more efficiently carried out in large, specially equipped laboratories generally unavailable to small firms; (3) improved transport and communication facilities affected the competitive position of small firms because
markets rapidly changed from local to national to international (export-
ing firms are larger than non-exporting firms); (4) improved managerial
practices enabled larger firms to become more efficient; (5) marketing via
the media strongly favoured larger enterprises, access to economies of
scale based on large scale marketing being 'The most important single
reason why the competitive strength of the larger firm has improved over
the last fifty years' (*ibid.*: 79) and (6) the growing role of the state
adversely affected the competitive position of small firms, due to
nationalization which prevented the entry and growth of private firms in
certain sectors, its massive bulk orders which favoured single large
suppliers, the growth of statutory education, health, safety, environmental, welfare and statistical regulations that increased overhead and
administrative costs, and taxation policies that limited access to the capi-

tal needed for expansion and damaged the viability of family owned firms.[3] Finally, the Bolton Report also pointed to the way in which increasing concentration and the emergence of the giant company contributed to the decline of small firms. Concentration of purchasing stimulated further concentration: e.g. concentration of food retailing favoured concentration of food production and supply. Domination of the giants in certain markets sometimes resulted in barriers to the entry of smaller firms and affected the survival of those already operating in the field. In short, the Bolton Committee argued convincingly that the prevailing environment for technology, managing techniques, communication, marketing, government intervention and business concentration was unhealthy for small businesses.

Though agreeing with these conclusions, Boswell, in *The Rise and Decline of Small Firms*, chided the Committee for its 'passive innocence' (1973: 22). Little men are not only pushed out, he argued, they are often complacent, lazy and/or poorly prepared. He demonstrated that the smallest and oldest firms showed the poorest performance and the greatest evidence of decline: 'Business energies and abilities tend to drop after the first generation' (*ibid.*: 130).[4] He also noted that because of steadily declining family size entrepreneurs were finding it increasingly difficult to locate possible heirs. Moreover, as Victorian patriarchalism was replaced by a less submissive and more egalitarian ethos, it was increasingly likely that 'even those theoretically available would opt out' (*ibid.*: 90). Thus, in addition to economies of scale it is likely that declining fertility, changes in socialization practices and shifting cultural values have contributed to the decline of the small firm.

In the early 1970s there were thus sound grounds for concluding, with the Bolton Committee, that the decline of small enterprises was a universal and continuing process (1971: 71). In spite of this generally sombre long term perspective, however, the report concluded, somewhat paradoxically, that the small firm sector was viable. Because their faith has proved well placed, it is worth giving their conclusions at some length:

> The sector is viable in our view, because the small firm is in many ways a highly efficient organism, better adapted to the exploitation of certain kinds of economic opportunity than larger units and having some special advantages which derive from the intense commitment of the owner–manager.
> 1) The small firm provides a productive outlet for the energies of that large group of enterprising and independent people who set great store by economic independence and many of whom are antipathetic or less suited to employment in a large

organisation but who have much to contribute to a vitality of the economy.

2) In industries where the optimum size of the production unit or the sales outlet is small, often the most efficient form of business organisation is a small firm.

3) Many small firms act as specialist suppliers to large companies of parts, sub-assemblies or components, produced at lower cost than the large companies could achieve.

4) Small firms add greatly to the variety of products and services offered to the consumer because they can flourish in a limited or specialised market which it would not be worthwhile or economic for a large firm to enter.

5) In an economy in which ever larger multi-product firms are emerging, small firms provide competition, both actual and potential, and provide some check on monopoly profits, and on the inefficiency which monopoly breeds . . .

6) Small firms, in spite of relatively low expenditure on research and development by the sector as a whole, are an important source of innovation in products, techniques and services.

(ibid.: 343)

The Bolton commissioners also provided a few scattered clues that suggested that the trend towards concentration might not be inevitable. They noted that technological developments sometimes favoured smaller units of production. The use of plastic instead of steel, electricity rather than coal, and electronic in place of mechanical or hydraulic units made small scale production an economic proposition. The growing availability of miniaturization and declining cost of accounting, data processing and mechanical equipment enabled the small firm to save on labour costs (*ibid.*: 75ff). In addition, Boswell (1973: 21) noted that software and computer time-sharing were also producing new opportunities for small enterprises. In the same vein, Gershuny (1978) pointed to the increasing cheapness and sophistication of production tools that are assisting the development of a do-it-yourself, 'self-service economy'. It is obvious that these small power tools can also bolster small firms.

Though, in retrospect, these observations may be viewed as prophetic, those writing in the 1970s did not foresee the end of the decline of small enterprises, much less that it would end before the decade was out. In fairness to the members of the Bolton Committee, their meticulous research produced an anomaly, which they duly reported. They were puzzled by the apparent increase in the share of German small establishments in total manufacturing employment. Between 1963 and 1967 this had risen from 33.5 per cent to 34.2 per cent. They wondered whether Germany provided an exception to their generalization that the decline of small firms was universal and continuing, though noting that the 'apparent increase is within the likely margin of error in the figures' (1971: 70).

Are small entrepreneurs increasing?

There is some evidence that the decline of small enterprises may have halted, and that their number may actually be increasing. Though the data is somewhat thin, a new trend is beginning to emerge. The aggregated figures for the Common Market countries show a steady decline in the proportion of non-agricultural employers, self-employed and family workers until 1977 (see Table 1), after which it rose slightly from 11.83 per cent in 1977 to 11.85 per cent in 1978. This was the first overall increase in the history of the Common Market.

There are other indications that the decline may indeed have bottomed out. A report of the Centre d'Etude des Revenus et des Coûts (CERC 1980: 121) noted that the proportion of independent workers outside agriculture had stopped declining and since 1975 had shown a slight increase. Recent OECD figures also indicated that the increase in the number of independent workers between 1977 and 1978 was not just limited to Common Market countries (see OECD 1980, Table III).

The number of small firms also appears to be increasing. In 1978, the Netherlands Association of Retail Traders noted that for the first time since the Second World War there was a slight increase in the number of retail outlets (Dieten 1980: 141). Van den Tillaart's massive survey confirmed this trend (1981: 426–30). Since 1976 the number of small enterprises and extent of employment in them has steadily increased, as the Confederation of British Industry recently pointed out (CBI 1980). Between 1930 and 1970 the number of manufacturing establishments with less than 11 employees fell from 160,000 to around 38,000. Since then the number has increased sharply, reaching 57,000 by 1976 (*ibid.*: 15). The number of firms with less than 200 employees rose by more than 2,000 between 1968 and 1976 (*ibid.*: see Table 3). This CBI study also showed that the contribution of smaller manufacturing enterprises to employment in the United Kingdom appears to be growing, though trends in the proportion of output provided by this sector are less clear (see Table 4). Saifullah Khan (1979: 131) also indicated that in London, partly in response to the economic recession, the number of homeworkers had increased. This trend is also apparent in Italy. While the proportion of manufacturing firms with less than 10 employees declined between 1961

Table 3. *Number of private sector enterprises in UK manufacturing*
1963–76

	Less than 200 employees	More than 200 employees	Total	Small* as percentage of total
1963	61.5	4.1	65.6	93.8
1968	58.2	3.5	61.7	94.3
1971	71.4	3.5	74.9	95.3
1972	69.0	3.3	72.3	95.4
1973	74.1	3.4	77.5	95.7
1974	81.1	3.3	84.4	96.0
1975	83.4	3.2	86.6	96.2
1976	86.3	3.1	89.4	96.5

*'Small' is defined as less than 200 employees.
Sources: CBI 1980: 14 (Reports on the Censuses of Production, Historical Record of the Census of Production 1907–1970).

Table 4. *Contribution of smaller enterprises* *
in manufacturing to employment and output **
in the UK

	Employment	Output
1971	20.9	17.9
1972	21.5	18.4
1973	20.7	17.1
1974	21.5	Na
1975	21.9	18.0
1976	22.6	18.2

*Enterprises employing less than 200 people.
**Output is defined as total sales and work done minus the cost of purchases and industrial services received.
Source: CBI 1980: 14 (Reports on the Census of Production).

and 1971, those employing between 10 and 250 increased (see Pettenati 1979: 75). It is also interesting to note that Hungary, Poland and East Germany have sought to increase the number of small shopkeepers and craftsmen by providing tax and administrative concessions. Their object is to stimulate more consumer products and services (*Economist* 1 January 1977: 49).

Table 5. *United Kingdom self-employment as a proportion of total employed, by occupational class 1921–71 (per cent)*

	1921	1931	1951	1971
Professional high	31.3	34.1	18.0	16.7
Professional low	11.8	11.7	4.9	4.3
Proprietors, administration, managers	66.6	66.0	48.6	35.4
Clerical	0.1	0.1	0.1	1.6
Skilled	5.3	4.8	4.5	6.5
Semi-skilled	1.5	1.3	1.1	0.8
Unskilled	2.3	2.5	1.2	3.1
Self-employed as percentage of total labour force	10.0	9.7	7.3	7.4

Sources: Based on Routh 1980: Table 1.1, pp. 6–7; and RCDIW 1979: Table 2.1, p. 30.

The factors behind the increase of small enterprises

The reasons for the apparent increase in the number of entrepreneurs and small firms remain obscure. Little work has been done on analysing this new trend, if indeed it is a new trend. At this stage ideas on the subject are highly speculative; they are working hypotheses for future research. The first thought that comes to mind is that the increase is somehow related to the prevailing economic recession. It seems logical that some of the persons made redundant should use the skills and capital they have accumulated, including any redundancy pay, to try to set up on their own. Saifullah Khan, as noted, suggests that some firms have increased the number of homeworkers and new outwork firms have been established in response to the current economic recession (1979: 131). But a comparison of the movement of the relative share of self-employment as a proportion of total employment in the United Kingdom between the censuses of 1921 and 1931 provides no evidence that self-employment increased during the 1920–30 depression (see Table 5). However, Light (1979) and Bovenkerk (1982) have argued that there has been a clear increase in the activity of ethnic entrepreneurs during periods of general unemployment in the United States and the Netherlands. Obviously more work must be done on this; it is more than likely, however, that the recession has been responsible for *some* increase in the number of self-employed.

On the other hand, the increase in the number of manufacturing firms and their contribution to employment and output was apparent before current recession began to bite in earnest (see Table 4). Thus, although the new trend coincided with the crisis, it might very well be related to other structural shifts affecting the very nature of post industrial society. The Centre d'Etude des Revenus et des Coûts recently expressed a similar opinion: 'Ce phénomène nouveau est apparu avec la "crise". Mais cela n'interdit pas de penser qu'il correspond, peut-être, à un tournant durable dans l'évolution des structures économiques et sociales' (CERC 1980: 121). There are at least five long term developments which help explain why the number of small entrepreneurs and their enterprises are increasing and are likely to continue doing so. There are unquestionably more. Hopefully, other researchers will also address the question. These five developments are increasing taxation, the growth of the service sector, decentralization, immigration, and concern for the quality of life.

The role of taxation

It has been suggested that the desire to avoid taxation is one of the reasons why larger firms split into smaller units (Scase and Goffee 1980). Other commentators have indicated that small entrepreneurs not only earn on average more than do their salaried counterparts, but that they also pay less tax on what they earn (*Economist* 25 February 1978: 46), or that the self-employed in general possess more consumer durables than wage earners with comparable (declared) incomes (Bechhofer, Elliott, Rushforth and Bland 1974: 106ff). The CERC study of the incomes of independent workers concluded that they earn 50 per cent more than their declared income (1980: 119), a figure which was arrived at after an extensive study of the consumer durables they owned. The desire to escape taxation and union dues also lay behind the sudden rise in the numbers of British small entrepreneurs in the late 1960s (RCDIW 1979: 42; Routh 1980). This was caused by the so-called 'lump', labour-only subcontracting in the construction industry. There were a number of fiscal benefits to be gained from registering as self-employed, including being able to pay tax later (and hence avoid it), exemption from the selective employment tax in force from 1966 to 1971, and avoidance of joining unions and paying dues. The unions in fact were the biggest opponents of the lump (Mordsley 1975: 507). Government introduced counter measures in the 1970s which brought the level of self-employment down again (see Table 1). In sum, the desire to avoid progressively heavier levels of taxation and contributions for social services (see Table 6) has stimulated larger enterprises to split up and people to start up on their own.

The growth of the service sector

The second long term development is the well documented expansion of the service sector of the economy of highly industrialized

Table 6. *Social security payments as proportion of total labour costs in Common Market 1972 and 1975 (per cent)*

	1972	1975
W. Germany	16.8	17.6
France	23.6	24.4
Italy	—	28.2
Netherlands	20.0	23.2
Belgium	20.7	22.7
Luxembourg	13.9	14.0
Ireland	—	10.4
Denmark	4.8	3.5
United Kingdom	9.4	11.7

Source: Eurostat 1979: Table 72.

countries (see, for example, Gershuny 1978: 53–70). Much of the growth in this sector is in personal services: entertainment, catering and repair of the increasingly complex consumer durables that are being acquired. As automation develops, so will the demand for services in which human beings are present. Personal services are by their very nature ideal niches for small entrepreneurs as will be apparent below.

Decentralization

The third trend favouring the increase of smaller enterprises is decentralization. Some large enterprises are finding it to their advantage to decentralize, not only for tax purposes, but also to avoid rising labour costs. The ability of labour to apply pressure is related to the scale of the enterprise; big business is matched by big labour. Given rising costs, any production unit that has access to labour willing to work longer hours, and do so without union-negotiated fringe benefits, will obviously have a competitive edge. Small enterprises, especially those employing a high proportion of family labour, are able to avoid fiscal control more easily than their larger competitors. They can also more easily side-step the increasingly heavy expenses associated with safety and avoidance of environmental pollution. Decentralization of industry has been given particular attention in Italy. This is not a coincidence: in Italy social security payments as a proportion of total labour costs are the highest in Europe. At 28 per cent they are more than double those of the United Kingdom (see Table 6). As noted, while the scale of industry grew from 1951 to 1961, the size of the average enterprise has declined since then (Pettenati 1979). Specifically, there has been a decline in the number of firms employing less than 10, an increase in those employing between 11 and 250, a slight reduction in the number of firms employing from 250 to 1,000 and a growth of the giants employing over 1,000. Pettenati notes that the return on capital is highest for firms which employ 21–50, because the cost of labour above this level increases more rapidly than productivity. Those costs are highest in the medium–large enterprise. Smaller firms run more profitably, not only because they can maintain better labour relations and are thus more flexible, but also because they can evade more easily labour regulations, social security contributions to government, taxes and contractual obligations. Hence many larger firms are making increasing use of subcontractors to carry out operations they performed previously. Since this trend may well become more pronounced in future, it is worth examining how this works in some detail.

Decentralization is particularly pronounced in the textile industry. It is also apparent among manufacturers of shoes and leather goods, furniture and certain domestic appliances (Lorenzoni 1979; Mariti 1977). Nowhere is this illustrated more strikingly than in the Prato textile industry.

The textile industry in Prato is reported to be booming.[5] This is in marked contrast to the state of the industry in the rest of Europe (cf. NEDO 1972; Day and Thies 1980). Between 1966 and 1976 the textile industries in Britain, France and Germany declined by 32 per cent; that of Italy by only 15 per cent. This decline, which has continued, represents the loss of hundreds of thousands of jobs. In Prato the industry expanded. The general North European attitude to Prato was summed up by an article in *The Times* (23 November 1979: 71):

> Prato . . . for nearly 30 years has been a thorn in the side of Britain. It exports woollen cloth made from reused woollens at such low cost that it has already virtually destroyed the woollen industries of Holland, Belgium, Germany and Scandinavia.
>
> It is suggested that low labour costs result from Prato being a cottage industry, but evidence is being gathered which points to the fact Prato workers belong to an army of some 6 million Italians who pay no taxes, no social security, no union dues and officially do not exist. Political fears of Communist domination defer government action. In the early 1950s Prato exported to Britain 10–12 million square metres of cloth. In 1974 it was 19 million square metres. This year it will exceed 50 million square metres.

A fortnight later the President of the Italian Chamber of Commerce for Great Britain replied (*The Times* 10 December 1979: 16). He attributed the success of Prato to three-shift work, quick write-off machines, reinvestment without loans, ability to follow the fashions and, above all, the speed with which orders are executed. He urged Britain to stop lamenting about unfair competition and to tap its own abundantly available hard work, ingenuity and enterprise. His views were foreshadowed by Britain's own National Economic Development Organization which observed that studies 'have produced no evidence of tax or financial concessions to Prato manufacturers or that they cheat' (NEDO 1972: 32; cf. Thies 1979).

What in fact has happened in Prato? The key figures in the Prato woollen industry are the *impannatori*, middle men who seek out customers, plan and set up production schedules and buy the raw materials. They also often carry out mid-stage processes such as warping, but mostly they subcontract. The success of Prato enterprises is due to innovation and the ability to disinvest and thus to switch rapidly to a new production line. This increases flexibility and ability to produce rapidly. Prato producers pride themselves on being faster and more inventive than competitors.

The size of the average Prato textile enterprise seems to have declined dramatically: from about 28 employees per enterprise in 1927 to 4.6 in 1976, though the number of employees per loom appears to have remained about the same. This decentralization occurred during the past 30 years in three stages. The first stage followed the crisis in 1950 that ended many of the larger mills. Workers took looms home and became self-employed, often remaining linked to their former employers, who continued to handle marketing. The initial reaction to the crisis was to decentralize to escape the fierce pressure of labour unions and to exploit price differentials; other virtues were then discovered. During the second stage, decentralization continued as a policy. The original motives, which were attacked by the unions, had given way to new motives (Mariti 1977). These are organizational flexibility, simplification of management, the sharing of different specialist skills and the rapid diffusion of innovations via the network of personal relations. Extensive managerial ability is not needed as production and marketing is broken down into simple steps.

There are three sizes of enterprise: enterprises with 1–5 looms, enterprises operating about 12 automatic looms; and enterprises with over 20 automatic looms. The smallest are most frequently dependent, poor, work the longest hours, exhibit little propensity to change and employ the most female labour. They work with at least two operations at the family level in single shifts of up to 12 hours. The productivity is low, the 'plant' is old and has been paid off. Profits are meagre, and little can be reinvested in modernizing, for automatic looms cost between 150 and 200 million lire (about £65–83,000 at late 1982 rates). There is little danger that these small enterprises will disappear, for they do not lack work.

Their operation is suited to weaving with coarse yarn that breaks easily and it is also suitable for older people who could probably not stand the high pace in factories. The trend, however, is for older looms to be replaced with automatic looms, which will increase their productivity. About 1,000 looms out of Prato's total stock of 15,000 are replaced annually. Much of the equipment in use in Prato is less than 10 years old (NEDO 1972: 31). Lorenzoni is silent about the source of capital for the new looms.

The third stage in Prato's postwar development was what Lorenzoni (1979: 57) calls 'pseudo-integration', the emergence of coalitions of enterprises that are beginning to work together more systematically than in the past. Prato's competitive edge remains keen and Lorenzoni comments upon the mania for work in Prato: 'Work is seen as an essential ideal, and a source of gratification in itself.' This attitude is present both in the more modern enterprises and in the undercapitalized ones. In the former, owners work hard to pay off the cost of the new plant; in the latter because they have to make up for the disadvantage of having obsolete machines (*ibid.*: 73). Employees work long hours to earn enough to start up on their own.

To sum up, Prato's success is due to its partial reliance on other people's research and design, the decentralization of most of the production, its involvement of other firms in marketing, and its ability to cooperate with competitors. Prato's story demonstrates that decentralization can prove economically successful, and can generate employment. Whether or not the experience there can be transferred to other areas as a development strategy remains to be seen. Much more must first be learned about the social organization of, and experience with, decentralized production in Italy.

The impact of immigration

The fourth long term development affecting the number of small enterprises is immigration, especially from Asia and Mediterranean countries. In the European core area there is a large population of immigrants from both the Mediterranean periphery and from former colonies. In the 1970s there were more than 43 million immigrant workers in France, Germany and Great Britain. Together they made up between 6 and 7 per cent of the labour force (Castles and Kosack 1973: 61–2).

While the number of foreign workers was declining, even before the most recent crisis, there is reason to believe that increasing numbers are becoming self-employed. Unfortunately, comparative studies on European migration have been strangely silent about immigrant entrepreneurs. There are at least three reasons for this. Firstly, until recently immigrant enterprises were relatively scarce. Secondly, many studies used a 'radical' perspective that focussed on 'workers' and ignored the petit bourgeois, perhaps because Marx predicted that they were destined to disappear; Castles and Kosack's monumental work on *Immigrant Workers and Class Structure in Western Europe* (1973) is a case in point. This exclusion is interesting, since so many migrants hope to start up on their own upon returning home with their savings. The third reason is the dearth of detailed case studies of immigrants. Where these exist, however, ethnic entrepreneurs figure prominently (cf. Sontz 1978; 1980a; Watson 1977). Studies carried out in the United States have constantly shown that small neighbourhood enterprises have served as springboards for upward economic and social mobility (Sontz 1980b: 7; see also chapter 3). White ethnic immigrants were more than ten times as heavily represented in small businesses as could be inferred from their numbers in the total population (Newcomer 1961; Andreasen 1971, Sontz 1980b: 7).

Beside the possible 'social springboard' motive, there are at least four reasons for the increasing self-employment among migrants in Europe. Firstly, immigrants have been disproportionately affected by rising unemployment and therefore have a particularly strong incentive to set up on their own. Secondly, migrants are now establishing roots in the host countries; they are settling down and raising families. It is unlikely that they will be returning to their countries of origin in the very near future. They are no longer migrants; they have become immigrants. Their specialized requirements for food, housing and credit, as well as those of the more transient migrants, are not adequately met by the host community. Increasingly these requirements are being met by ethnic entrepreneurs. Thirdly, as racial tension mounts, employed ethnic minorities may increasingly experience discrimination at work. Hence the idea of starting up on one's own becomes more attractive. Thus, growing tension generates both the pull of demand for the services of more ethnic entrepreneurs and the push of incentive to become one's own boss. Finally, because of certain cultural attributes, Asian and Mediterranean immigrants have been successful in setting up small enterprises. They are willing to work longer hours, are able to draw on family labour, and have an intense desire for economic independence.

The Italians in London are massively represented in the restaurant sector (see chapter 6); more than half the Italian households Palmer (1977: 251) traced in London were associated with private business. All but eight of these were in the catering trade and their employees were frequently close relatives. Greeks and, to a lesser degree, Turkish Cypriots, demonstrate a similar interest in self-employment (Constantinides 1977;

see chapter 7). Ethnic entrepreneurs succeed not just because European demand for exotic food is growing. The hard work, long hours and family labour with which they have developed ethnic catering throughout Northern Europe are important resources when they compete directly with their hosts. For example, Chinese in the Midlands and North-West in Britain have taken over much of the traditional British fish and chips business. The Chinese work longer hours and offer a wider variety of food than their British competitors. Watson (1977: 191) explains why the take-over is inevitable:

> In Manchester, for example, the established friers with their traditional opening hours cannot compete. A typical English owned fish and chip shop in that city maintains the following hours: closed all day Monday and most of Sunday, open for lunch Tuesday through Saturday 11.45–1.30, closed for tea every day except Friday 4.45–6.30, open evenings 8.45–11.15 except Monday and Thursday; closed during all public holidays. A Chinese takeaway shop in the same neighbourhood is open 14 hours a day, every day of the year except for Christmas.
>
> Another advantage that the Chinese bring to the take-away trade is their exclusive reliance on family labour, thus avoiding high wages and overtime problems.

In London, East African Asians are taking over shops incorporating sub-post offices. In Sweden there has been a dramatic growth of Chinese restaurants and Yugoslav hairdressers in the past few years. Both Asians and Cypriots are active in the outwork clothing business in London and Manchester (see chapters 7 and 10). The examples can be multiplied.

The activity and growth of ethnic entrepreneurs has not, however, been uniform. Some immigrant groups produce few entrepreneurs, and immigrant entrepreneurs in some countries are not active outside their own ethnic communities. For example, Africans and West Indians in Britain are not noted for their entrepreneurial success (see chapter 8). On the other hand, in Holland there are many entrepreneurs among migrants from its ex-West Indian colony of Surinam, but few among the long established Moluccan immigrants. Why there should be this unevenness is intriguing. Wallman (1979), in a study of migrant workers in Toronto, has pointed to the economic consequences of the attitudes that different ethnic groups had to work. Her Trinidadian informant 'did not aspire to buying a house, to moving up the job hierarchy or out of the central city; to a better credit rating; or to saving for his retirement' (Wallman 1979: 2). In contrast, Mediterranean migrants, at least in the eyes of Wallman's informant, dedicated their lives to work, to saving, to buying heavily mortgaged suburban houses, and to acquiring consumer durables. (For the views of Italian Canadians about 'lazy spendthrift' French Canadians, see Boissevain 1970: 57.) Differing life goals may thus influence the effort invested in work; these goals to a large extent are culturally conditioned. Most Mediterranean migrants and many others have come from peasant societies, characterized by thrift, hard work and a strong desire for independence.

Differences in culture also affect the ability of would-be entrepreneurs to mobilize family labour, which has been seen to be an important resource. For example, Marris and Somerset (1971: 132–50) described the competitive advantage that joint family ideology gave Asians over Kenyan entrepreneurs. Whereas the former could draw extensively on family labour and capital, the more egalitarian inheritance system of the latter and their competitive relationship with kinsmen precluded cooperation. It is probably not coincidental that the takeover by immigrants of traditional enterprises, such as corner grocers, has been particularly pronounced in Britain (see chapter 11). This country has the lowest proportion of small businesses and self-employed in the Common Market and, after Sweden, in Western Europe. In a certain sense this indicates an empty space in the service sector which ethnic entrepreneurs are filling. The relations between such cultural and structural variables are considered elsewhere in this book.

The quality of life

The fifth long term development influencing the increase of small enterprises is the growing concern with the quality of life. Not surprisingly, this preoccupation often shelters under the slogan 'Small is beautiful'. There are a number of ways that this manifests itself.

First, increasing awareness of environmental pollution has furnished a niche for entrepreneurs able to provide natural products, whether for the stomach, the body or the mind. Enterprises selling macrobiotic food, natural perfumes and soaps and authentic crafts are sprouting up all over Europe.

Secondly, the increasing size and power of firms during the past two decades has brought about growing pressure for democratic consultation. This has increasingly politicized decision making which, in turn, has reduced the relative autonomy of managers. These developments have decreased the job satisfaction derived from employment at the managerial level in large firms and many dissatisfied managers in large corporations strike out on their own. As Boswell (1973: 30) observed, there may be something in the view that 'Giantism breeds entrepreneurship . . . through the emigration of frustrated men with useful experience who subsequently start up on their own.' Thus the increase in disenchanted managers may well be a function of the growing scale of sections of the economy. Hence the increase in the number of small enterprises is partly a function of the increase of scale.

Thirdly, there is a growing realization that the quality of life in urbanizing Europe is adversely affected by the disappearance of neighbourhood shops offering varied products, repair services, flexible opening hours and credit facilities. Finally, related to the realization that increase of scale generates problems is the belief that a reduction in scale provides satisfaction. Many have stepped out and down. Little is known about the numbers involved or their degree of success, but evidence that it is occurring surrounds us.

One manifestation of those disenchanted with increase in scale is the rapidly growing Dutch MeMo foundation. MeMo describes itself as follows:

> MeMo is the abbreviation of *Mens en Milieuvriendelijk Onderneman* (Enterprise Friendly to People and the Environment). MeMo is earning your daily bread in your own enterprise honestly and in a way that is useful to society. There are as many ways of performing enterprise that are friendly to people and environment as there are MeMo enterprises. Persons in MeMo enterprises have first of all realized a series of personal aspirations and wishes. All these persons have one thing in common: they have succeeded, alone or with others, in creating their own work in their own enterprise with which they can earn an income. They have thereby become independent from the dole and from employment at which they were no longer able to work with pleasure. They can now independently provide for more than just material needs. Many have made a profession from their hobby.   (*Memokrant* 8 May 1980, translation J.B.)

Founded in 1977, MeMo had over 1,200 associates by 1982 providing work for over 3,000. The foundation has an active administration that continually stimulates communication between members by means of a regular newspaper (on recycled paper, of course), an annual market and periodic meetings and courses for aspiring entrepreneurs. It also offers suggestions for new enterprises such as the need in most communities for jack-of-all-trades centres for house maintenance and repair of domestic appliances, signals material shortages, such as the increasing demand for woven linen and wooden buttons, and pinpoints locations for new enterprises. It also promotes the exchange of experience, expert services and products among members. Finally, in August 1980, it established a fund of some Hfl.300,000 (£63,830) to provide loans of up to Hfl.10,000 (£2,128) to members. The foundation to date has received no government help, although it hopes to receive a subsidy. Its activities are obviously stimulating small scale enterprises. By its offer of help and linkage to a wider community of persons who have recently made it on their own, it removes some of the uncertainty from starting up on your own. MeMo is a movement. How widespread it is, its rate of growth, the actual motives and attitudes of the members, the problems they encounter, how they cope and the relative importance of assets brought from former employment are all unknown. The growing activity of its members, however, is very much a part of our time.

Conclusion

Thus increasing redundancies, the growing burden of taxation, the expansion of the service sector, industrial decentralization, the consolidation of immigrant minorities and a mounting concern with the quality of life are interrelated trends which favour the growth of small as opposed to large scale enterprises. Small entrepreneurs in Europe are growing in economic, social and political importance; ethnic entrepreneurs form a particularly dynamic category. It is not unthinkable that they are the forerunners of tomorrow's commercial elite. Our knowledge of them is clearly inadequate. Policy decisions affecting small entrepreneurs are made almost daily at all levels of government, commerce and industry, but because understanding of this entire field is so incomplete, the basis for such decisions must often be questionable. This chapter has sought to broaden our understanding of the complexities of the contemporary position of small businesses in the economies of Europe.

3

Small business vulnerability, ethnic enclaves and ethnic enterprise

ELLEN AUSTER and HOWARD ALDRICH

After a brief flurry of interest following the Second World War, social scientists in the United States almost completely neglected small businesses as a research topic. Many theorists, Marxists and functionalists alike, assumed that the petit bourgeoisie's position on the margins of the economy indicated that they were merely a residue of the pre-capitalist mode of production that would disintegrate as capitalism matured (Lipset and Rokkan 1967; Marx 1964; Nielsen 1980). For several decades, OECD figures documented a relative decrease in the proportion of the economically active population in Europe which was self-employed, but this trend appears to have reversed around 1978, as Boissevain has noted in the previous chapter. Although recent increases in the small business population are not large, they certainly undercut the pessimistic forecasts made after the Second World War, as economic concentration was increasing.

In this chapter we consider the intersection of the social category of small business ownership with that of ethnicity. We are particularly concerned with ethnic and racial minorities in the United States, mainly Asians and blacks, while drawing on information about majority-group (white) business owners in Britain and other Western societies for comparative purposes. Our discussion is organized around the theme of the vulnerability of small business, a topic for which some evidence has already been advanced (see chapter 2). We focus on the ways in which particular ethnic groups have responded to economic vulnerability in societies where small businesses face the greatest difficulties.

The vulnerability of small businesses in advanced industrial societies

Small business owners, like other capitalists, own their means of production. Unlike owners of larger businesses, however, owners of small shops and other businesses are extremely *vulnerable* to the vicissitudes of the market. Hundreds of thousands of small businesses are founded every year in the United States, and over 50 per cent fail within two years. The Small Business Administration recently estimated that 75 per cent fail within five years and 90 per cent within ten years (*New York Times* December 6 1981: 138). Birch's (1979) studies show that a business's chances of survival are more strongly related to its size than its age, with small young businesses the most vulnerable, and large older businesses the least vulnerable. In spite of high individual mortality rates, the small business sector in the United States is quite vital in the aggregate, accounting for a large fraction of net jobs added in the past decade (Birch 1979). Dawson and Kirby (1979: 22) noted that during the 1960s and early 1970s, the number of retail shops in Britain was declining by a little over 1 per cent per year. The largest decreases were among the smallest shops, with actual increases recorded for the largest shops. Survey data from three British cities (Bradford, Leicester and London) revealed that about one third of the small shops owned by whites in ethnically changing areas were vacated between 1978 and 1980 (Aldrich, Cater, Jones and McEvoy 1982).

Vulnerability, as a defining characteristic of 'smallness' in the business sector, can be examined at three levels: that of the world system, the nation-state and the industry in which the business operates.

(1) The world system level

Vulnerability can be assessed as the differential survival and growth prospects of small businesses across societies. In particular, divergent development of the means of production across societies may help explain the persistence of a larger proportion of small business in some nations and a smaller proportion in others. The position of small businesses, compared to other classes and strata, may be viewed as a consequence of a nation's position in the world capitalist system and the history of class relations within that nation.

Burris (1979) argued that core countries, such as the United States and Great Britain, are characterized by a uniform pattern of capital accumulation and expansion. In these nations small business owners represent less than 10 per cent of the labour force, as large firms monopolize economic resources. Small businesses are pushed to the economic periphery because of their inability to achieve market power in the face of the dominance of larger firms. They are left in an extremely vulnerable market position.

In contrast, small business owners in semi-periphery nations such as Italy or newly emerging core nations such as Japan are less vulnerable than small business owners in core nations (Burris 1979). The late development of capitalist industry and the somewhat weaker position of capitalists in periphery nations has produced a less uniform pattern of capital accumulation and expansion. Because of their subordinate position in the world system, these countries have oriented their industrialization towards export markets, leaving their domestic markets unevenly developed. Uneven capitalist expansion has left in its wake many reservoirs of resources, which small business owners have managed to manipulate into economic strongholds. Large firms, which can create barriers to entry and survival in core countries, are unable to dominate domestic markets in semi-periphery countries. State investment has been directed towards the development of export markets, leaving transportation and communication facilities underdeveloped, and thus inhibiting larger firms' ability to penetrate and exploit domestic resources. Hence, small businesses are less vulnerable in semi-periphery countries than core countries.

(2) The national level

Governments' actions can inhibit or facilitate the formation and survival of small businesses, and can dramatically affect their relative vulnerability. State infrastructural development largely determines the extent to which capitalists can infiltrate previously isolated regional markets (O'Connor 1973). State investments in communication and transportation facilities extend capitalist penetration into local markets previously dominated by small firms, as in the United States and Britain.

In Italy, Spain and Japan, the international market is segregated, to a large extent, from the domestic market. Large amounts of capital have been invested in the infrastructure necessary to compete in overseas markets, whereas little investment has been directed towards domestic markets. Consequently, small businesses have maintained strong positions in domestic markets, and they have flourished as dispersed markets and high transportation and communication costs prevent larger national firms from dominating the economy (Berger 1981; Burris 1979).

During economic crises, differences between national infrastructures produce divergent outcomes for small businesses. In the United States, depressions and recessions have caused a higher rate of failure among smaller firms than larger firms. Larger firms, with substantial assets, are able to weather the ups and downs of the market and their access to transportation and communication networks allows them to absorb the market of smaller firms.

In semi-periphery countries, where state infrastructures are less developed, periods of economic crises often produce increasing reliance on the small business sector. Berger (1981) argued that in Italy, economic crises have produced shifts of production and employment out of large scale, capital intensive plants into small enterprises. Piore and Sabel (1981) have also noted recent patterns of decentralization in Italy. Large firms faced with rigid employment and work guidelines from unions and increasing social welfare taxes are, as was shown in chapter 2, relying on small firms to cut costs. Small firms provide efficient, cheap output due to their ability to organize work flexibly in responding to market conditions, free of union – or state – imposed restrictions on hiring and firing. Large firms in Italy are subcontracting with small firms to fill the gaps in their production, and these vertical interorganizational relationships stabilize the market for small firms.

Burris (1979) proposed that the persistence of small commerce in periphery and semi-periphery countries stems from the desire of the state to use the small business sector as a 'shock absorber'. Costs of economic fluctuations are also reduced in the modern sector through the use of the small business sector as a vast reservoir of jobs, where the labour force can expand or contract. Whether this is a planned or accidental by-product of state policies is unclear.

In Italy, the state has provided a variety of subsidies and legislative restrictions on hypermarkets to ensure that the small business 'buffer zone' continues to survive. These supports also strengthen the cohesion of small business owners and maintain their allegiance to the anti-communist coalition. In France, small businesses are also dependent on the state to a large extent. Infrastructural development and legislation has been oriented towards ensuring the survival of small business owners, particularly in recent years.

In the mid 1970s, two significant pieces of legislation were passed in France which were designed to protect small scale commerce. In 1973, the Royer law established local commissions with the authority to regulate competition and forbid entry by certain businesses into particular trades. In effect, this law constrained the expansion of supermarkets. In 1975, the tax system was reformed, and the taxes paid by shopkeepers and artisans were decreased substantially (Burris 1979: 15). Burris (1979: 14) argued that the state supports small business owners in semi-periphery countries because, 'in most cases, the petite bourgeoisie provides a political counter-weight to the expanding strength of the working class, which impedes the tendency towards class polarization and allows the state to more effectively stabilize the contradictions of the capital accumulation process'.

In the United States and Britain, however, where small business vulnerability is much higher because of their position in the world system and the nationalization of their internal markets, small business politics are the 'politics of survival' (Bechhofer and Elliott 1968: 187–93). The state, while ideologically bound to the continuation of the small business sector, has done little legislatively to ensure their persistence. The small business sectors in the United States and Great Britain are volatile political groups, shifting their allegiances opportunistically. High business failure rates (Aldrich and Fish 1981), and militant individualism and heterogeneity of social origins (Bland, Elliott and Bechhofer 1978) have undermined the formation of clearly defined political stances. The state in these two core countries is only marginally concerned with manipulating the small business sector politically, for the impact of small business political mobilization would be minimal, although as Ladbury argues in chapter 7, this may be changing in Great Britain.

(3) The industry level

Vulnerability at the level of industries and firms is assessed by analysing a firm's market and the extent of competition for the resources it needs. In the United States and Great Britain, the dominance of large firms and economy-of-scale barriers to entry inhibit business creation in many markets. Increasing capital accumulation and expansion in the United States has accompanied the routinization and specialization of tasks and the mechanization of production. Crafts and services which were once the domain of small entrepreneurs have been absorbed and transformed into factory production. In France, Italy and Japan large firms tend to compete in the export market, while leaving domestic markets to smaller firms.

Capital availability affects businesses' access to technological innovations, research and development, advertising, and other potential competitive advantages. In the United States, large firms do not spend proportionately more on research and development, but they do acquire a high proportion of the innovations developed by small firms and can more easily use innovations to block competition from small firms. In periphery nations, lack of capital availability is less of a handicap. Strong regional ties and weaker penetration by large firms make local customer demand more reliable.

Having discussed the context of extreme vulnerability which small businesses in general in the United States face, we turn now to how ethnic groups respond to the restricted range of opportunities within this context.

Ethnic groups' entry into small business

The early sociological literature depicted small business owners as political conservatives who put in long hours and worked hard to maintain a sense of autonomy and independence (Bunzel 1955; Mills 1951; Trow 1958). Consequently, many social scientists assumed that a need for autonomy and independence explained *why* people entered small business – small business satisfied a social-psychological need to be one's own boss. Others argued that small business was an avenue through which those who lacked educational qualifications could attain marginal middle class status (Mayer 1975). What these approaches have in common is their assumption that entrepreneurship reflects the decisions of isolated individuals to enter small business. An entrepreneurial approach fails to account for why members of particular ethnic groups in the United States – Eastern European Jews, Japanese, Chinese, Koreans and Cubans – have contributed high proportions of their members to small business proprietorship, whereas other ethnic groups have been under-represented. In 1900, 13.7 per cent of the immigrant Chinese, Japanese and Indians in Chicago were retail merchants and dealers compared to only 3.7 per cent of the native white population. In Los Angeles in 1920, 12.2 per cent of the immigrant Chinese, Japanese and Indians were retail merchants and dealers, compared to 7.7 per cent of foreign-born whites, 4.4 per cent of native whites and 1.5 per cent of the black population (Light 1972: 13). Japanese over-representation in small business continued into the 1960s, as 51 per cent of second-generation Japanese (the Nisei) on the Pacific coast were employed in this sector (Bonacich and Modell 1980: 176). Koreans are the most recent Asian immigrants to the United States to gain a toehold in self-employment. In 1976, 25 per cent of the Korean families in Los Angeles County were in small business, a proportion three times higher than the rate for the total non-agricultural workforce (Bonacich nd: 1; Kim and Choy Wong 1977; Light 1980). A random sample of 2 per cent of all the restaurants in the three largest New York City boroughs found that 60 per cent in 1980 were immigrant owned (Bailey and Freedman, 1981). Lovell-Troy's work in Connecticut on Greeks in small business indicates that 'up to 80 per cent of the Greek immigrant families in the Greek communities in that state are self-employed in small businesses, with as many as 76 per cent of them in the pizza business' (Lovell-Troy 1980: 61).

In contrast, blacks in the United States have historically been under-represented in small business ownership (Light 1972). Markwalder (1981: 303) argued that recent evidence shows black business has stagnated over the past few decades: 'the deepening recession of 1980, as well as the release of the newest census statistics on black business, are casting serious doubts on [those] who believe that the sales of black firms would continue to grow more rapidly than the overall economy. The new evidence clearly leads one towards the views of Andrew Brimmer (Brimmer and Terrell 1971), who contended that the potential of "black capitalism" was limited.' Blacks now constitute approximately 11.6 per cent of the US population and receive 7.5 per cent of personal income, but they own only 1 per cent of all income-producing wealth.

Part of the reason for optimism over 'black capitalism' in the mid 1970s stemmed from a mistake in the 1972 census. Between 1969 and 1972, the real increase in black business was insignificant, and between 1972 and 1977, once appropriate adjustments are made, the real increase in sales of black businesses was 1.5 per cent. Over that period, the real gross national product increased 14.4 per cent. In 1977, even if all employees of black-owned firms were black, black business could have provided jobs for less than 2 per cent of all black employees. Black-owned firms account for less than 0.2 per cent of total business sales.

What accounts for the higher proportions of some ethnic groups' members found in small business? The deficiencies of explanations based on personality or achievement motivation are highlighted by a consideration of models stressing social structural conditions. Following Bonacich and Modell's (1980: 24–30) scheme, these approaches fall into four subtypes. *Pure prejudice* theories focus on how societal values and norms push particular ethnic groups – the targets of discrimination – into small business. These theories claim that discrimination rooted in a society's ideology prohibits ethnics from securing jobs in the mainstream economy. Ethnics enter small business because few other options are available. *Cultural* theories explain ethnic over-representation as a product of special features of minority subcultures. Light (1972) stressed the role that rotating credit associations – an institution that both the Chinese and Japanese imported to the United States – played in assisting the financing of their businesses. Extensive kin networks and the family structure of the Chinese and Japanese also would be viewed as cultural assets.

Contextual and *situational* theories will be discussed simultaneously, as the distinction between them seems minimal. According to Bonacich and Modell, contextual theories emphasize the societal 'context' – the configuration of social, economic and political institutions – which immigrants encounter upon their arrival. 'Situational' theories stress how historical circumstances shape the opportunities and constraints facing ethnic minorities. These two theories are intrinsically intertwined. The social, economic and political institutions at any time are grounded in the historical circumstances surrounding their development. Similarly, the opportunity structures faced by ethnic groups are created by the way in which history has moulded these institutions. The early opposition towards Japanese immigrants on the west coast of the United States by labour unions, which feared that Asians would replace them at lower wages, obstructed Japanese entry into the mainstream economy. In response to this segregation, the Japanese pooled their resources and ultimately captured a significant portion of California's agricultural sector until their internment. The strong ethnic solidarity formed by union hostility generated ethnic networks which supported subsequent generations (Bonacich and Modell 1980). Blacks in the United States faced constraints in every institution – political, economic, social, residential and educational – as they attempted to climb the socio-economic ladder (Hirschman 1982; Lieberson 1980). Societal antagonism towards blacks created overwhelming barriers and deficiencies which are difficult for contemporary blacks to surmount. In both of these cases, situational and contextual factors faced initially by the ethnic group directly affected the situational and contextual factors the minority confronts today.

The opportunity structure

From a world system perspective, the flow of ethnic groups between nations represents the reallocation of labour resources between peripheral and core economies, as core nations have imported labour from less developed nations to meet the needs of their expanding economies. Clearly no core nations set out to recruit small business owners from the world's labour pool, and so ethnic enterprise is probably an accidental product of the restricted opportunities ethnic groups encounter and their own inherent organizing capacity.

Two types of opportunities condition ethnic groups' chances of entering small business: economic (employment) and residential (locational). Employment opportunities for minorities are often restricted because of their limited education, lack of training in the skills required in higher paying jobs, and poor facility in the majority group's language. From the 'human capital' perspective, Asian immigrants in the late nineteenth and early twentieth centuries and Southern black immigrants in this century lacked the resources to compete for the best jobs in the core economy of the United States. Prejudice and discrimination were often powerful obstacles to gainful employment, even when minorities possessed the relevant 'human capital'. Lieberson (1980) has documented the powerful institutional discrimination blacks faced in urban labour markets around the turn of the century.

Residential opportunities were also limited for many of the groups migrating to the United States in the late nineteenth and early twentieth centuries, as migrants competed for sites in cities that were already residentially developed. Discrimination often limited minorities to particular quarters of a city, and high rents pushed them to the cheaper dwellings vacated by the white majority as it moved out from city centres. Residential succession was a frequent occurrence as financially weak and disadvantaged groups replaced whites in many neighbourhoods (Aldrich 1973). Although it is unwise to overstate the case, residential segregation partially limited employment opportunities for minorities (especially blacks); as business and industry began decentralizing in many US cities around the turn of the century, non-white ethnic minorities were left behind in central cities where few 'core' jobs were available.

Thus, lack of education and skills, discrimination and spatial segregation limited economic opportunities in the mainstream economy for minorities, in both the US and Great Britain, forcing them to consider other options. Many (but by no means all) took poorly paid jobs in peripheral firms characterized by a high degree of job insecurity and few benefits. For others, self-employment was an attractive alternative to low income employment in a white-owned business. We have seen that the opportunity structures in employment and residential succession have severely restricted the access of minorities to the better paying, more secure jobs in the labour market. How then do we account for the highly variable rates of movement by ethnic minorities into self-employment and small business?

Organizing capacity

Opportunities are irrelevant unless taken advantage of, and people vary widely in their ability to seize opportunities and make the most of them. Bonacich (1973), Light (1972) and others have argued that the possibility of exploiting opportunities is linked to a group's internal organizing capacity. Ethnic groups with a high level of self-organization provide co-ethnics with a collective capacity for organizing new ventures. Mutual aid, in the form of capital, credit, information, training opportunities and the regulation of competition gave Chinese and Japanese immigrants to the USA a strong base on which to develop small businesses. In contrast, black migrants to Northern cities had few collective organizational traditions to follow, except for religion (Frazier 1957; Glazer and Moynihan 1963; Light 1972).

Most small businesses are capitalized from the owner's savings, but other sources of funds are often sought. Light (1972; 1980) pointed out that the Chinese *hui*, the Japanese *ko* and *tanomoshi*, and the Korean *kye* – rotating credit associations clothed in their respective cultural traditions – provided simple mechanisms for Chinese, Japanese and Korean immigrants to raise business capital.[1]

Blacks in the United States lacked cultural traditions which they could rely on to raise capital. Light (1972: 40–4) contended that slaves' dependence on owners, relief provided by slave owners during crises, minimal absentee ownership of Southern plantations and unfavourable post-emancipation conditions severed the potential cultural tie between American and African blacks. In times of crisis, slaves relied on slave owners for support rather than establishing ties with other slaves. While potential organizing capacity existed, the intervention and surveillance by slave owners made networks difficult to establish or maintain. Strong ties based on regional differences did not develop among American blacks migrating North, either. As Glazer and Moynihan (1963: 33) noted: 'There was little clubbing together of the South Carolinians versus the North Carolinians versus the Virginians – life in these places was either not different enough, or the basis of the differences was not attractive enough, to create strong local groups with local attachments.'

Without a means of generating funds, blacks in the United States were forced to turn to banks for external funding. Black banks were more receptive than white banks, but their contributions were minimal because of their inability to recruit qualified officials, venality and misappropriation of funds, and faulty and inadequate records (Light 1972: 44–61).[2] By comparison, Ward and Reeves (1980), on the basis of interviews with bank managers and West Indian small businessmen in Britain, found that there was substantial variation in bankers' views of the credit-worthiness of West Indians. Asian entrepreneurs can count on bank managers being favourably predisposed to their applications, whereas West Indians had to put up a strong case for a loan.

Most ethnic businessmen employ co-ethnics (often relatives) at long hours and low wages under a tradition of eventually assisting their employees to enter business for themselves. Young people employed at low wages are encouraged to think of themselves as serving apprenticeships, and they thus tolerate working conditions which would be intolerable from a short range perspective. Bonacich and Modell (1980) noted that Japanese youths' enthusiasm for long hours at low pay waned after the Second World War, as opportunities opened up in the non-ethnic sector.

Small business in ethnic enclaves

The concept of 'ethnic enterprise' *could* be applied to any small business owned by a member of an ethnic minority, but that usage robs the term of much of its meaning. The most salient feature of early business efforts by immigrant groups is their dependence on an ethnic community for support. Support is provided at two levels: informal support from the friends and relatives of aspiring business owners, and support from the larger networks of ethnic institutions, including religious associations, fraternal organizations and other small businesses (Light 1972; Wilson and Portes 1980). Strong community support, based on ethnic ties, allows small firms some degree of independence from the core community. Wilson and Portes (1980) labelled these social forms 'ethnic enclaves'. Bonacich (1973) also noted that ethnic groups often form solidary communities, when confronted by host group hostility, to overcome the handicaps facing them.

For the Japanese in the United States, denial of citizenship, exclusion efforts and laws prohibiting ownership of land promoted in-group solidarity and cooperative efforts in agricultural production and marketing. While their evacuation and incarceration during the Second World War strengthened their ethnic bonds, it also fragmented their position in the market and disrupted the ethnic continuity which might have arisen from that resource base. After the war occupational patterns looked very different from pre-war patterns. Had their internment not occurred, generational ethnic continuity in small businesses owned by the Japanese might be more pronounced.

Ethnic enclaves benefit greatly from residential segregation and concentration, as for example in the Chinatowns found in many large US cities. Residential concentration brings several advantages: an initial 'cushion' of customers is available, white shopkeepers may move out and leave their white customers with little choice but to patronize ethnic businesses, and a number of agglomeration economies arise when many co-ethnics start business in the same area. Agglomeration economies occur, for example, when retailers offering complementary products locate next to each other, such as ethnic butchers, greengrocers and bakeries or sweet shops. Customers drawn to the area by one merchant may stay to patronize the others.

The importance of a 'protected market' is difficult to establish, for, as Light pointed out, there were far more Chinese and Japanese businesses in California in the 1920s and 1930s than could possibly have been supported by their co-ethnics. They must have conducted most of their business with the white population. However, it is also the case that in certain lines of trade, for example clothing, restaurants and groceries, co-ethnics would have an advantage over white merchants in dealing with distinct ethnic tastes. One explanation offered for the failure of blacks to build a viable small business community is the lack of a distinctly 'black' market with unique consumer demands that only black shopkeepers could serve (Light 1972).

We propose that ethnic enclaves provide much more generalized support for ethnic businesses than a potential protected market of customers. To the extent that they are in competition mainly with other ethnic enterprises, ethnic firms may not be exposed to the cost barriers facing them in industries dominated by white-owned businesses. Formal organization through guilds enabled the Japanese, for example, to regulate competition through negotiation and collective decision making. Informal politics, bargaining and compromise reinforced control over internal competition (Bonacich 1973: 586).

Light (1980: 51), studying the retail liquor industry in Hollywood, found strikingly high levels of ethnic homogeneity of business transfers among Asians:

> 79% of Korean sellers found Korean buyers even though Koreans represented only 15% of all buyers. Similarly, 70% of Chinese sellers found Chinese buyers even though Chinese represented only 7% of all buyers. Conversely, 'all other' persons were 74.4% of buyers but this 74.4% accounted for only 7.5% of purchasers of Korean businesses and 11.1% of purchasers of Chinese businesses.

Results from a two-wave panel study of small businesses in Bradford, Leicester and London show a similar pattern (Aldrich, Cater, Jones, McEvoy and Velleman 1982).

Rotating credit associations, and the possibility of building on *trust* relationships within the ethnic enclave, could provide a protective shield for small businesses in raising capital away from the high interest credit markets dominated by whites. Relations between ethnic firms would tend toward cooperative mutual adjustment and self-regulation, rather than competition, when backed by a strong ethnic economy. This implies lower ethnic business failure rates than in the economy at large, but unfortunately there are few longitudinal studies of ethnic businesses. In preliminary analyses of data from Bradford, Leicester and London, Aldrich and McEvoy (1983) found a strikingly low failure rate for Asian-owned businesses between 1978 and 1980: only about two in ten failed or moved away, compared to one in three white-owned shops. Between

1980 and 1982, however, the rate of failure was about the same – three in ten – for both groups.

Within an ethnic firm, the organization of production may be considerably different from white-owned businesses. Waldinger (1982), in his study of 90 immigrant-owned firms in the New York City clothing industry, found that kinship and ethnicity played an important role in reducing managerial, technical and capital costs. Ethnic workers tolerate working conditions that many white workers would consider inexcusable in exchange for the initial hiring and the paternalistic support of their employer. The employer benefits from cheap, loyal, easily recruited and trained labour. Family participation and extremely long working hours are often viewed as expected responsibilities rather than arbitrary impositions, further promoting the survival of these labour intensive businesses. Studies of Turkish Cypriots (chapter 7) and Pakistanis (chapter 10) in the rag trade in Britain show that this analysis has widespread application.

The strength and structure of the obligations and support provided by the ethnic enclave varies across ethnic groups. For Chinese, Japanese and Koreans, clans are an ascriptively based, tight-knit unit of collective solidarity. Ethnic obligation applies equally to all members and their economic behaviour is oriented towards the collective interest of the ethnic community. The structure of support in the Asian enclaves often mimics support structures found in their homeland.

According to Lovell-Troy (1980), clans among Greeks, in contrast, are based on combinations of nuclear families formed through ties created by ethnic sponsorship of immigrants' entry into the United States, rather than on ascribed identification with a village or region in their home country. Collective economic obligations for clan members are secure. Unaffiliated Greeks, however, must rely on their own individual initiative in order to establish ties with others and benefit from resources their ethnic group offers.

For Greeks, the nuclear family is the primary responsibility and obligations to the nuclear family override collective ethnic responsibility. Consequently, the support and resources provided by the Greek community assisted the immigrant Greeks temporarily in acquiring training and capital to open their own businesses, but did not generally provide direct continued support. Thus, Lovell-Troy (1980) labelled Greeks as 'quasi-collective' economically, compared to their Asian counterparts. The strength and structure of obligations in the Greek enclaves are more individualistically based than in the Asian enclaves.

The extent to which ethnic solidarity persists, once a minority group has achieved prosperity, is important in understanding the link between small business and the persistent salience of ethnicity. Rosentraub and Taebel (1980), in a study of Jews in the Dallas–Fort Worth area, found evidence of declining ethnic collectivism, solidarity and patronage among prosperous Jews. While Jews were still involved in Jewish organizations, often holding positions of authority, the nature of these activities had shifted from the economic sphere to the political and social sphere. Koreans with higher educational and income levels, by contrast, are more likely to belong to the *kye* (the Korean rotating credit association) than Koreans with lower income and educational levels (Light 1980: 43).

While some might propose that cultural predispositions explain the ethnic differences we have discussed, structural explanations which emphasize the different situations these groups have faced in the United States should not be overlooked. The central question embodied in this framework would be: under what conditions do ethnicity and small business reinforce each other? The salience of ethnicity and the persistence of small business would be viewed as a product of the structural conditions of the immigrants' home country and the structural conditions the immigrants face upon entry.

The structural conditions of the immigrants' home country would influence who emigrates, the human capital of the immigrants, the strength of their ethnicities and their likelihood of entering small business. The pattern of ethnic small businesses in the US would be considered 'emergent phenomena', emerging out of the structural conditions and constraints faced by immigrants upon entry (Yancey, Erikson and Juliani 1976). The length of time minorities have been in this culture, their educational and skill levels and how they mesh with the occupational structure in the United States, the extent to which jobs, education and training can be obtained without reliance on the ethnic group, the nature of the discrimination the ethnic group currently faces in this country, their residential stability and concentration and their dependence on common services and institutions would be important factors to examine in assessing the impact of structural conditions on ethnic small businesses.[3]

Summary and conclusions

Ethnic enclaves provide some stability and security from forces increasing the vulnerability of small businesses in advanced industrial societies. Ethnic firms which rely on the ethnic community for loans, business sites, supplies and other services as well as customers are at a distinct advantage. Like small businesses in peripheral nations, ethnic small businesses in ethnic enclaves, it is argued, have a greater probability of persistence.

(Note that 'ethnic enclave' refers not to a place but to a network of communal solidarity which can encompass widely separated areas.) Small
owners operating on the margins of the core economy, reinforced by
ethnic support systems, are likely to have an advantage over militantly
individualistic white owners.

Several extensions of this line of argument are possible. The degree to
which this depiction of small businesses in ethnic enclaves can be
generalized to other 'ethnic' small businesses may shed light on the
general phenomenon of the persistence of the small business sector in
advanced capital economies. Do family, friends and community support
count for more than we might have imagined in the small business sector?
To the extent that ethnic enclaves ensure the continued survival of
'ethnic' businesses, small business owners have a stake in the persistence
of ethnic identities. Ethnic shopkeepers' participation and leadership in
community events, whatever their motives or degree of foresight, help
preserve the ethnic basis of economic solidarity.

Our analysis and propositions are based mainly on ethnic groups'
experiences in the United States, but our arguments apply to the prospects facing ethnic minorities in other core economies, such as Britain.
We have cited a number of British examples which appear similar to the
ones drawn from the United States, and succeeding chapters in this
volume will present others. A major uncertainty clouding our ability to
draw parallels is the future shape of British governmental policy toward
small businesses *and* toward ethnic minorities, particularly from the New
Commonwealth. Neither small business nor New Commonwealth
minorities have presented a politically united and coherently organized
challenge to government policies which give low priority to their needs,
suggesting that the two nations' experience might begin to diverge soon.
In the United States, black representation has increased dramatically at
all levels of government, and strong anti-discrimination laws are backed
by a number of government agencies and departments. In Britain, 'race
relations' is still politically sensitive, and national legislation is less
encompassing and coercive than in the United States.

Although the United States has a specific agency devoted to 'small
business', and another to 'minority business development', it is not clear
that their efforts have been of great consequence. General economic
policies have been much more important for the fate of small business,
and recent developments are not favourable in that respect. With the
Conservative Party's victory in the 1979 general election, small business
in Britain appeared to have gained a voice in government economic policy
making – or so certain small business interest associations thought – but

things have not worked out as expected. In both nations, ethnic small businesses will continue to struggle for a toehold as the world economy moves towards increasing integration.

PART TWO

Diversity in ethnic business

4

Ethnicity and the rise of capitalism in Ulster[1]

RICHARD JENKINS

All of the other papers in this collection deal with ethnic groups which constitute a subordinated minority in the societies of which they form a part. In this chapter I intend to explore the ways in which a politically dominant self-conscious ethnic *majority*, in this case Northern Irish protestants, and particularly the Northern Irish protestant bourgeoisie, mobilise and manipulate ethnicity in the realm of economic transactions. Given that, for much of the history of English colonialism in Ireland, the protestants constituted a numerical minority within the island, this may seem rather an inaccurate view of the situation. There are, however, three senses in which Ulster protestants can be seen as a majority. First, they are, and have been since the state's inception, a majority within Northern Ireland. Secondly, for most of the history of 'English' Ireland they were a political majority, in the sense that they held power. Thirdly, within the overall context of the British Isles, they formed an organic part of the dominant, metropolitan Anglo-Saxon majority (Hechter 1974).

In adopting this problematic I am following anthropologists such as Fredrik Barth (1969) and Sandra Wallman (1978) in viewing ethnicity as a resource to be drawn upon or exploited in varying interactional contexts. However, inasmuch as most studies of ethnicity in urbanised or industrialised societies which have been carried out in this tradition have looked at majority situations, they have tended to overlook the salience of other factors, such as class and the social construction of power relationships. At best, factors such as these have been treated as external 'structure', impinging upon the group in question as a more or less constraining factor in their lives (Davis 1975; Grillo 1980). This paper, in looking at Northern Ireland, where the state and the economy were constructed by and in the social relationships between a dominant ethnic group and a subordinated ethnic group, will allow a less abstract dis-

57

cussion of the state and the economy than has been typical of most anthropology.

Another central focus of the anthropology of ethnicity has been its concern with the maintenance of boundaries between ethnic groups: 'The location and reasons for the maintenance of a we/they dichotomization becomes the crucial goal of research and theorizing' (Cohen 1978: 385). This research orientation has lead to many insights, not the least of which being that ethnicity is revealed as an essentially relative phenomenon, its nature shifting with the contexts of its mobilization. However, while accepting that ethnicity may be a resource (or, of course, a liability) in inter-group relations, and that in the absence of such relations and their concomitant group boundaries ethnicity is literally unthinkable, in this paper I intend to examine another aspect of ethnicity: its mobilisation as a resource by a dominant elite in their strategies for the internal control of their own class-stratified ethnic group.[2] Thus the focus of attention is shifted from *inter*-group to *intra*-group relationships. In passing, I hope also to add something to the debate surrounding the role of the 'protestant ethic' as a causal factor in the development of capitalism in Western Europe.

There are other reasons for looking at Ulster protestants in the context of a volume such as this. One important consideration is that the Northern Irish protestant community illustrates some of the limiting conditions for the economic mobilisation of ethnicity by an ethnic majority. If these limiting conditions are not specified, one might then be tempted to describe the Anglo-Saxon business establishment in Great Britain as 'ethnic business'. Although there is a relatively trivial sense in which such a description might be accurate, it is helpful to restrict the scope of the notion of 'majority' ethnic business to a limited range of situations. If we do not restrict the use of the concept, then, it may be thought to apply to all situations, in which case it actually applies to *no* situation.

There are two limiting conditions in this case. First, there is the dominance in the political arena of *ethnic conflict* as opposed to *class conflict*; in other words, the class politics of industrial capitalism are overridden by a stronger ethnic political struggle. This, of course, is very much of a simplification: ethnicity and class are neither necessarily, nor even consistently, oppositional principles. Depending on the particularities of the situation they may complement or contradict one another.

Secondly, there is the *scale* of the situation under examination. For the business of an ethnic majority to be truly 'ethnic', I would suggest that it must be carried out within a small scale political and economic arena, though clearly not one without links to the wider world economy. The bigger the arena of operations becomes, the more 'open' it is to the penetration of external capital and political control. More important, perhaps, with that penetration may come new organisational and institutional patterns which will undermine the local ethnically based relationships of production and distribution.

In summary, therefore, for the business activity of an ethnic majority to remain ethnic, these conditions must be at least partially satisfied; it is, perhaps, arguable that one is contingent upon the other. Northern Ireland is, of course, not the only such situation. Other examples of majority ethnic business might be found in French-speaking Canada, pre-invasion Cyprus, certain post-colonial African states or white South Africa in the late nineteenth and early twentieth centuries.

The other reason for looking at Ulster protestants here is that, precisely because of the dominance of ethnic, or sectarian, issues in the politics of the province, ethnicity in business extends (or extended) as an important principle of organisation to all levels of business activity, big business as well as small. Thus, alongside the chapter by Pollins on Jewish business, this piece may serve as a useful corrective to the open-all-hours corner shop image of the ethnic business.[3]

The roots of ethnicity in Ulster: the Plantation

For our purposes, the history of the Northern Irish protestant community may be traced back to the Ulster Plantation of the first decades of the seventeenth century. Although there had been some earlier colonisation of the counties of Antrim and Down by Scottish settlers (Stewart 1977: 37), the Plantation marks the beginning of the process which resulted in the present 'troubles'. Originally envisaged as an essentially military adventure, to secure the hitherto rebellious earldoms of Tyrconnel and Tyrone for the English crown by 'planting' a new and loyal population, the scheme acquired a commercial orientation very early on. Following an agreement between the crown and the corporation of the City of London, the latter set up a joint-stock enterprise:

> to plant the country of Coleraine, and to rebuild and fortify its two main towns, Coleraine and Derry. In return, they were to receive extensive privileges, including the patronage of all churches within their territory, the fisheries of the Foyle and the Bann, and a long lease of the customs at a nominal rent.
>
> (Beckett 1966: 46)

The links of commerce thereby established between the province and the mainland were to set the pattern for much of Ulster's subsequent history. The relative geographical isolation caused by the Irish sea, on the one hand, and the differences from the rest of Ireland which I shall discuss below, on the other, were also to set a pattern for the north-eastern counties, however. The history of the province since the Plantation is a curious mixture of insularity and backwardness contrasted with varying degrees of incorporation into the political and economic mainstreams of the rest of the Kingdom.

Throughout the rest of Ulster, the Plantation took on a similar character to that described above, either directly initiated by the government in London or encouraged by them at one remove through 'undertakers' or agencies such as the London company. In Antrim and Down, however, following a government-approved dismemberment of Con O'Neill's Clandeboye estates, the Plantation became more a matter for private adventurers. Here in particular the Plantation acquired a distinctly Scottish character, in contrast to the strong English influences at work further west.

As a result of this colonisation there developed a series of marked differences between Ulster and the rest of the island. There one saw the development of an essentially *rural* and *agricultural* society, based on commercially oriented tenant farmers, with a subsistence peasantry on the western margins. In the north-east there eventually developed, by contrast, an *urban* and *industrial* society, based in the first place on small-holdings leased from the undertakers by the colonist yeomanry and small tenantry, many of whom had a background in the textile industry then emerging across the Irish sea (Crotty 1966; Cullen 1969; Gibbon 1975: 9–12).

One of the original aims of the Plantation, and in this its military origins reveal themselves, was the physical removal of most of the native Irish population from the best areas in the north and their replacement with a politically loyal English and Scottish population drawn from all the social classes. In this aim the Plantation failed, however, and this for at least two reasons. First, the colonists, in particular those holding large estates, were happy to find tenants available on the spot. Secondly, those that were to be moved frequently resisted, as is witnessed by the planter's need for fortified houses or 'bawns'. The 'final solution' to the Ulster problem was not to work as well in practice as its architects in London had expected.

Nonetheless, although many or most of the former inhabitants remained, things had changed for them, and changed for the worse. Within twenty years, at the beginning of the seventeenth century, all of their customary rights to land and property vanished; in effect, they became aliens in their own country. A few, very few, either retained their status or were granted new lands, but they constituted a tiny minority.

> The great mass of Ulster Irish remained on their former lands,
> but degraded to the status of tenants-at-will. As they became
> increasingly impoverished, economic pressure tended to drive
> them out of the more fertile and into the worst lands, where their
> descendants are still to be found. (Moody 1974: 5)

In 1641 the fruits of this policy towards the native Irish ripened into
rebellion. Led by Sir Phelim O'Neill, and spurred on by fear of a puritan-
dominated House of Commons at Westminster, the Ulster catholics rose
up in revolt. Eight years later Oliver Cromwell arrived in Dublin and by
1652 the rebellion was over. The Irish were punished severely, by confis-
cation of most of their remaining land or deportation to the West Indian
plantations; the result of the 1641 rebellion was the consolidation of the
original aims of the Plantation and the commercial domination of Ireland
by the settlers, particularly in the north-east and the towns.

The end of the century saw further violence, most notably the siege of
Derry in 1689 and William's defeat of the Jacobite army at the Boyne in
1690. The Treaty of Limerick in 1691 and the flight of the 'Wild Geese' to
France signalled the final collapse of the Stuart cause. For the Irish
catholics the major results of the Williamite wars were the Penal Laws of
the early eighteenth century, which, although gradually relaxed,
remained in force until catholic emancipation was granted in 1829. In
addition to the already severe restrictions on Irish trade, catholics were
excluded from the army, barred from politics at both local and national
levels and deprived of access to education. Protestant estates could not be
sold to catholics, catholics were not allowed to lease land for more than
thirty-one years and the inheritance laws encouraged the minute sub-
division of catholic-owned land. Nonconformists suffered to some extent,
but in the north they were somewhat protected by the 'Ulster Custom'
which meant that they could sell their farms to their successors and could
not be evicted so long as they paid their rent.

The history of seventeenth and early eighteenth century Ulster has two
important features for this discussion. First, two contrasting ethnicities
were established: native catholic Irish, on the one hand, and Ulster
protestant settlers, on the other. The latter category was subdivided in
turn into the mainly presbyterian Scots of the east of the province and the
mainly Church of Ireland (i.e. Anglican) English of the western counties,
although the nineteenth century did see a significant migration into
Belfast of members of the Church of Ireland.[4] This distinction remains
important today, but the primary ethnic cleavage has historically been
between the native Irish and the settlers, with religion providing one of
the main boundary maintaining mechanisms.

The second point to note is that ethnicity in Ulster has had economic consequences from the earliest days of the Plantation. Catholics were first of all alienated from the land and eventually, via the Penal Laws, debarred from professional or political careers, and so further isolated from the possibilities for entrepreneurial activity. Thus were laid in the seventeenth and eighteenth centuries the foundations of protestant capital accumulation and catholic exclusion from most levels of commerce and business.

The consolidation of ethnic domination: the Industrial Revolution

The protestant colonists had their roots in areas of England and Scotland with traditions of both capitalist commodity farming[5] and domestic textile industry. The potential for industrial development which this implied was given a further boost in 1698 by the arrival at Lisburn, Co. Antrim, of Louis Crommelin and his fellow Huguenots, refugees from religious persecution in France. Their sudden appearance is at least partly explained by the fact that Huguenots had been among William's best troops in the campaigns of ten years earlier. The significance of their immigration rests mainly in the fact that they brought to Ulster the craft of weaving damask, a very fine, patterned linen fabric; plain linen cloth was already a well established manufacture in the province by the time of their arrival. Following the abolition by the British government, in 1696, of the tax on plain linens from Ireland,

> many English dealers began to buy Ulster cloth because it was cheaper than the Dutch and German linens. Since it continued to sell very well more weavers throughout Ulster began to weave for the London market and the industry spread to places as far apart as Strabane, Antrim and Monaghan before 1710.
> (Crawford 1972: 1)

Thus we can see several reasons for the rise of the textile industry in Ulster. First, there is the knowledge and skill of the settlers, both the original planters and the later Huguenot refugees. The importance of their craftsmanship, combined with some experience of small scale capitalist production, in a word, *business*, cannot be underestimated.

Equally important, however, in encouraging the harnessing of this entrepreneurial potential was the economically privileged position of the protestant settlers, particularly their secure land tenure system, as discussed earlier. This might have served in some cases to encourage small scale capital accumulation, encouraging farmer-manufacturers to expand by either employing weavers, or 'putting out' extra work. Finally, inasmuch as, for obvious political reasons, their case had the ear of the London government, Ulster protestants were in a position to petition for, and achieve, important economic concessions such as the withdrawal of the tax on plain linens in 1696. It is on these foundations, the technical know-how of the settlers, their secure relationship with the land and their links with the mainland (based on what was, in the local context, a bond of shared political ethnicity) that the Ulster textile industry was built up.[6]

It was this industry, originally domestic in its nature, which provided the necessary base from which industrial development stemmed in north-east Ireland. The trend in the rest of the country, with some important exceptions in urban centres such as Dublin or Cork, was increasingly towards large scale agriculture, with the emphasis being on both dairy and beef cattle. Until the famine years of the 1840s the western margins and the less fertile upland areas continued to be characterised by the small-holdings of the native Irish peasantry.

Once linen manufacture had been firmly established it became less reliant on the land tenure customs of Ulster and evolved into an independent industry in its own right. This had important consequences for the industrial and social future of the province:

> the linen industry affected the character of Ulster society . . . It not only gave employment to manual workers; it produced a substantial middle class of bleachers and drapers, many of whom acquired considerable wealth . . . It also promoted urban development, for the towns were the natural centres for marketing the cloth woven by rural weavers; and at least in some areas, there was a tendency for weavers to concentrate in the vicinity of these market towns. (Beckett 1973: xii–xiii)

Thus in the wake of capitalist industrialisation, albeit on a small scale at this time, we have the concomitant development and elaboration of class stratification within the protestant ethnic community. Manufacturing, far from being a reflection of prosperity rooted in the land, was rapidly becoming a source of capital accumulation in itself.

Further economic stimulation came as a result of the agitation by the Volunteers for free trade and other reforms. In 1779 many of the restrictions remaining on the Irish export trade were lifted and in 1782, following a political meeting in Dungannon, Co. Tyrone, the Dublin parliament was largely emancipated from control by Westminster. In the years immediately following, the Dublin government of Grattan's parliament did much to stimulate grain production, brewing, woollen manufacture and the cotton industry. The north-east counties, inasmuch as they had a head start on the rest of Ireland, benefited disproportionately from these reforms.

The new parliament failed, however, to grasp the nettle of catholic emancipation, a cause which was attracting some sympathy at this time in nonconformist quarters. The organisational expression of this sympathy was Wolfe Tone's 'Society of United Irishmen', founded in Belfast in 1791. Once again, however, as so many times before and since, self-interest and ethnicity successfully undermined the movement's radical ideals. In County Armagh, an area dominated by the textile industry and distinguished by an approximate demographic balance between catholics and protestants, a violent encounter occurred in 1795 which lead to the formation of an 'Orange Society', which spread quickly in the country-side. With it went increased attacks on catholic weavers, many of whom fled. There is considerable evidence of sympathy and support for the society among landlords and the magistracy; when a yeomanry was established to counter the United Irishmen's 1798 rebellion, the Orange Society provided many of its members. The protestants may have been increasingly stratified along class lines; nonetheless, ethnicity remained the major axis of political mobilisation (Senior 1966).

By the beginning of the nineteenth century Belfast had come to rival Dublin in its importance as a mercantile and financial centre. In terms of manufacturing the north-east had established a predominance it has yet to lose. The expansion of the textile industry, new technological developments (McCutcheon 1977: 51–5, 59–66) and the boom in cotton production stimulated by the Napoleonic Wars all combined to encourage systematic mechanisation, both in yarn spinning and weaving. By the 1830s factory production was rapidly becoming a commonplace, with linen manufacturing eventually reasserting itself as the market for cotton became increasingly competitive again in the conditions of peacetime.

The mechanisation of the labour process in textiles led to the development of the local engineering industry, based in the first instance upon the market for machinery and repair services among the local mill owners. This development was heavily dependent upon the mainland, particularly for specialist expertise. However, despite the influx of entrepreneurs possessing such expertise, the enterprises set up during this period were local companies which were not accountable to external sources of control.

> Few of the early engineering works in the north of Ireland were established by local men; Joe Rider, John Hind, Stephen Cotton, George Horner and E.J. Harland came from England, James Combe and James Mackie from Scotland. From the middle of the nineteenth century, however, local men trained in the

original works began to set up business for themselves or to take over the management of existing firms when founders retired or got into financial difficulties . . . It seems clear that the early entrepreneurs were attracted to the north of Ireland, not by the local market for small metal goods, but by the opportunity to exploit new techniques, such as iron founding, the making of steam engines and textile machinery, and the provision of a machinery repair service . . . the region was kept in touch with progress in industrial organisation in Britain not only by the political union of the two countries but also by periodic infusions of new blood from the British engineering industry.

(Coe 1969: 193, 194, 196)

Business or other economic links with the mainland were not all one way, however. In addition to the inward flow of technology and entre-preneurial personnel, there was also a flow of investment capital, in par-ticular – though not exclusively – a flow of local capital out for investment in England and Scotland. Due to the restricted scale and scope of the local economy, the local economic elite's links with their fellow businessmen 'across the water', sometimes the close links of family or marriage, pro-vided a useful avenue for diversification and investment (*ibid.*: 190–2). From the middle of the nineteenth century onwards, Ulster rapidly became incorporated into the developing industrial economy of the rest of the Kingdom.

The increasing importance of large scale manufacture, which required easy access to the sea for the import of the necessary raw materials and the export of its finished products, resulted in Belfast becoming the centre of industrial and commercial activity. The situation developed for three reasons. First, there was the city's centrality within the predominantly protestant area east of the river Bann; second, its ease of communication, via the natural corridor of the valley of the river Lagan, with the smaller textile towns of the rest of the province; and third, its position as the major deep-water port on the north-eastern seaboard, providing ready access to the markets of the Empire and the rest of the world. Belfast's position was strengthened by the establishment of the steamship services to Glasgow and Liverpool in the 1820s. In 1800 the city had been smaller than either Limerick or Waterford; by 1891 Belfast had overtaken Dublin in both size and commercial importance.

Naturally enough, the industrial development of the Belfast area drew in many immigrants from the rest of the province. Although it was already happening before the Famine, rural distress in the 1840s and the sub-sequent flight from the land accelerated this population movement. Many of the new city-dwellers were catholics from the southern and western districts of Ulster, attracted to Belfast by the availability of employment. They tended to take unskilled jobs in textile production or as navvies, building the new town. Skilled work, particularly in engineering, remained the preserve of the protestant working man; industry and commerce were controlled by the local protestant bourgeoisie – either local or newly arrived – and hiring practices reflected the traditionally sanctioned hierarchy of catholic and protestant.[7] Relations between an employer and his workforce were often paternalistic and a firm recognition of the relationship between employment and ethnicity structured the emergent labour market in the city, although this did not prevent the emergence, from the 1870s, of labourism and union organisation (Patterson 1980). Historians of this period leave us in no doubt as to the systematic manipulation of ethnicity by the local elite, both in furtherance of their political ends (the maintenance of protestant supremacy and the link with Britain) and, more indirectly, their economic goals. The link between the political and the economic was clearly recognised by both workers and employers and formed the basis of the Unionist class alliance.

With the increasing importance of shipbuilding and marine engineering from mid-century onwards, the present industrial structure began to emerge. The development of the shipyards was the result of a number of factors: the presence of a deep-water harbour, the large numbers of skilled men, such as boilermakers, in the engineering industry locally (although many more were brought in from Clydeside), and the enthusiasm of the Harbour Commissioners in developing the Queen's Island site. As the century drew to its close, the Belfast region became incorporated more and more into the wider United Kingdom economy, particularly that region of it which includes the other major Irish sea ports, Glasgow and Liverpool. Both employers and men participated in national and regional industrial negotiations and disputes and the commercial life of the city drew ever closer to that of the rest of the Kingdom, much local capital continuing to be invested on the mainland (Coe 1969: 191; Lyons 1973: 270–86). By 1900 the economy was provincial no longer.

In this section I have sought to develop a model of the industrialisation of Northern Ireland which allows us to examine some of the links between culture or ethnicity, on the one hand, and economic activity, on the other. During this period the linked processes of urbanisation, industrialisation and mechanisation served to reinforce the economic and political dominance of the local protestant bourgeoisie in at least two respects. First, their economic position was made more secure, and their sphere of activities expanded, through the importation of technological resources from the mainland. Their access to external investment markets when the local opportunities for capital accumulation became too limited further consolidated their economic base. Both of these strategies were facilitated by their links of shared ethnicity – in the religious *and* political sense – with the English and Scottish bourgeoisie, who were a source of technologically innovative entrepreneurs and provided opportunities for Ulster protestant businessmen to invest money in their enterprises. Secondly, the economic and political interests of the local businessman – and the two are inextricably linked – were well served by the stratification of the working class along ethnic lines. Class issues were never forgotten in local politics, and the distinction between the skilled and unskilled protestant worker remains important to this day, but the increasing orchestration of ethnic solidarity by the Orange Order as the nineteenth century wore on ensured that sectarian issues – particularly following the Home Rule crisis of 1886 – dominated the political arena. The important connection between ethnicity and access to work would probably have seen to that if nothing else did and this tendency was reinforced by the preeminence of elitist craft unions amongst organised labour.

Sectarian ethnicity was not the only factor, of course. It must not be forgotten that the underdevelopment of the rest of Ireland was a powerful argument against Home Rule; a real fear of losing a relatively prosperous life style informed both politics and industrial relations. The outcome of these fears for the Ulster employer, occasional disputes notwithstanding, was the continuing control of his workforce and a high degree of industrial harmony.

It must be stressed, however, that 'Ulster Unionism emerged as the product neither of a conspiracy of landed notables and industrialists to "dupe the people" nor from the spontaneous convergence of a set of forces without prior political relations' (Gibbon 1975: 145). The important thing to grasp is the systematic interconnections which are revealed between ethnicity, economic activity and politics in Ulster since the Plantation; these interconnections are, however, neither accidental nor 'structurally' determined. They are the result of the pursuit – not always consistent – of rational political and economic goals by the government in London and the Ulster protestant establishment. They became finally systematised with the rise to importance of the protestant industrial and commercial elite of Belfast in the second half of the nineteenth century. Their roots, however, lay very much earlier.

Organised labour and the manipulation of ethnicity

We have seen how the foundations of a hierarchical ethnic division of labour were laid in the military subjugation of the Ulster Irish and the subsequent Plantation; this division of labour was further consolidated as the industrial revolution progressed in north-eastern Ireland. I shall conclude with some discussion of the subsequent development of the capitalist economy in Ulster, in particular during the life of the Northern Ireland state, between 1921 and the prorogation of Stormont in 1972.

Before the First World War, the remarks of the above section notwithstanding, there had been some class-based political organisation and industrial action, most notably Jim Larkin's organisation of unskilled labour, both protestant and catholic, in Belfast in 1907. Industrial unrest rose to new heights, however, in the wake of the war, as it did throughout the United Kingdom.

> Industrial militancy was growing among Belfast workers. There had been a massive engineering strike at the beginning of 1919 which had brought Belfast industry to a halt for four weeks. Ominously for the Unionists the leader of the largely Protestant strikers had been a Catholic, Charles McKay. The workers' new class consciousness seemed to carry through to the local elections in January 1920, for twelve Labour councillors were elected to Belfast Corporation, one of them topping the poll in the Protestant stronghold of Shankill.   (Farrell 1976: 27)

In the appalling social conditions of working class areas of Belfast during this period the labour movement should have found fertile ground to take seed and flourish. However, this was also a period of intense sectarian conflict, stemming from the pre-war Ulster Volunteer Force crisis and the Civil War in the rest of the island. The troubles of this period, combined with the blatant playing of the 'Orange Card' by local employers and, later, by the new Stormont government, played a substantial part in undermining inter-ethnic or cross-sectarian socialist activism.[8] It was during this period that the identification by protestants of the necessary identity of interests between socialism and Irish nationalism was first formulated, opposition to the latter generating rejection of the former. The Northern Ireland Labour Party has struggled on under this electoral handicap ever since.[9]

The upshot of this was the wholesale expulsion of Catholic workers from many areas of Belfast industry, most notably the shipyards, a state of affairs further encouraged by the fact that differences in skill levels between catholics (a majority of whom were unskilled) and protestants (a high proportion of whom were skilled) led, in some respects, to the reproduction of the ethnic division of labour among the trade unions. There was no General Strike in Belfast in 1926, and the unique events towards the end of 1932, when catholic and protestant workers marched together to protest at their unemployment and destitution, were put down by the

Royal Ulster Constabulary armed with rifled and armoured cars. In the wake of this dangerous display of class politics, Unionist politicians were swift to realign politics and public violence along the more familiar lines of sectarianism. In 1934 and 1935 there was a return to the *status quo ante*: violence erupting on the streets between the two groups (Farrell 1976: 125–40).

After the Second World War, the Unionist government, newly incorporated, albeit somewhat reluctantly, into the Westminster Labour Party's welfare state, resolved to revitalise the Ulster economy, suffering now from over-concentration upon textiles and heavy engineering in its formative phases. The main development strategy was the attraction of outside companies to the province by means of generous capital subsidies. Most of the new enterprises set up were sited in protestant areas east of the river Bann and most of the new jobs correspondingly went to protestants. This was particularly the case in engineering, which required skilled men. Furthermore, the new capitalism accepted quite readily the practices of the old. The toleration of local practices was a small price to pay for good industrial relations.[10]

> A good many new businesses conformed without protest to the practices of old capital. In 1965, when new industry provided about 60,000 of 190,000 manufacturing jobs, the first Development Plan complained that only 10 per cent of new vacancies were being filled through labour exchanges. Evidently Orangeism was becoming absorbed into the new workplaces.
>
> (Bew, Gibbon and Patterson 1979: 189)

Thus we see organised labour effectively split along ethnic lines, the protestant section of it 'bought off' by the Unionist government and the local business elite. The arrival of the new multi-national enterprises served only to strengthen this state of affairs, inasmuch as it suited their best interests – the maintenance of a quiescent workforce and easy access to subsidies – not to resist it.

How this mobilisation of ethnicity was managed can only be understood if one appreciates the interpenetration of the political, legal and business spheres in Northern Ireland prior to the imposition of direct rule from Westminster in 1972. Between 1921 and 1972 the Northern Ireland state was the institutional embodiment of this interpenetration; the main integrating organisation holding the system together was, and even, to some extent, remains, the Orange Institution (Buckland 1980; Harbinson 1973).

The Prime Minister said in 1932: 'Ours is a Protestant Govern-

ment and I am an Orangeman'. . . In the House of Commons the
Prime Minister said: 'I am very proud indeed to be Grand Master
of the Orange Institution of the loyal County of Down. I have
filled that office for many years and I prize that far more than I
do being Prime Minister. I have always said I am an Orangeman
first and a member of this Parliament afterwards.'

(Mansergh 1936: 240–1)

Unless it is appreciated how closely overlapping were economic and political power in Northern Ireland, coming together in the Orange Institution and the Unionist Party, the working of the informal network of
political patronage, one of the lynch pins in the maintenance of ethnic
domination, cannot properly be understood.[11] As suggested earlier, the
small scale of the local political and economic arena, and its relative
autonomy prior to 1972, are vital to any explanation of the workings of
this system. Since the suspension of the local state in 1972, and particularly since the downgrading of local government in Northern Ireland in
1973, the situation has changed somewhat. There is no reason to suggest,
however, that incorporation into the British state has undermined the
informal apparatus of protestant control (O'Dowd, Rolston and
Tomlinson 1980).

Protestant ethic or ethnic domination?

In this chapter I have attempted to show the manner in which a protestant
ethnicity was initially established in Ulster and subsequently manipulated
within the domain of economic activity. This has, incidentally, illustrated
the relative impossibility of maintaining hard and fast distinctions
between the economy and other areas of social reality.

The economic distinctions between catholics and protestants in Northern Ireland which I have drawn attention to remain important today.
From the 1971 census data it is immediately apparent that catholics are
more likely to be unemployed than protestants, more likely to be
employed in the tertiary (service) sector than in manufacturing and are
over-represented in semi- or unskilled occupations (Aunger 1975; Fair
Employment Agency 1978). In the business world, the only occupation in
which catholics are over-represented is that of publican or inn-keeper
(Osborne 1980: 210), an 'ethnic niche' which dates back to the nineteenth
century and may have something to do with the stigmatised nature of the
occupation in 'respectable' protestant eyes (Gibbon 1975: 92). This ethnically skewed occupational distribution is likely to persist, according to
projections of future occupational mobility (Miller 1979).

The reasons for the persistence of ethnic economic domination should, I hope, be clear from the evidence I have discussed. For example, it probably has little to do with different levels of formal educational achievement: although protestants did 'better', educationally speaking, in the past, this is a trend which is rapidly being reversed (Osborne and Murray 1978). Furthermore, this historical under-achievement is probably best viewed as a *result* of ethnic domination, not one of its *causes*. Similarly, a study designed to elicit responses indicating attitudes to work could find only negligible differences between the two ethnic groups (Miller 1978). There would, therefore, appear to be no ready 'cultural' explanation for the striking differences in the pattern of employment described above.

This, however, is not the protestant folk view of the situation; in their eyes their economically privileged situation is a just reward for their hard work, thrift and 'hard-headedness' in business. Thomas Wilson, an Ulster protestant and an economist, has eloquently summed up this point of view as follows:

> As for business life, Presbyterians and Jews are probably endowed with more business acumen than Irish Catholics . . . For generations they were the underdogs, the despised 'croppies' the adherents of a persecuted religion, who were kept out of public life by the Protestant conquerors. They were made to feel inferior, and to make matters worse they often *were* inferior, if *only* in those personal qualities that make for success in competitive economic life.   (Wilson 1955: 208–9)

The view of protestantism as encouraging economic enterprise has found its way into other academic analyses (e.g. Baker 1973: 803). That this is so should not be surprising in view of the continued academic debate surrounding Max Weber's thesis concerning the connection between the 'puritan asceticism' of the Reformation and the development of capitalism (Weber 1968: 615–23). While recognising that this article, with its limited geographic scope, can do little to confirm or deny the fundamental points of the 'protestant ethic' thesis,[12] there has, I hope, been established a firm case for resisting the notion that protestant economic supremacy in Northern Ireland has anything to do with the cultural norms of protestantism. The contemporary level of economic achievement of the protestant ethnic community must be traced back to the Plantation and the systematic dispossession of the economic resources of the indigenous Irish population. This act of initial domination, creating as it did two ethnicities in conflict, was consolidated during the Industrial Revolution and has yet to be seriously challenged. The evidence of this paper is that the nature of the opportunity structure for catholics – itself the result of protestant political domination and the intimate relationship between Unionism and the local business elite – is sufficient explanation for the present ethnic division of labour.

Conclusions

This has been a necessarily superficial account of Northern Irish history and, as such, it has two major weaknesses. First, in my desire for economy in length, I have presented a more tightly functionalist model of the situation than I would otherwise have wished. The contradictions and inconsistencies of history have necessarily been lost in a smooth flow of generalisations. The protestant working class, for example, was not as easily or comprehensively 'bought off' as my account suggests. Second, I have largely ignored the role of local and national state institutions, in particular the security forces, in providing employment for protestant workers and contract for protestant businessmen. It is to be hoped, however, that these lacunae do not undermine the argument to severely.

The mobilisation of ethnicity as a resource in the pursuit of business success and capital accumulation may, if the Ulster situation is any guide, take many forms. In particular, in the second phase described above, the period of industrialisation and urbanisation, protestant ethnicity was a resource which encouraged and facilitated links with the British mainland, technology being imported and capital exported for investment elsewhere. From the late nineteenth century ethnic ties were increasingly, and, apparently, self-consciously recognised to be, a part of the local bourgeoisie's strategy for dealing with organised labour. The management of the class-stratified protestant community was achieved in a number of complementary fashions, the two most important being the control of recruitment into employment, in a labour market with more job seekers than jobs, and the creation of political unity, a class alliance, through the periodic manipulation of the external threat of catholic nationalism. It is upon these foundations that contemporary protestant commercial and industrial supremacy in Ulster today rests.

5

The development of Jewish business in the United Kingdom[1]

HAROLD POLLINS

A study of Jewish business in Britain provides a useful addition and a counterpoint to the majority of contributions in this book. For one thing the time-span is longer: there has been a continuous Jewish presence in Britain since the readmission in 1656 (the medieval community which was expelled in 1290 after some two centuries of existence is also worth a mention). Moreover, over 1,000 years of Jewish minority status in numerous countries have produced a variety of adaptations in different sets of circumstances. Although the evidence is patchy and ambiguous, it is reasonable to speak of a tendency for Jews to be more highly represented in business, widely defined, than other groups. A common finding of numerous studies of the Jews of America clearly indicates a higher rate of upward social mobility in the twentieth century than with other immigrant groups (e.g. Glazer and Moynihan 1963).

The Jewish community in Britain, as elsewhere in the Diaspora, was built up through immigration and natural increase. Converts to Judaism have been minimal, but losses have occurred through conversion to Christianity, outmarriage, or mere secularisation, as well as emigration. The various waves of immigrants brought with them a combination of religious doctrines and customs, attitudes acquired in their countries of origin, and traditional patterns of economic activity. These were powerful determinants of their occupational distribution in Britain. With these predisposing qualities Jewish immigrants and their descendants faced changing economic, social and political conditions in Britain (Kosmin 1979; Pollins 1982).

In general Jews migrated to escape discrimination and persecution. While some came for better economic possibilities, the 'push' element was normally greater than the 'pull'. The greatest expansion of the community came with the mass migration from Eastern Europe, between the 1870s and the First World War. From that group is descended most of today's Anglo-Jewry. At the start of that period, around 1870, the community probably numbered 60,000–70,000; perhaps 100,000–150,000 migrants settled in Britain during those four decades. The two previous centuries of growth from the 1650s had been slow: from 1,000 in 1700 to 25,000 in 1800. It had begun with the Sephardim, the Jews who, whatever their immediate country of emigration – Holland or Italy for example – were part of the once large Spanish and Portuguese Jewish group. They were soon surpassed by the Ashkenazim, the Jews of Northern Europe (Germany, Holland, Poland and Russia). The great migration from Eastern Europe at the end of the nineteenth century radically transformed the community, but its subsequent population growth was less dramatic with a low birth rate and reduced flow of immigrants. The immigrants in the 1930s were refugees from Nazism and after the Second World War they came from a variety of countries, including 'black' Jews from India, Pakistan, the Arab world and Africa (even the occasional Falasha from Ethiopia). The peak population of some 450,000 was reached after the Second World War; it is now less than 400,000, the decline being a consequence of a low rate of natural increase, emigration, especially to Israel, and 'losses' to the non-Jewish world.

Circumstances of origin

Jews in Britain are a heterogeneous collection of people and although the term 'community' is commonly used, it is no more than a convenient shorthand. There were and are numerous divisions among them; nor did they possess a uniform set of predispositions on their arrival. Moreover, the various migrants came at different periods of British history and the conditions and opportunities they encountered necessarily varied. The most important conditioning fact is that the Jews were always in a minority in the countries of their dispersion and their economic structure was not 'typical' (Gross 1975). In most places they were divorced from the land and from an early period they were more accustomed than most to money and an exchange economy. Moreover, they were often excluded from many pursuits, e.g. where Christian guilds controlled entry to their crafts, though where the Jewish population was large, as in Poland and Spain, separate Jewish guilds were established (Wischnitzer 1965). The extreme cases of exclusion and specialisation occurred in those medieval countries – England was one – where, according to the available records, moneylending was virtually the Jews' sole occupation. In effect they were the tax-collectors, the interest they received on monetary advances finding its way as revenue to the crown. For that reason they were formally under the king's protection but when they were no longer needed they were expelled. In many other countries, however, in the medieval and early modern periods, their activities were much more diverse. Where there were large numbers of Jews, specialisation was less possible. Often they were left with low status and degraded jobs, although others were engaged as silversmiths and the like in the production of luxury items.

There is no need to pursue explanations for all these different activities – why Jews were often in the drink trade in Eastern Europe or in tobacco manufacture or the diamond business in Holland. The numbers in various occupations are seldom known but the occasional statistics for a few places show that a higher than average proportion of Jews were in some form of business, some of them magnates and merchants, but the majority craftsmen-traders or petty pedlars and hucksters. The implication of the discussion so far is that the propensity of the Jews to be found in business can be accounted for by the nature of the relationships between Jews and non-Jews as well as by the stage of economic development in the various countries. In addition there was the body of religious teachings which covered all aspects of life, including the economic. How powerful they were in establishing attitudes and behaviour patterns is by no means clear and it is unrewarding to examine the religious texts for this purpose. Despite the emphasis on study and the prestige accorded to men learned in religious matters, it is hard to establish if the majority of Jewish males were familiar with the teachings or, if they were, could apply them. It was one thing, for example, for the rabbis to advocate teaching one's son a craft, it was another to realise it. More to the point, when Jews came to Britain from the seventeenth century onwards they brought with them attitudes which were already formed and, especially, their traditional economic activities.

The earliest arrivals, the seventeenth-century Sephardim, came from an environment of, on the one hand, commercial capitalism and, on the other, a high degree of secular interaction with the non-Jewish world. Indeed, their forced conversion to Christianity in the fifteenth and sixteenth centuries in the Iberian Peninsula had paradoxically been of help. Although many remained secret Jews (and reverted to Judaism in tolerant countries), as formal Christians in Portugal they were broadly acceptable as equals, even if officially designated as a separate group, 'New Christians'. Those who came to Britain were accustomed to the modern world and its ways, and many to the practices of international trade.

Apart from a few men of similar experience, the larger numbers of Ashkenazim who arrived in the eighteenth century were generally of low status, both economically and socially. This was true for most Jewish immigrants up to 1914, although their backgrounds were diverse. Those from Holland came from a country which, in the seventeenth century, had probably been the first to allow Jews a high degree of toleration, according them an unaccustomed life of freedom. They had little difficulty in adjusting to a similarly free British atmosphere. For those, the majority, living in much of the rest of Europe emancipation came later, in the Napoleonic period, when French influence and conquests swept away old restrictions. Thus German-Jewish immigrants had previously experienced segregation and discrimination, with familiar consequences for their occupations, but emancipation in the early nineteenth century enabled them to enter hitherto closed activities. A few of them came to Britain as men of substance, some with a good secular education in scientific subjects. The great immigration at the end of the nineteenth century, however, was of people from countries in Eastern Europe which had been untouched by emancipation; indeed the Jews' condition had deteriorated during the century. They had known residential segregation, persecution, numerous restrictions, physical violence and pogroms. Rapid population growth had added to the pressures.

Opportunities in Britain

Whatever their varying predispositions and backgrounds, the immigrants all found greater freedom in Britain. They were emancipated *de facto* on their arrival. From the seventeenth century formal religious discrimination was minimal and growing economic liberalism reduced restrictions on occupational choice. Popular antisemitism was always present, if fluctuating in degree; but it did not have the intensity that it manifested in other countries. Religious freedom was important. Despite the dominance of the Church of England after the Cromwellian interlude – which meant that all religious groups outside the Church suffered certain disabilities for nearly two centuries (and during which the arch-enemy was Roman Catholicism) – the general trend was towards toleration. Some restrictions were strictly maintained but administration of others was lax. Jews were, in law, merely one among many groups outside the Church and suffered the same loss of rights, such as the inability to hold public office. The one field which affected Jews (and other non-Christians) specifically was the obligation to swear a Christian oath. This prevented them from taking up certain occupations, some of the professions for example, and joining certain institutions, such as guilds and some overseas trading companies (Henriques 1908). This requirement was abolished piecemeal mostly by the middle of the nineteenth century but it had not been a racial barrier. People of Jewish origin who were prepared to swear the oath could enter these activities, some becoming

Members of Parliament and others obtaining commissions in the armed forces.

In any case the growing liberalisation of the economy meant that, in fact, many formal restrictions were ignored. The guilds, unlike those on the continent, were moribund by the eighteenth century and even the City of London companies, which had the right to control entry to City trades, constantly complained of 'foreigners'; 'interloping' was a persistent feature of overseas trade, and many trade routes were outside the province of chartered companies. Similarly there were no restrictions on residence. Jews were not required, as they were in many European countries, to live in certain districts or in defined parts of towns. Most lived in London, especially in the City and the East End, but they soon began to live in provincial towns. There is no solid evidence that the eighteenth-century provincial Jewish settlements came about because Jews were debarred by the City authorities from opening shops or pursuing their crafts and so had to go elsewhere.

Alongside this unusual freedom, from the seventeenth century, must be placed the economic opportunities available to the diverse sets of immigrants. During the period since 1656 Britain changed from being somewhat on the periphery of the European economy to become the first industrial nation and the major world power of the nineteenth century. New products, new markets, rising standards of living and a growing population all provided openings for more people. In general Jews did not arrive, as has largely been the case with the post-1945 black immigrants, to fill niches vacated by the indigenous population.

The historical development of Jewish business in Britain

The results of the combination of predispositions and opportunities can be observed in the varying business activities entered into by Anglo-Jewry since the readmission (reference to the majority who were not in business will be minimal here). The wealthier among the early arrivals, mainly Sephardim, were occupied in such activities as the army commissariat services (this was an era of war); as brokers of various kinds, including dealing in government and company stocks and shares, even before the Stock Exchange was established; as government loan contractors; as bullion and foreign exchange dealers; and in foreign trade and shipping. These were often activities undertaken by Jews on the continent and transferred to Britain. In some cases the numbers involved were small, a handful in the commissariat service or in loan contracting but rather more in the others. Even so they were usually a minority except in one particular field, the diamond trade, particularly the Sephardim for whose elite it was the main, single occupation. The diamonds were exported from India, with Jewish agents at Fort St George (Madras), imported by London Jews and exported to Amsterdam for finishing, often by Jewish firms. The diamond imports from India were paid for, in part, by coral which was imported from the Mediterranean to London and then exported (Yogev 1978).

It was not at all unusual in the eighteenth century for economic links to be along religious lines and within families. Jews traded with Jews and Christians with Christians. Jewish loan contractors raised funds for the government from the Jewish community in London and also in Amsterdam. It was common for a family firm to send one of its members to another country to open a branch agency for trade – Dutch Jews in London, for example, or London Jews in Madras or in America. Such religious separation can be seen in the developing domestic banking in Britain. One looks in vain for Jews among the London banks, which were protestant enclaves; the immigrants who entered them were Dutch Christians or Huguenots, some of their descendants still being found as major City figures.

It may be though that there was another reason for the absence of Jews from banking, i.e. their tendency to restrict themselves to the occupations and channels of trade they knew. There is little evidence of their moving into different spheres: they did not take much part in the rapidly growing overseas trade of the eighteenth century, to North America for example. Their total contribution to commerce was a mere few per cent. However, despite these undoubted separate economic groupings along religious and ethnic lines the segmentation was not rigid. There was much economic intercourse across the lines. Jews obviously banked with non-Jewish banks and it was by no means uncommon for Jews and non-Jews to form partnerships in such fields as shipping adventures.

Even less separate were the more typical eighteenth-century Jewish businessmen, the low status pedlars. They were part of the great congregation of itinerant sellers who thronged the market towns, villages and seaports and sold door-to-door. But the Jews sold direct to the public; they did not act as manufacturers' agents, selling to retailers. It was a time of growing retail trade but distribution was as yet undeveloped, fixed shops being usually for the rich. The ubiquity of the Jewish pedlars is known from the frequent references to them in many parts of the country. Alongside the literary allusions to Jews as stockjobbers ('jobbers' being a word of abuse) were the equally well known pedlars, often captured in pottery figurines. In London, too, they were street-sellers, of fruit for example, and, especially, old-clothesmen, collecting the discarded clothing of the rich for sorting and resale (Shepherd 1981). The latter lived on the margin of criminality, Jews as fences being another popular image.

Peddling was an immigrant trade, not especially a Jewish one, although it was common enough for Jews on the continent. The job required no fixed capital, and stock could be obtained on credit; little skill was needed; and knowledge of a few words of English would serve. Presumably some of the pedlars were transferring their trade from one country to another but there is occasional evidence of occupational downgrading. Surprisingly, British-born Jews also took up street-selling; one of the features of the diagnoses of the 'degraded' social condition of London Jews in the late eighteenth and early nineteenth centuries (when Jews were among the criminals transported to Australia, and were notable among the prizefighters) was that they did not take up more suitable occupations than selling in the streets. Efforts were made to educate the children and to apprentice them. When Henry Mayhew wrote about the London street Jews around 1850, he observed that they were moving out of these trades, sometimes ousted by the newer Irish immigrants. And although some of the children went into manual employment, a familiar progression was from peddling to shopkeeping and, for some, subsequently further up the social scale: the family of the Liberal statesman Viscount Samuel followed this course. Others, less successful, fell on hard times or turned to crime (Williams 1976: 62–71). The growing numbers of shopkeepers were sometimes pure sellers, of food for example; others were slop-sellers, retailing cheap clothes. A high proportion, notably in the provinces, were silversmiths, goldsmiths and watchmakers. Some of these made their products; others, whatever their title, were probably really pawnbrokers.

It is evident that in the eighteenth and early nineteenth century Jews tended to concentrate on particular fields, where they usually comprised a small proportion of those in a particular occupation. Most of their economic dealings were extra-ethnic: they sold to the general public. This was so even in the densest area of Jewish population, the City and East End of London. It was obviously so for the tiny numbers scattered among some of the many provincial towns.

For much of the nineteenth century the rate of immigration was low and some of those arriving stayed only temporarily before moving on to America. So the community, in the first 60 or 70 years, came to comprise a native-born and acculturated majority. Popular hostility was not especially great and antagonism towards minorities focussed on the larger numbers of Irish catholics, notably in Lancashire. They were the social problem of the mid-century. It was possible for the wealthier Jewish stratum, aiming to be fully integrated into British society, to become gentlemen, sometimes to the extent of marriage into the highest levels: it had begun earlier (Endelman 1979). The families of many of the eighteenth-century Sephardi elite thus disappeared during the nineteenth and some of today's aristocracy have a Sephardi ancestor.

The features of Jewish settlement in the nineteenth century are identifiable: the growth of both a middle class and a working class, composed of the native-born and immigrants. The businessmen were occupied in the trades already mentioned, especially the expanding ones, as stockbrokers, retailers and wholesalers, and overseas traders. The newly developing manufacture of cheap ready-made clothing was another area, the employees, including outworkers, often being non-Jews. Workshops making slippers, furniture, caps, and a variety of other products became more common. These were usually on a small scale, typically in poor conditions, often run by low-status immigrants, anticipating the much greater incidence of such businesses later in the century. Slightly more substantial were the cigar-makers, many of them from Holland, who settled in the East End of London to produce for a growing market. In that location the industry was largely Jewish-owned and Jewish-manned, cigar-making providing the main single source of employment for the London Sephardim. The enterprises were somewhat larger than workshops, the work was skilled if badly paid and the first ethnic strike – Jewish workers against Jewish employers – took place in this industry in 1858.

It is to be expected that the industrial expansion of Britain in the nineteenth century should attract to the country all manner of foreign businessmen, the vast textile industry in particular being their target. They included men who had been importers in their own countries and now became exporters and in some cases manufacturers. Some of these immigrants were Jews, sometimes a representative of the family business, but they eventually formed their own businesses here. Thus Jews as traders or manufacturers went to Lancashire (cotton), Bradford (wool), Nottingham (lace) and Dundee and Belfast (linen).

Others participated in the rapid development of London as a major financial centre. Its growth too attracted numerous foreigners who tended to specialise in merchant banking, acting as acceptance houses and channels for overseas investment. German-Jewish bankers were a significant part of this development, Rothschilds being the best known. They, like the non-Jewish Barings – the other main name in Britain – had originally been merchants (among other things) and it was a familiar move from overseas trade, where experience had been gained in international transactions, to banking (thus the name 'merchant banking'). In the case of the German Jews there was a further explanation for their importance in this activity. The numerous Germanic states in existence before the country was unified had led to many financial transactions across boundaries in a variety of currencies; experience was thereby gained. Moreover, in some of them the rulers had employed 'Court Jews' to act as their financial experts, the novel *Jew Süss* (Feuchtwanger 1925) bringing the matter to popular attention in the twentieth century. It can be argued that, because overseas financing was risky, it was helpful to have agents in the other countries who were known and reliable; to be of the same religious or national group, particularly in the same family, was a distinct advantage. The Rothschilds, with five brothers in five different cities, acting at first as one firm, were clearly in a strong position. Similar connections can be discerned for other families, the Seligmanns and the Speyers, for example. But two considerations are relevant which modify any conclusions about the importance of such networks. Many of the Jewish bankers soon left the religious community; and many banks were successful but had no such connections (Greenberg 1974).

Most Jews lived in London and their occupations necessarily reflected the capital's economic activities. Most enterprises were small, factories were few. The staple industries were mainly elsewhere and apart from the textile manufacturers one comes across the occasional colliery owner, and immigrant chemists, like Mond, in the north-west of the country. Probably the largest industrial entrepreneur was Samuda in London, a major shipbuilder. It is unlikely that he employed any Jews in an industry where the unions were strong and exclusive, and on his death in the 1880s the yard closed; the London shipbuilding industry in any case was declining. In addition there were a handful of Jews on the boards of the biggest companies of all, the railways.

There is no profit in trying to explain the reasons why a particular individual took up any of these 'unusual' trades. There was nothing 'ethnic' in their choice and it is noticeable too that many of the immigrant businessmen were only Jewish in origin, some having given up their Jewish connections before arriving, others soon afterwards. This was as true of some of the bankers, for whose occupations one can supply explanations from Jewish history, as of such people as Wolff, of the Belfast shipbuilding firm of Harland & Wolff, for whom one cannot (unless this is seen as part of the response of German-Jewry to the sudden emancipation of the early nineteenth century which resulted in a great outburst of activity in many directions).

In sum, there is no doubt at all about Jewish upward social mobility in the first three-quarters of the nineteenth century. Numerous indices point to it: more Jewish children went to middle class schools, even to the great public schools; there was a move to the suburbs. An attempt was made at the time to quantify the social class composition of London Jews in the 1880s, when the immigration from Eastern Europe was in its early stages. The compiler divided the population into eleven categories which he summarised as four classes: upper, middle, lower and pauper. His estimated 46,000 London Jews included 15 per cent in the upper class (professionals and merchants in West London). About 37 per cent were middle class (professionals and merchants in other parts of London, together with shopkeepers; the largest element in this section was the shopkeepers, amounting to some 25 per cent of the grand total). Just under 25 per cent were 'petty traders recently on Board of Guardians' who were placed in the 'lower class' along with 'servants and assistants'. Despite the heroic efforts of the compiler to check these figures from a variety of sources, he made no claim for precision. The numbers of paupers who had come to the attention of the Board of Guardians were exact but the other categories he described as 'probable' or 'about which there can be any serious departure from the actual state of the population'. He himself thought his proportion of the wealthy was too high. Nevertheless the impression of a large middle class segment is undoubtedly valid (Jacobs 1891: 10–17).

This position was rapidly changing as he wrote. The highly acculturated community – its English trappings including the adopting of such names as 'Boards of Guardians' for its welfare bodies, the Chief Rabbi wearing bishop's gaiters, and the ministers wearing clerical collars – having witnessed the removal of the last vestigial restrictions, now found large numbers of foreigners in its midst. It is true only in part that the newcomers' passage into British society was facilitated by a pre-existing community with its own institutions. Between the Yiddish-speaking aliens and the native-born there was much suspicion and hostility: the latter indeed tried to discourage the former from coming to Britain and arranged repatriation. The existing institutions were often shunned by the newcomers. They seldom joined, for example, the more sedate United Synagogue in London or the similar 'anglicised' synagogues in the provinces, preferring their own insanitary establishments.

Nevertheless, most of the immigrants settled in towns where there were Jews already. Not many pioneered new areas. London, Manchester, Leeds, Glasgow, Liverpool and Birmingham were the main cities of residence, and particular districts within them. This was for a variety of reasons. They kept together, as immigrants do, and also for religious reasons and for fear of the non-Jewish world. Chain migration ensured a cumulative process whereby not just families but people from the same town in Eastern Europe settled near each other, even setting up their own institutions, such as the Poltaver Synagogue for people from that place. Synagogues of this nature were not denominationally different from each other. The immigrants settled in their various districts not because they were areas where accommodation was most widely available; on the contrary, they lodged in houses already occupied by Jews, adding to severe overcrowding. It is not likely either that their location was primarily determined by local economic opportunities. Boot and shoe workers did not go to Northampton or Norwich, major centres of the industry, presumably because few if any Jews lived there.

There was an expansion in the provision of communal services – religious functionaries, the provision of religious equipment, and food shops. Jews were found in a great variety of occupations. But most were in a few limited areas: peddling or the clothing, footwear, headwear and furniture industries, the largest single one being clothing. The Population Census of 1901 shows over 60 per cent of males who were born in Russia and Poland (almost all of whom were Jews) as being employed in clothing or the making of hats and furniture, two-thirds of them in clothing. Many of the immigrants had previously been in these industries. But there was much movement between jobs, for most of them were seasonal and people would sometimes take up others in the slack periods.

Apart from those working independently, Jews normally worked for other Jews, usually of the same immigrant wave. Some worked with or for non-Jews but frictions were not infrequent. Many jobs, moreover, were not available to Jews, or were not in their tradition. They were not usually found in the staple industries – mining, engineering, textile manufacture or the railways. For most the occupational as well as the residential environment were entirely Jewish, including separate trade unions (at a time when there were numerous new unions), but the majority of economic relationships were with the outside world. The Jewish clothing workshops in Leeds were complementary to the 'English' factory section, supplementing the latter's output in the busy season (Buckman 1983). The East End clothing trade supplied goods for West End shops. There was certainly some competition between the immigrants and the native British, and many complaints were broadcast, including resolutions at the Trades Union Congress to halt immigration; but there were some Jewish niches. They made caps but not silk hats, for example. In general, their trades were not those which had been vacated by British workers. In some cases, such as the making of women's dresses, the immigrants were innovators, these garments having been imported previously.

The basis of Jewish success in business

The success of Jews in penetrating the business structure in Britain so effectively can be attributed to a combination of factors. First, Jews normally worked independently or in workshops, not in factories: this was not surprising in London, where large enterprises were few in number, but it was also the case in the provinces where factories were normal. In the small scale industries it was common for workers and employers to move between those positions. Given the large number of small units, the proportion of employers was higher than in those industries where the scale of production was greater. By and large, most of the industries they entered were expanding, and growing numbers of all manner of people worked in them.

But it was not only their concentration in certain sectors of the economy that facilitated their advancement. The immigrants, it is often said, possessed various characteristics which impelled them then, and later on, towards improvement. One of the first to essay an analysis was Beatrice Webb (then Potter), researching in the late 1880s for the Booth survey. She stated, as a fact, that the immigrants were 'placed in the midst of the very refuse of our civilization and yet . . . whether they become bootmakers, tailors, cabinet-makers, glaziers, or dealers, the Jewish inhabitants of East London rise in the social scale' (Booth 1902: 185). She suggested a number of reasons for this success, including a hint of Darwinism: 'the brutal persecution of the Middle Ages weeded out the inept and the incompetent' (*ibid.*: 192). Her evidence is impressionistic but it may have been valid in the more prosperous years of the late 1880s. If she had done her research a little later she might have needed to take into account the strikes of Jewish workers and the unemployment among them. However, the main, general point refers to the immigrants' intentions and motivations: to work hard, to save, to become a master. It is a description repeated and summarised for comparable New York immigrant Jews as, 'sobriety, temperance, frugality, willingness to defer gratification, and commitment to education' (Shapiro 1978: 216).

Such generalisations do not allow for the great variety within the East European group – the failures as well as the successes, the acceptance of fate rather than battles to overcome it. Beatrice Webb, it is true, referred to the Jews' propensity to gamble. But there is much to be said in favour of the analysis; this approach, as well as helping to explain Jewish social mobility in subsequent twentieth-century generations, usefully supplements and counterbalances the perhaps excessive nostalgia for the old immigrant areas and their way of life. However lively that history appears now, their inhabitants' aims were to ensure that their children did not work in the workshops, and to move away from those inner districts.

Such ambitions did not necessarily include an escape from the Jewish world. In general they maintained their religious culture, however modified, while acquiring a British one. The more overt East European parts were discarded. Thus Hebrew was taught in religious classes but

Yiddish, except in a few cases, was not. The children went to local schools and were quickly anglicised, acquiring the local accent. They used Yiddish for family conversation, but grandchildren knew it not. This rapid anglicisation was accompanied by one demographic effect of the immigration process: it was not uncommon for immigrant grooms to marry British-born wives (Prais and Schmool 1967: 157–8). To have a parent accustomed to British mores was a significant factor for it enabled their children 'to enter the general social milieu with comparative ease for first generation British' (Kosmin, Bauer and Grizzard 1976: 25).

Jewish business in the twentieth century

The consequences of all this for upward social mobility were delayed by the economic circumstances of the years between the wars, as the slump and unemployment prevented rapid changes. But the recovery in the 1930s was significant. It occurred mainly in the south of the country where most Jews lived. Standards of living rose and there were innovations in taste and new products. While the 'East Ends' of various cities still contained a large number of Jews until the Second World War, and a sizeable working class persisted, it was possible to take advantage of the improved opportunities. The number of independent shops grew and the Jewish ones among them were probably mainly in the traditional fields – food, clothing, furniture and jewellery for example. Others, though, went into newer activities like radio and consumer durables. Manufacturers too remained in the same industries which, despite some increase in unit size, still retained a majority of small workshops, as in clothing and furniture. Important areas of expansion often grew out of traditional economic activities: thus women's dresses for the growing mass market attracted not just the children of the East European immigrants but also German refugees of the 1930s.

In the inter-war period few of the East European group grew beyond family firms, to add to the larger scale immigrant enterprises which had been founded before 1914, such as Marks and Spencer's variety chain stores, or Montague Burton's clothing manufacturing and retailing chain (Emden 1944). One family, the Ostrers, primarily financiers, were important in the film and cinema business, their Gaumont-British (and other companies) forming one of the two major enterprises in the industry. Another large newcomer was the grocery firm of Tesco, which originated in street trading after the First World War. The few Jews who went into some of the newer industries like aircraft operation, motor-car manufacture or radio and electrical manufacture were not usually from the East European group. A somewhat unusual set of industries was set up by German refugees in the depressed areas, making products for the motor, steel and building industries among others.

Since the Second World War the picture has been one of a growing middle class community, upward social mobility being assisted by a quarter century of full employment. The handful of sociological studies of Anglo-Jewry of the period[2] indicates the pattern quite clearly, as do general knowledge and experience as well as the large number of studies of American Jewry, similarly descended from the East Europeans. To find a large middle class component is not unexpected in those surveys which were done in middle class districts, where indeed the proportion of Jews in social classes I and II was found to be higher than among the local population (Krausz 1969). However, in lower middle class and working class suburbs the proportion of Jews who were found to be self-employed (with or without employees) was high. In the London Borough of Redbridge in 1978, while almost two-thirds of the economically active Jews were employees, just over a third were self-employed or employers, five times the national average (Kosmin and Levy 1981). Even in lower status Hackney the proportion of Jews in self-employment or employers was 21 per cent (Kosmin and Grizzard 1975).

The findings of these local surveys are confirmed by a more comprehensive study relating to the position in 1961. As many as 38 per cent were in social classes I and II. This leaves 60 per cent in classes III and IV, but none in class V (a few were unclassified). These figures indicate the continuation of an employed class of some size but the proportion who were in the two top classes, many of them employers or self-employed, was more than double that of the national average which in 1961 amounted to 16 per cent (Prais and Schmool 1975).

The majority of enterprises remain on a small scale and, surprisingly, usually in the 'traditional' fields. Yet at the same time, and in conformity with general trends in industrial structure, there has been a growth of large scale enterprise, often through mergers. These big companies have gone beyond the traditional types of activity, as a consequence of acquisition. Thus Sir Charles Clore's interests encompassed shipbuilding and road transport. One particular new area, property development, is especially noteworthy. After the war Jews came to be disproportionately involved in this activity. The people attracted into it needed the skills of risk-taking rather than the expertise of the building industry; all manner of people therefore came into it (Aris 1970: 186–206).

Within this general field, since the Second World War, there have been many changes. One is the marked decline in independent retailing in addition to the normal coming and going in the small scale sector – the ever hopeful new entrants and the demises through death, retirement or the absence of an heir to take over the family business. The same applies to large scale enterprise. Firms founded by Jews, with a long or a short history, have disappeared through mergers. During the preparation of this paper Associated Communications Corporation, the television and entertainments company founded in the 1950s and run by Lord Grade, was taken over following financial difficulties. Even such an old firm as J. Lyons & Co. in the catering and food industry was absorbed by a non-Jewish firm. Ironically, in 1981, the second largest property company, MEPC, which had been founded by a Jew, was judged by a majority of an Industrial Tribunal to have unfairly dismissed a Jewish employee, its lawyer, 'because of his racial origins'.

Clearly with large scale enterprise we are in a different world. The logic of change suggests that eventually big companies become 'naturalised', like ICI or Unilever or Shell, all originally Jewish in part. Problems of succession are common to family firms in general: they are not a peculiarity of Jewish business; and the great majority of shares come to be held by outsiders.

A final point about the postwar world has been the expansion in the number of Jewish students at universities and other institutions of higher education. The total is unknown: in the 1970s the university Jewish societies recruited about 2,500 members but various unreliable guesses put the figure as high as 10,000 Jewish students. Medicine used to be the favourite profession ('My son the doctor') but nowadays the choice is wider. Lawyers are more common as well as engineers of various kinds, accountants, and lecturers. The survey of 1961 (now out of date because of the great growth of higher education in subsequent years) showed that 10 per cent of Jews were in the professions, just over twice the national average (Prais and Schmool 1975).

The effects of the economic problems of the late 1970s and early 1980s cannot yet be assessed. The decline of the clothing trade is one which must have greatly affected the picture. The recession may well drastically change the traditional story. It is too early to know if unemployment has altered the very interesting attitudes expressed during the survey of Redbridge Jewry in 1978, when local unemployment was very low. The respondents in that district, it was found, did not have high expectations for their children. A large majority of parents, in answer to the question 'What careers would you like your children to follow?' stated 'Whatever they want.' The authors of the survey commented: 'Redbridge Jews do not want to push their sons into industry and commerce . . . there appears to be a concern with the quality of life of their children' (Kosmin and Levy 1981: 34).

How widespread such views are is not known and it would be improper to use this study as a basis for generalisations, but changes are under way. Small business has been in decline, even if hopefuls are ever ready to try their hand, and the recent emphasis on the beauty of smallness may reinvigorate the sector. At any rate the openings may be less than in the past. Expansion, of course, entails bureaucratisation which, it is often said, does not attract Jews who are reputed to prefer independence. Given the larger number of Jews pursuing higher education we might expect a greater move to the independent professions.

If these trends were to continue and these possibilities to be realised, perhaps the historical move into business might decline. An analogy, a little far-fetched perhaps, might be made with the history of the Jewish labour movement in many countries of the Diaspora during and immediately after the period of the East European migration (and including too the countries of Eastern Europe). Nowadays the existence of Jewish trade unions and socialist and anarchist bodies as well as the electoral attachment of Jews to political parties to the left of centre – all this is seen as a historical eposide, specific to a set of conditions, relevant to a particular period. How far a comparable interpretation can be applied to Jewish business remains to be seen.

6

The rise of the Britalian culture entrepreneur

ROBIN PALMER

This account is based on anthropological fieldwork in London and Italy among those I have called the Britalians.[1] The scope of the inquiry was broad; the aim was to document as much as possible of the experience of this particular minority beyond the more intimate levels of domesticity and kinship, an area of investigation which was only excluded because Garigue and Firth's excellent study (1956) appeared to leave little to add. The field thus defined included the world of work and of occupations. Since, for approximately 3,000 of the breadwinners among the 250,000 Britalians in Britain, work means running private businesses, an important sub-field was the entrepreneurs (Marin 1975: 103).

In this chapter the business activities of a network of Britalians from one Central Italian parish (Palmer 1977; 1981) are seen against the background of the past forms of Britalian entrepreneurship encountered in an earlier attempt at Britalian historiography (Palmer 1972). Basic to the model that I developed to organise the historical and contemporary data is the concept of the *culture entrepreneur*.

Ethnic strategies in immigrant entrepreneurism

Following Barth (1963), following Belshaw (1955), the entrepreneur emerges as 'someone who takes the initiative in administering resources, and pursues an expansive economic policy' (Barth 1963: 5). In return for his independent efforts at management and innovation in business, the entrepreneur may expect either profits or the less welcome consequences of the risk-taking which is so much a part of entrepreneurship. Barth warns against regarding the entrepreneur as a whole person, or even as a whole status or role, conceding only that this is an *aspect of the role* played by one who, even in the occupational sphere, might only be entre-preneurial part of the time, and without official recognition.

89

But for all his subtleties of definition, and his subsequent manifest interest in ethnicity (Barth 1969), there is no suggestion in Barth's definition of the entrepreneur that the *emigrant* entrepreneur can, under certain conditions, steal a vital march on his fellow entrepreneurs, either in the society of origin or that of destination. His ethnicity, or culture – its distinctive products and orientation – may be employed as a vital part of his stock-in-trade: it represents, as far as his patrons are concerned, an innovation, a novelty; yet it is one the entrepreneur only has to transfer (from where it is common to where it is scarce), not invent. Since this kind of entrepreneur has always had its exemplars in the empirical world, it is appropriate that it should receive due recognition as a sub-type of entrepreneur, the *culture entrepreneur*.

Implicit in the above is the great limiting factor in culture entrepreneurship. If the culture entrepreneur is to be construed as an entrepreneur who, among his other business practices and innovations, brings goods and other less concrete items (such as *style*) from where they are commonplace to where they are scarce, then it is necessary that the items be scarce in both senses of the word. That is, they must be of *value* to the consumer as well as merely scarce in numerical terms. An item's value is a function of its association with a particular culture, frequently a particular artist, craftsman or manufacturer of that culture. The Cellini centrepiece, for example, is worth more than its weight in gold, and that surplus value is a function, in part, of the item being in a *particular* tradition launched by the unique Italian Renaissance.

In large scale culture entrepreneurship, involving the international transfer of items such as fine art, *objets d'art*, designer furnishings and clothing, cars, folk arts and crafts and suchlike, nationals of many countries, and specialist dealers in the products of specific cultural traditions, conduct a lucrative trade in the modern period as in all the ages of civilisation.

But in confronting the *Britalian* culture entrepreneurs one finds that the type is not exhausted by the entrepreneurs and representatives of large firms who are engaged in large scale trade between Italy and Great Britain: that is, people of a relatively high level of education, training and general sophistication, drawn from the Italian middle and upper classes, who are not likely to have settled in Britain, but are merely based there, temporarily. The great majority of Britalian culture entrepreneurs are true immigrants, settlers more than sojourners, workers and 'self-made men' with the lower class, usually rural, origins of most Italian migrants. As with most migrant entrepreneurs of this kind of background, they have used ethnicity in the launching, sustaining and expanding of their business enterprises. This is a strategy so rational and obvious to the actors that it is almost a reflex. Latterly, its advantages have become apparent to those economists, historians, sociologists and anthropologists who have increasingly interested themselves in 'the ethnic factor'. In the economic sphere it is frequently of greater explanatory value than the more obvious, and therefore most often cited, factors of prejudice and discrimination. Take, for instance, the fundamental issue of starting capital.

> Some have argued that the very different 'representation' of various ethnic groups among business owners or managers reflects differing availabilities of capital needed to start a business, due to discrimination by banks. In fact, however, owner-operated businesses are seldom started with bank loans, regardless of the race or ethnicity of the businessman. The crucial information needed for assessing the prospects of an owner-operated business is information about the kind of person he is, and this information is much more readily available to the businessman's family and friends than to a bank . . . Accordingly, we find that most small businesses begin with capital supplied by the individual businessman and those closest to him.
>
> (Sowell 1981: 63)

Since those closest to an immigrant would-be entrepreneur are almost invariably his co-nationals or co-ethnics as well, there is intra-ethnic dependency from the inception. At the same stage or later, and in response to similar imperatives, the entrepreneur turns to his family and friends for the staffing of his enterprise, and for wholesalers if he is a retailer and retailers if he is a wholesaler – trust and mutual obligation are equally important in these areas.

There is another way in which immigrant entrepreneurship and ethnicity have supported each other in the United States which has received a disproportionate amount of attention in the literature, to say nothing of the mass media. Hannerz (1974) has analysed the situation most succinctly. It concerns the criminal entrepreneurs of mainly Sicilian origin who rose to prominence with the Prohibition in the 1920s, and became known collectively as Cosa Nostra (also, erroneously, as the Mafia). According to Hannerz, their Italian ethnicity had important advantages for these transplanted *mafiosi*. In the first place, the Italian-American criminal entrepreneur had access to extra-territorial resources in Italy: he could draw on an Italian-based network for assistance with the narcotics trade, for shelter when a fugitive and for recruits to the American network. Secondly, ethnicity provided the Italian-American criminal entrepreneur with a basis for cohesion, a unique idiom:

traditional Sicilian kinship, fictive kinship and cultural codes such as local definitions of honour and manliness (see Blok 1974; Schneider and Schneider 1976) were employed to great effect in the integration and articulation of the 'families' of America. Thirdly, the criminal entrepreneurs were able to exploit the hermetic nature of the American 'little Italies' in whose working class neighbourhoods the *mafiosi* were respected by many for their material success: in these urban ethnic enclaves they found support, cover and recruits from their youthful admirers (Hannerz 1974: 51–2).

There is no shortage of examples in the literature of migrant entrepreneurs of the 'self-made' variety advancing their careers through the manipulation of ethnicity and extra-territorial networks, whether criminal or legitimate (see e.g. Whyte 1955; Price 1963; Ianni and Reuss-Ianni 1972; Watson 1975). The tendency, however, has been to document the phenomenon in countries which have been the recipients of the greatest numbers of immigrants, and to specialise in the best-represented nationalities – hence the strong interest in the Italian-Americans. But the entrepreneurs who have emerged following mass immigrations have a characteristic which is *sui generis*: among business operations of smaller and medium size it has not been necessary to go beyond the ethnic market, since it is so massive. 'Trading with the natives' has been an option many immigrants have exercised, especially the more expansionist among them, yet in the New World and in Australasia it has never been required in the way that it has been for the smaller Britalian community in Britain.

Among the Britalians the ethnic factor has supplied starting capital, staffing, commodities and business connections, as well as 'Italianness', the Britalian entrepreneur's most important stock-in-trade, but by and large his co-nationals have not been his market – he has had to essay the difficult course of persuading Britons to 'buy Italian'. In short, for six centuries, he has had to practice culture entrepreneurship as a *marketing strategy*. That is, whether he had business premises or not, whether he had a licence or not, whether or not he or his patrons regarded his role as entrepreneurial, a disproportionate number of Britalians have found themselves, over the centuries, giving prominence to their culture in the hope or expectation that they will derive profit or advancement thereby.

Why should formal or informal entrepreneurism of this kind have so characterised the Britalians? One consideration – the relative absence of co-national consumers – has already been taken into account. But there are other, unique, historical considerations which must also be taken into account.

Historical incentives for Britalian culture entrepreneurism

The principal determining incentives are two-fold. One of them is more of a constraint than an incentive – a negative incentive – but it has been as important in determining the occupations of the Britalians as the other. This is the 'exclusionist spirit' noted by Foerster (1919: 206) for British labour. More than any other nationality the British worker has sought to maintain in native hands, and in those of the Irish, working class jobs which have been filled by immigrants in other countries – jobs in agriculture, mining, construction and manufacturing. The only area of the economy to which protectionism has not been extended at some time or other has been the tertiary sector, and the expansion of the tertiary sector in Britain is a relatively recent phenomenon. Thus, while Britain's relative proximity to Italy has made it a 'natural' focus for Italian emigration over the centuries, restricted opportunities channelled the emigrants into specific areas of the economy and occupations which were quite different from those they filled in other European countries and overseas. Whereas, elsewhere, Italians were the archetypal labour migrants, in Britain, until the 1950s when postwar reconstruction necessitated the relaxation of the TUC's restrictive policy, the Britalians either dealt in skills and commodities unavailable locally, or entered service occupations. Either way, a proportion found it expedient to give prominence to their ethnicity, the opposite of the strategy recommended to labour migrants.

This is where the other incentive comes in. It is the essential precondition for culture entrepreneurism – the historical precedent. In general, until the 'ethnic look' in clothes and decor became fashionable among younger elements of the bourgeoisie in the affluent countries of the West, it was difficult if not impossible for the immigrant from a less developed country or region to interest the populace of a more developed country or region in the less sophisticated artifacts or cuisine he purveyed. But in the case of the Britalian, no matter what his circumstances had been in Italy, he was an 'Italian', and many Britons, especially moneyed Britons, had expectations of 'Italians' which were frequently naive but usually high – at least in the artistic, musical and culinary fields. In circumstances of constrained employment opportunities it made culture entrepreneurism a viable alternative or adjunct. How did this unique favourable climate originate?

The positive incentive existed long before the negative one, and was centuries in the making. It was inculcated over that extremely long period in history, from 55 BC until the Reformation, when the British were in many ways the dependants of the successive and various powers that came into existence in the Italic Peninsula. Finding themselves by turns under the political and military domination of the Romans, the religious domination of the Vatican, and the economic domination of the Genoese, Venetians, Lombards and Tuscans, the response of the Britons was to be drawn inexorably into the cultural ambit of the ascendant Latins. Shakespeare made Richard II express a widespread Elizabethan sentiment when he declared:

> . . . proud Italy
> Whose manners still our tardy apish nation
> Limps after, in base imitation.   (in Marin 1975: 18)

The cultural dependency of the British on the Italians did not end with the loss of the 'Lombard' bankers' privileged position at court and the displacement of the Britalian wool merchants in the fifteenth century. A hundred years after the decline of Italian political and economic influence, the official diplomatic language at the court of Elizabeth I was Italian, and Shakespeare's palpable Italophilia was receiving endorsement from his contemporaries as it has ever since. That Italian culture in a variety of fields should have been an important reference point for the British elite in the Elizabethan period, tending to become more important in the centuries that followed, testifies to the effectiveness of 1,500 years of groundwork under the Romans, the Vatican, and the mercantilists. But while the accession of Elizabeth marked the beginning of the expansion of the British political economy, the same period in Italy harkened in centuries of chaos and foreign despotism which was only partially resolved by the Risorgimento. Yet despite the total role-reversal in terms of power, Italian culture has continued to influence and inspire the British, whether in its most sublime or more mundane manifestations, from Dante and Palladio to Mario and Franco. This is the precondition on which Britalian cultural entrepreneurism depended.

The first Britalian culture entrepreneurs

Foreign domination and economic failure in a partitioned Italy impelled Italians from all walks of life to emigrate, and communications were such that until the mid nineteenth century the British Isles were the furthest most migrants would venture. Until the Aliens Act restricted their entry in 1905, they came in steadily mounting numbers, mainly to London, but the more proximate countries – France, Switzerland, Germany and Austria – must have taken more of the earliest migrants. (Certainly, their share has been much greater throughout the modern period.) Once pioneer migrants had made a thorough reconnaissance of what Britain had to offer Italian immigrants, the word began to be passed back along the migration 'chain', and kin and *paesani* (fellow townsmen) began to make the long walk too (see Palmer 1977; on chain migration see Price 1963; 1969: 210).

From the fourteenth to the eighteenth centuries the migrants were more frequently well-educated or highly skilled *maestri* in the best tradition of Italian 'high' culture, including the advanced technology (for its time) of the Italians. Marin (1975) has described in detail the characteristics of these professionals, or 'elite migrants' as he describes them – the scholarly humanists and *literati*, the artists and sculptors, the architects and engineers and masons, the craftsmen in mosaic and terrazzo, the musicians and opera-singers, the merchants. Subsequently, in the nineteenth century, Victorian enthusiasm for the Italian Renaissance and for elaborate decoration in its neo-gothic architecture meant 'elite migrants' had scope and patronage as never before.

Whether or where the elite migrants settled – if they settled at all – depended on their terms of reference and status. The scholars, artists and musicians seem to have had a very close relationship with their upper class English patrons, frequently becoming part of their households for the duration of their appointments. The architects, engineers and masons stayed as close to the site as they could. Scholars and musicians, who were academics more than tutors, became part of the English universities from the earliest days of Oxford and Cambridge (Marin 1975: chs. 1 and 2). But the lowlier craftsmen, who were also the longest sojourners, even settlers, had congregated in Clerkenwell and Holborn (which lie between the City and the West End of London) since the eighteenth century. These were the clock and instrument makers, the *gesso* modellers, the carvers and gilders, the importers, wholesalers and retailers who dealt in Italian produce, and the proprietors of bars and cafes which catered to the growing Britalian population of the area.

Into this already populated and growing niche (in every sense of the concept), the Italian rural proletariat immigrated in increasing numbers for the first time between 1850 and 1905. There was no employment for them other than occupations in the service sector (which only began to be important after mid-century), but their entry was not controlled until after 1905, so, in their optimism and desperation, they came, swelling what is now known as the 'informal sector', after the manner of present-day migrants to the cities of the Third World (see Hart 1973). Those who were not attracted by domestic service or hotel and restaurant work, could find employment in asphalting and ice-hauling, which the British and Irish eschewed.

By 1893 there were at least 2,500 Britalians informally occupied in a kaleidoscope of street trades in London. From specialised barrows they fashioned crude thermometers before the eyes of passers-by, or sharpened cutlery, or sold ice-cream or hot chestnuts. Others displayed exotic animals or mechanical novelties, or entertained with several kinds of musical instruments, including the mechanical barrel-organ. Still others hawked *gesso* statuettes, or swept chimneys. Most of the itinerants had juvenile helpers, whom they hired from their parents in Italy for a few ducats a year. This practice later offended the growing liberalism in Britain and was one of the motivations for control of Aliens, especially the itinerants, in the latter part of the nineteenth century (see Farley 1972).

None of the itinerants' trades required any formal training, and so they were open to illiterates and semi-literates who had formerly herded sheep and goats or tilled the soil. But some of these independent pursuits required relatively large amounts of capital. Exotic animals, mechanical novelties, barrel-organs and those barrows equipped for knife-grinding or thermometer making, to say nothing of stock-in-trade, did not come cheaply. Farley records an 'exhibitor of mechanical figures' from Parma who had, from his former income of three shillings a day, accumulated the £35 necessary to purchase his set of mechanical figures. Employing these novelties he managed immediately to double his income and employ two assistants (1972: 24–5). (Lodgings in Clerkenwell were about a shilling a week at this time.)

Clearly, what is being described is a primitive form of entrepreneurship. But the itinerants were also culture entrepreneurs, not so much because the character of their business was always strictly and literally Italian, like the tradition in which the elite migrants had largely worked, but because there were so many of them, and they were so conspicuous, that to the British public 'Italian' became that which the itinerants trafficked in, as much as the characteristic cultural forms of the Italian great tradition. By 1893 there were in excess of 2,500 itinerants, and there were still under 10,000 Italian-born in Britain (Foerster 1919: 204).

That the itinerants were culture entrepreneurs is more obvious at this time than the catering workers (especially the waiters). The itinerants were self-employed, and frequently had their own staff, even if these were only children. In order to make a living in a sector where there has never been fiercer competition, before or since, they had to innovate and use their ethnicity as part of their stock-in-trade; they bore risks, but sometimes extracted small profits; some of them, most notably the knife-grinders and the ice-cream sellers, were able to acquire fixed premises and join the formal private sector, sending work permits to their relatives and friends in Italy after 1905 and subsequently.

Yet the catering workers who were in a position to use their ethnicity in their own interest (as opposed to having it used against them by their employers and fellow workers, which is the usual experience of immigrants) also became culture entrepreneurs, albeit in the sense that culture entrepreneurship was merely an *aspect* of their occupational role.

By 1901, after a period of heavy immigration from Italy, there were 1,317 restaurant waiters, 547 hotel waiters and 543 cooks born in Italy, according to the British census. Italian sources have estimated that there were altogether 5,000 Britalians in catering at that time (Marin 1975: 59). For the cooks and kitchen porters, who did not deal with the public but rather with the chef whose ethnic stereotype was inescapably French, there was almost no scope for the part-time entrepreneur. But among the waiters it was another situation entirely. Up to now the role of waiter had not been made the prerogative of any particular nationality. Furthermore, the waiter dealt directly with the public, and so there was more scope than in the behind-the-scenes roles to manipulate a positive stereotype in which 'waiter' and 'Italian' became inseparable; an ethnic hegemony in this occupation thus became possible.

The fusion took no more than fifty years to achieve. Before the First World War the phrase Sir George Smith, first chairman of the prestigious Savoy Hotel Group, had coined ('Dans la salle les Italiens, dans la cuisine le Français') became a kind of maxim. How did the Britalian waiters acquire such a privileged position in this occupation?

In his autobiography, Peppino Leoni, who began as a waiter in London in the early years of the century, opines that, as a result of their collective experience of feudalism and post-feudalism in an only recently centralised Italy, 'they had learned to be servile without loss of pride, to be humble without fawning, and they applied this knowledge to their work' (1966: 83) – in short, they had been moulded by culture and history for this particular task, and their elevation was merely the consequence of the growing recognition of innate and unconscious qualifications.

There may be something in this, but I would add that, like Leoni himself, many of the recruits to this particular role in British catering nurtured ambitions for an independent, entrepreneurial future, and they sought to maximise earnings and tips. The recruits tended to come from small rural communities in North and Central Italy, where the populace supports itself less on labouring, for a wage, than on petty proprietorship, or rented land, or *mezzadria* (sharecropping), or combinations of the three. Only the poorest 'work under others' in the direct sense. The majority work for themselves, or as part of what has to be seen as the rural counterpart of the urban small family business – the peasant farm. Against this background, it is understandable that the Britalian waiter does not always wish to be a waiter all his life, and is impatient to accumulate the experience and capital needed to open 'a place of his own'. So if the Britalians appeared to be more eager to please and to work extra shifts, it was often because waiting was construed as the means to a much more valued end, in terms of the value system they had brought with them. The process by which the Britalians were endowed with 'natural' qualities to account for their relatively better performance in their field was something they tended to encourage, by playing up to the stereotype, because any preferment they were given as a result hastened the day when they could make the transition from partial culture entrepreneurs to full-time culture entrepreneurs, as proprietors of their own restaurants.

The rise of the self-made culture entrepreneur

Leoni eventually became a 'self-made man'. He was also a culture entrepreneur. From his autobiography, he appears to have been very conscious of his ethnicity, its drawbacks and its advantages, and to have used it, in an occupation where it was already an advantage, to prepare himself for independent entrepreneurship. Thus, in 1926, at the age of 31, with 17 years accumulated experience in restaurants and hotels and £800 in savings, he opened a small restaurant in Soho with seven tables. His aim was to make Italian cuisine as 'snob' as French cuisine, and after 40 years as a restaurateur in expanding premises in the same street, he and his Quo Vadis (for that is what he called his restaurant) had become institutions. His competitors, Oddenino's and Gennaro's, together with his Quo Vadis, were all *ristoranti* in the grand style, catering to the same sorts of Britons who also dined at the Savoy and the best French restaurants. It was a considerable achievement, but it was not within the reach of every peasant son who emigrated to London with dreams of eventual independence. Even for Leoni, a man of exceptional motivation and energy, real success only came when he was well into his fifties, and at considerable cost to his health.

A self-made culture entrepreneur is one who, like Leoni, acquires all his skills, experience and capital after emigrating, from scratch, and invests them in an enterprise with 'Italian' characteristics, which he proceeds to expand. The son or daughter of an immigrant, born in Britain, or educated and socialised in Britain, may also be regarded as a self-made culture entrepreneur if he or she makes an entrepreneurial career independent from that of the parents. By Leoni's time there were many exemplars of both kinds of self-made culture entrepreneurship, as well as those who were continuing in a tradition, making small innovations when and where these were appropriate. In this manner the ice-cream trade and the cutlery business, with their itinerant roots, persisted, the former especially enjoying a great expansion between the wars, when there was, as yet, no competition from any large British firms. Firms with less proletarian origin, but strong Britalian identities, also continued (and continue). Negretti and Zambra, Annello and Davide and Gamba were all originally founded by Clerkenwell craftsmen who made instruments and ballet-shoes, respectively. The most popular form of Britalian enterprise, however, both with the relatively unskilled, undercapitalised immigrants and with the British public, was the small retail establishment which offered cold and hot drinks, ice-cream, snacks and meals in various combinations and in every kind of locale, all over the British Isles. Some were patently 'Italian'; in others the policy of the proprietor was the antithesis of the culture entrepreneurial. These latter are discussed later; for the present we are concerned with entrepreneurial forms in which ethnicity or culture were 'active ingredients'.

Before the war Britalian firms of all kinds flourished, and the entire ethnic group took on an entrepreneurial aspect. This was partly because those who had immigrated before 1905 had achieved their goals, in many cases, and there had been very little immigration since 1905 to provide examples of occupations typical of earlier stages of settlement; and partly it was because Mussolini's representatives in Britain were spending millions of lire on the advancement of Britalians who conformed to the corporativist ideal, namely the emergent entrepreneurial and professional middle class. 'Italians living abroad were wheedled at great cost to the exchequer into becoming [Mussolini's] most blatantly enthusiastic fans and propagandists' (Smith 1959: 399). The amount of attention and investment directed towards the emigrants abroad had more to do with the strategic location and capacity for rapid transformation of the collectivities than their size. The London collectivity, already corporate and 'embourgeoised' to a remarkable degree, and sited in the capital of the power Mussolini most needed to win over if his foreign policy was to succeed, benefited per capita more than any other. The charismatic 'first hour' Fascist, Dino Grandi, was sent as Ambassador to work the transformation. Strategies included Christmas parcels and free seaside holidays for every Britalian child, the first Italian school in London since Mazzini's in the previous century, and a large and lavish social and cultural centre, the Casa Fascio, which was also the headquarters of an umbrella organisation, the Circolo Cooperative, whose scope was to coordinate and develop extant professional and voluntary associations. Small wonder that most Britalians were won over to Fascism.

Nemesis followed swiftly, however, and the entrepreneurs along with all other Italian-born Britalians between 16 and 70 were interned for the duration following Mussolini's declaration of war in 1940. It was a great trauma, and for the first time since the Roman Conquest Britons and Britalians found themselves on opposite sides. But there was no question of repatriation after 1945, especially for the entrepreneurs. Italy was in ruins, and all their assets were in Britain. As soon as these were released by the Custodian of Enemy Property, the task of reconstruction during a period of rationing ensued.

Any strong assertion of Italian culture was liable to be misconstrued at this time, and so for the first decade after the war the tendency was to keep a very low profile, in business as in private life (see Garigue and Firth 1956: 69). Surnames and the names of businesses were changed or modified. The long-standing basis of culture entrepreneurship had been severely undermined. But this did not mean that ice-cream, the milk-bar or particular kinds of small cafe-restaurant were still the targets of native anger. And of course the more sophisticated Quo Vadis with its upper class clientele went on as before. Culture entrepreneurship was not dead, merely waiting for a new generation of patrons, and the 'coming of age' of the new immigration – the young men and women who in the postwar period expanded the Britalian minority from about 30,000 before the war to 250,000 in the early 1970s.

The new impetus to the Britalian culture entrepreneur in the postwar period began modestly enough. During the period of rationing, when eating out was an infrequent experience, marred by the shortages and austerity for both patron and restaurateur, the milk-bars and coffee-bars began to take on a new significance, especially among the young. You could pass a whole morning, afternoon or evening there, and spend no more than a few shillings. If the war had alienated you from your elders, and for the first time there was the possibility of financial independence from them, you needed somewhere to meet that was your own. The beginnings of the youth revolution and the milk-/coffee-bar converged as the period of austerity gave way to the boom. In order to make these venues as attractive as possible, the Britalians invented an idiom that was unmistakably modern, yet Italian as well, drawing their inspiration from the all-purpose urban Italian bar, except that in Britain they would never be allowed to serve liquor. But the laminates, spindly wire-legged bar stools and chairs, *terrazzo* floors, hissing *espresso* machine with its glass cups on top, and travel posters on the walls captured something of the atmosphere, and it was 'foreign' enough to appeal to the young.

The wives of the Britalian proprietors of these places claim it was they who upgraded the snacks that were also sold to full meals in the Italian lower class tradition: the *pizza*, and the numerous variations on *pasta*. They tried out the kind of food they made for their own families on the young people who seemed to stay and stay, consuming nothing more than endless *cappuccinos* and cigarettes. This innovation went with the rest, and received instant acceptance. Some of the coffee-bars expanded, opening kitchens and dining areas, but always the accent was on the food that appealed to young Britons, including *pizza* and *pasta*.

Towards the end of the 1950s (they say the Trattoria Toscana which opened in Soho in 1957 was the first) the dining component of the coffee-bars came to be recognised for what it was, an evocation of the Italian *trattoria* (the Italian equivalent of the French *bistro*), and was tried out on the evening trade divorced from the coffee-bar component. But the *trattorie* did not compete with the full-blown *ristoranti*, such as Leoni's Quo Vadis, any more than the *pensione* competes with the grand hotel. It remained an unpretentious eating-place, catering to the young, now a little older and capable of affording a full meal with a carafe of wine. The ambience typically consisted of plain white or check gingham napery, a trellis draped with plastic vines and empty *chianti* bottles, and murals of characteristic Italian scenes. At the time the *trattorie* represented something new and 'different' yet affordable to the 'salariat', an equally new and *arriviste* element in the bourgeoisie. Raban has suggested that since this class had no direct role in *production*, yet was acquiring great economic power as the boom took Britain into the post-industrial phase, it could only identify itself in terms of its power to *consume* – to consume conspicuously. With the spread of affluence the salariat was structurally prone to inherit the tendencies, at a lower level and on a smaller scale, of Veblen's original upper class conspicuous consumers (Raban 1974; Veblen 1934).

The self-effacing *trattoria* idiom in its 1950s form could not satisfy the salariat for long, however. The nascent architects and supporters of the 'swinging sixties' phenomenon required something more sophisticated of the Britalian culture entrepreneur, just as they called for constant innovation and reinterpretation on the part of other stylistic entrepreneurs at this time.

Two aspirant restaurateurs who did not have the means, at the time, to found a full-blown *ristorante* were Mario Cassandro and Francesco Lagattola. They had both been waiters at a number of top hotels, restaurants and clubs, but they were also accomplished amateur chefs, and both were interested in Italian provincial cuisine. When they had enough saved for a *trattoria* of their own, they took one in Soho, as close to the theatres as possible, and hoped a reputation for first-class Italian food would attract the patrons they had come to know personally at their former places of employment, as well as the passing trade. It was a formula that had been repeated over and over in the history of the Britalians. But Mario and Franco's career was to turn out somewhat differently.

Enzo Apicella emigrated to Britain in the latter 1950s when the newspaper he was working on in Naples went into liquidation. He managed to find a job in the advertising department of Schweppes, since he was an accomplished designer as well as a journalist, and not much English is needed to design. Subsequently he moved to the BBC. An engaging eccentric, who submitted (successfully) cartoons to Punch and other leading magazines, he soon acquired a wide circle of friends and acquaintances – 'personalities' and 'celebrities' whom the salariat looked up to and tried to emulate. A middle class emigrant, well-educated and highly skilled in a field that has long been associated with Italians, Apicella was the modern equivalent of the old 'elite migrants' who were also culture entrepreneurs.

It was coincidence that Apicella met Mario and Franco. He was recommended to the Trattoria Terrazza. He was not disappointed in the food – on the contrary, he became a regular patron. But he found the decor hackneyed and depressing. One evening he brought designs he had prepared of how the restaurant could be transformed. Nothing Apicella ever did was unoriginal, and the proposed renovations were revolutionary in concept. They included rough-cast stucco for the outside; enlarged, arched windows; hand-made ceramic tiles on the floors and set into the walls; hand-woven napery in warm colours; rush-seated carved and painted chairs; plenty of indoor plants and spotlights. The design was an amalgam of visual clues betokening individuality, sophistication, escapism and 'taste'. Although Mario and Franco could not afford the transformation at the time, Apicella convinced them that it was essential, and he was vindicated. The Trattoria Terrazza became the 'in' place for a generation which invented 'in', and the first of a chain of fourteen restaurants and clubs which became a public company and made Mario and Franco and Apicella millionaires. (So many Britalian culture entrepreneurs sought to emulate the originals that Apicella went on to design 40 other restaurants.)

This phenomenon of the 'trat' undoubtedly gave a stimulus to ethnic Britalian entrepreneurship in London and in the provinces, sparking off a minor revolution in catering. Many of the imitations were vulgar and the food they served execrable, but the point had been made, and the fashion took a long time to run its course, involving a great many patrons who did not know the difference between the imitation and the 'real thing'. Just when it became necessary to innovate again, and find some form that went beyond, behind or beneath the 'trat', the British recession began to bite, and with the better organised catering unions of Italy having improved conditions in that part of the tertiary sector to the extent that potential Britalian waiters (and hence entrepreneurs) came to Britain in sharply reduced numbers, Britalians repatriated themselves. It is quite possible that the 1970s saw the end of the proletarian and self-made forms of Britalian culture entrepreneurship in the British Isles.

Culture-suppressed entrepreneurs

When I came to examine Britalian occupations in microcosm by survey-ing the 184 households of the Abbazzini in London (a section of the 'dia-spora' of Abbazzia, a parish in the Emilian Apennines), I found people in all kinds of employment and entrepreneurs of the kind discussed in this paper; but there were also entrepreneurs who denied their ethnicity for business purposes. These were 'culture-suppressed' entrepreneurs. They ran anonymous-looking cafes, restaurants and snack-bars in various parts of London. If some prospered and others did not, this could be accounted for in terms of such universalistic criteria as siting and management, for there was no discernible difference between these establishments and similar ones run by other nationals and the British. More importantly, the culture-suppressed establishments, taken as a whole, compared very favourably as profitable concerns with the establishments which were unmistakably Italian in terms of decor, menu, and even the conduct of the staff.

There is another detailed, published autobiography of a Britalian entrepreneur, that of C. Cavalli (1972). He was born the year after Leoni (1894), and he also entered the restaurant trade after a spell as a waiter. At one time he had four cafe-restaurants to his name. In his private life he was a fervent patriot and did much for his local Britalian community in Southwark. Whereas Leoni's book is published in English by an English publisher, Cavalli's is published in Italian, by *La Voce degli Italiani*, the Britalians' newspaper. Yet Cavalli's business practice from the outset was to aim for the British working class market and serve them nothing that was not in the native lower class culinary tradition (except, presumably, ice-cream). He even employed British waiters and waitresses. Cavalli lost his enthusiasm for expansion after the war: his other interests came to take precedence. But he could have continued to exploit this end of the market as the Abbazzini have done in the more recent period.

Another case: in 1913 a boy of five emigrated to Britain from a rural district near Rome, and spent the remainder of his youth in Scotland, where his father and other relatives were in the cafe-trade. When he was 26, he struck out on his own and moved to London. By 1945 he had nine milk bars to his name and he had been interned. Up to this stage it is a familiar case history, conforming to the culture entrepreneur model. But subsequently this man began acquiring hotels and important sites in London. By 1962 he was in a position to 'go public', offering shares in his company on the Stock Market, a stage very few Britalians ever reach. In 1970 his company took over Trust Houses, Britain's largest hotel group. The group is now one of the world's greatest multi-nationals in the catering field. The entrepreneur is, of course, Sir Charles Forte, the greatest tycoon the Britalians have ever produced. His private life is very Italian indeed, and he has worked tirelessly for the London collectivity from the beginning, resuscitating the historic Mazzini-Garibaldi Club after the war, and chairing the Italian Chamber of Commerce for years. But his business practice has emphasised universalistic values, and the comparison is thus more with Carnegie, Morgan, Hearst, Clore, Getty and the other great capitalists of history than with, for example, Mario and Franco (see Davis 1978).

From these examples of culture-suppression – at least in the business sphere – it appears that the strategy I have defined as culture entrepreneurship is not a *necessary* strategy of the Britalians. Even in circumstances that positively *invite* culture entrepreneurship on a full-time or partial basis, such as the historical Italophilia of a section of a society formerly dominated by Italian culture, universalistic entrepreneurship may be as effective as the strategies I have identified in this paper. On the other hand, through the subtle and not-so-subtle manipulation of their ethnicity over six centuries, immigrants from Italy have been able to create opportunities for themselves and a niche for their successors where none would have otherwise existed.

7

Choice, chance or no alternative? Turkish Cypriots in business in London

SARAH LADBURY

The decision of the European Parliament to make 1982 the 'Year of Crafts and Small and Medium Enterprises' (*Guardian*, 8 January 1982: 15) is significant in the European and the British context. As Scase and Goffee note, small businesses[1] in Britain were neglected throughout the 1960s and 1970s, when the concern of both Conservative and Labour governments was to bolster large scale production units in the belief that it was only these which could utilise, and therefore derive maximum benefit from, new technological systems (1980: 13). It took, not surprisingly perhaps, a Conservative government – elected in 1979 under the leadership of Mrs Thatcher – to acknowledge that this policy was a failure and to announce the only alternative in the Tory repertoire: a return to the practice and ethics of classical capitalism. This involved, among other things, a restatement of the old Tory contention that the economic future of the country lay with individual initiative and enterprise. 'The aim must be to change the atmosphere and environment for the business community, to create anew conditions in which men and women of independent spirit will see it as worth their while to use their skill and enthusiasm to start or expand profitable enterprises'(Conservative Central Office 1977: 3). Thus, well before the official unemployment figure in Britain passed the three million mark (January 1982), as Boissevain discusses in chapter 2, the 'small is beautiful' notion had been revived. Even though there was no evidence to suggest that increased activity in the small business sector could reduce unemployment, the government maintained 'If they [small businesses] were encouraged to do so they could become the main source for new jobs' (*ibid.*). In stark contrast to this romantic ideology, the most recent research at that time indicated that the opposite was in fact true.[2]

The revival of the small business ethic by the government cannot therefore be explained solely in economic terms. Initial moves to implement a Small Business Policy in 1980 and 1981 suggest that the government's real concerns were not small business *per se*, but those on the economic periphery – blacks, for example, and those recently made redundant as a result of massive plant closures in the manufacturing industry. The publicity given to the increased availability of financial loans and advice to these and other groups suggested that the main objective of the government's Small Business Policy was to win over those most likely to feel disaffected with, and directly impoverished by, Tory economic policy – a political rather than an economic concern on the part of the government.

That the small business sector should be seized on by a government in a period of escalating unemployment, and put forward as an escape route into work for the unemployed, is a strategy which is not unique to the Tories, or to the present. But the small businessman or woman is worthy of attention by the Tory Party for another reason: he or she, conceived as a hard-working, individualistic entrepreneur, whose aim is to succeed without state assistance, embodies the spirit of Conservative dogma and, it follows, of Western capitalism. Given this natural association between small business and Tory ideology (practice is somewhat different), it is initially surprising that the Conservatives, like Labour, have not tried in the past to understand or respond adequately to the needs of small business people. Presumably, one of the reasons is that those who work in small businesses as owners and employees have no representative voice; their level of unionisation is low and their cause is never championed. Ironically, it is this very silence which, in 1980, made it possible for the government to revive the 'small is beautiful' ethic. If owners and, more significantly, employees in small businesses were able to speak, would they endorse this idealised, romantic government view? Would settled immigrant populations – our focus in this volume – go along with it?

The immigrant's actual experience of small business is certainly different from the government's visionary conception of the same. For most people, and for immigrants in particular, 'small business' does not mean making leather belts in Cornwall, or overseeing an art gallery in Hampstead. It means working in a small factory or at home for long hours, with no job security and low or variable wages. Most immigrants in the small business sector probably took jobs there because that was all they could get. There was no question of choosing this sector in preference to better paid white collar or manual jobs in the open labour market. It is very important in discussing ethnic minority involvement in small business to be aware of these conflicting visions of what small business is about. In this chapter, as in the rest of the volume, the concern is with the unglamorised vision – the reality which immigrants actually experience.

My focus is on one particular ethnic group: Turkish Cypriots. In the pages that follow, I shall first discuss Cypriot, and particularly Turkish Cypriot, employment patterns in London. The questions with which the remainder of the paper are concerned arise naturally out of this initial discussion. The political implications of the government's concern with small businesses are returned to at the end of the paper, where they are discussed in the light of the immigrant experience in general, and the Turkish Cypriot experience in particular.

Turkish Cypriot settlement patterns and economic activity

It was not until 1955 that Turkish Cypriots began migrating to Britain in any number. By that time, a small Greek Cypriot community was already established here (Oakley 1971: 241ff).[3] From 1955 until the 1962 Immigration Act came into force, approximately 12,000 Turkish Cypriots migrated to Britain, the majority arriving in 1960 and 1961. They were outnumbered by their Greek Cypriot counterparts by about 5:1 at that time, though proportionately more Turks settled in London than Greeks. Indeed, except for a few Turks who settled in the Home Counties, Birmingham and Manchester, the Turkish Cypriot population was almost exclusively London-based, and it has continued to be so. The ratio of Greek to Turkish Cypriots in London today is probably in the region of 3:1. Approximately between fifty and sixty thousand Turkish Cypriots now live in the United Kingdom according to the Turkish Consulate (personal communication).

Within London itself, Turkish Cypriot settlement is quite dispersed. On the basis of the 1971 Census and more recent statistics which give an indication of changes in Cypriot settlement patterns,[4] it seems that the areas of most concentrated Turkish Cypriot settlement in North London are Haringey, Newington Green and Stoke Newington, and in South London, Elephant and Castle, New Cross and Peckham. Turkish and Greek settlement overlaps, though the Greeks have tended to settle to the west of the Turkish zones in the North London boroughs. Although Haringey was the borough with the greatest number of Cypriots in 1971, there were already indications that both Greeks and Turks were gradually moving northwards, out of Inner London to the more residential areas of Enfield and Barnet.

As other contributors to this volume stress (see, for example, chapter 11 on Asian retailing in England) settlement patterns are significant in accounting for the concentration of ethnic businesses in any one area. Proximity of residence creates a demand for ethnic services and provides labour for the business set up to meet this demand. Thus, although

Turkish Cypriots are quite dispersed within Greater London as a whole, the fact that enclaves of Turkish Cypriots have become established in the areas mentioned means that ethnic businesses have flourished here. Indeed, in areas where Turkish or Greek Cypriots have settled in any number, they tend to be a 'visible' minority, not on account of their skin colour or style of dress – in these respects they resemble their English neighbours – but on account of their business activities. A relatively large proportion of Cyprus-born working men are self-employed – 20 per cent in 1966 – more than twice the national average (Oakley 1970: 101). The majority of the remainder work as employees in Cypriot-owned factories or for Cypriot firms. The range of business entered is considerable; most are in the service sector, with clothing being the most notable exception (see Table 6 in chapter 8, p. 135).[5] Nowadays, Cypriots – Greeks and Turks – work as employers and employees in restaurants and cafes (including kebab houses), grocers and greengrocers, dry cleaners, mini-cab operators, hairdressers, garages, travel and estate agents, and a host of other types of service occupation.

In clothing, most Turkish and Greek Cypriots are employed in the section of the industry which makes women's outwear garments – skirts, dresses, blouses and suits. The Cypriot-owned factories vary in size and most employ between 10 and 30 people, the majority – though by no means all – of whom are Greek or Turkish Cypriot. Most women work as machinists, most men as cutters or pressers, though the latter may also machine. Some work as menswear tailors.

Work in the clothing industry is less 'visible' insofar as it does not involve the provision of a directly marketable product and the workplace is either a small dress factory or, for some women, their own homes. However, in any area of concentrated Cypriot settlement, it is possible to find small showrooms selling women's fashion garments direct to the public, with many small factories advertising for machinists, cutters and pressers. The operation of businesses in both the service sector and the clothing industry tends to be on an ethnic basis – though in this context 'ethnic' means 'Cypriot' rather than 'Turk' or 'Greek', as the two populations are closely linked in most economic areas. Indeed, although the focus of this paper is specifically Turks, much of what is said applies also to Greek Cypriots.

Recent research which has focussed on London's Greek and Turkish Cypriot populations is useful in indicating employment trends (Ladbury 1979a: 57ff; 1979b; Berk 1972; Leuwenburg 1979). Although the percentage of Cypriot – and particularly Cypriot women's – involvement in the clothing industry has declined proportionately since the 1950s,[6] the number involved is still considerable. Indeed, on the basis of my own research carried out between 1975 and 1977, I would suggest that at least 50 per cent of Turkish Cypriot working women continue to be employed as machinists.[7] This is a higher proportion than for Greek Cypriots, who have been quicker to move out of clothing and into secretarial and clerical work.

The proportion of Turkish Cypriots employed in the service sector remains high. The trend towards an expansion in the range of services entered began in the 1950s, when most Cypriot men were employed in catering (Oakley 1971). Nowadays, as mentioned above, the range of services involved is so wide that it is usually unnecessary for Turkish Cypriots to go outside the Cypriot community for their provision.

Despite this concentration in the service sector and clothing industry, a considerable proportion of Turkish Cypriots have not entered this ethnic business sphere, instead finding employment in the open labour market – in local factories and light industry, as well as in professional capacities. One might expect this movement away from traditional occupations to be gradually increasing as those born and educated here join the labour market. The working conditions and terms of employment of those employed in local industry or in a professional capacity are likely to be very different from those experienced by Turks employed in Cypriot-owned and -staffed businesses.

In the remainder of the paper I attempt to answer three questions which arise out of this brief discussion of Turkish Cypriot economic activity:

(1) Why is there a concentration of Turkish Cypriot business in the service and clothing industries?
(2) Who has found employment in the open labour market, and in what circumstances?
(3) What, in cultural terms, defines economic success for Turkish Cypriots? Is this definition changing and, if it is, how can it affect the employment patterns, or at least the aspirations, of the young?

Turkish Cypriot business activity: the clothing and service sector

The structural and cultural models referred to in chapter 1 are relevant in explaining why Turkish Cypriots, like their Greek Cypriot counterparts and other immigrant populations, have entered the clothing industry and service sector.[8] The economic and political situation in Britain at the time of migration constrained choices on the one hand and presented opportunities on the other, thus effectively rendering some types of employment inaccessible while facilitating entry into others. These structural constraints, imposed on Turks and other immigrants by the economic order and the xenophobic attitudes of the indigenous population, were compounded by what I will call cultural constraints. The work experience, expectations and socio-economic aspirations of the migrants themselves incline them towards certain types of work within the range of opportunities open to them while defining other types as less appropriate or agreeable. Both these factors have been significant in determining Turkish Cypriot employment patterns. However, it is clearly the case that structural constraints have been paramount insofar as they have defined the sphere in which cultural choices have operated.

According to Oakley's detailed study, Turkish Cypriots migrated primarily for economic reasons (Oakley 1972: 22, 144). Both 'push' and 'pull' factors were at work. On the one hand, there was the lack of economic opportunities in Cyprus following independence in 1960. At that time, 64 per cent of the island's population were villagers, and population growth had out-stripped the country's capacity to produce jobs and the required standard of living (Oakley 1972: 130). Significantly enough, it was not the farmers who tended to migrate, but the service and white collar workers, those who had received a primary education but who came from rural areas where employment opportunities, apart from farming, were non-existent (Oakley 1972: 79). In Britain meanwhile, there was a demand for labour and, on a personal level, those in Cyprus were doubtless encouraged by reports received from relatives in London about employment prospects there. The fact that Cyprus had been ruled in effect by Britain for over 80 years (1878–1960) undoubtedly made both Turk and Greek feel familiar with the British and their way of life, even before they entered the country.

(i) The clothing industry

Those Turkish Cypriots who entered Britain during this period found that some jobs were closed to them while others could be entered easily. The clothing industry is an example of the latter. This had been vacated by the English over time, and particularly by English girls who had been drawn to the better pay and conditions offered by office jobs. Cypriots entered the clothing industry, in a similar fashion to immigrants from South Asia (see chapter 10), because vacancies were available, especially for women, who make up 85 per cent of the workforce in the industry.

A second reason for early Cypriot involvement in the trade is that the industry was, and continues to be, pressured to use a cheap labour source, due to the increasing competition from abroad. Immigrants were the most obvious source as they usually lack formal qualifications and, as a result, the bargaining power which would give them access to 'better' employment.

A third contributory factor was that the production units – the small factories which make up the garments – were small enough to remain situated in Inner London, when other firms were having to move out in order to expand. Thus Turkish Cypriots were able to remain relatively concentrated in certain areas – areas where they lived and worked and, it follows, created a demand for ethnic services.

The clothing industry, then, effectively 'pulled' Turkish and Greek Cypriots into its service. Since both groups were barred from more congenial and high status employment by their lack of knowledge of the language, their lack of formal qualifications and white majority prejudice, they responded positively. But there was a separate element to this response, with both structural and cultural dimensions, deriving from the nature of the sending society and this is important to understand if one is to explain why Cypriots entered the clothing industry in such numbers rather than, say, shopkeeping. First of all, tailoring and dressmaking were traditional Turkish Cypriot occupations. Oakley notes that 80 per cent of women who migrated and who were economically active in Cyprus worked as dressmakers, either on their own account or for small manufacturing firms (1971: 85).

A second 'advantage' from a Turkish point of view was that the skills necessary for machining, pressing or cutting could be learnt by demonstration. Thus, a knowledge of English, and the educational qualifications essential in other jobs, were not necessary.

Thirdly, the trade has several 'advantages' relevant to the employment of women. For example, it provided them with the choice of working in the factory or as a machinist in their own homes. This was important since, at the time of Turkish Cypriot arrival, women had not been used to wage-earning in Cyprus, unless this was in a family business or shop. Indeed, many women spoke of the opposition they encountered from their husbands and families to the idea of their working when they first arrived. But the financial expediency of women working soon became apparent. When it was realised, for example, that an experienced machinist could earn at least as much as her husband who was a presser, attitudes to women working changed considerably. The fact that recruitment to a factory was usually on the basis of personal recommendations, and that employees therefore tended to know each other or to be related, facilitated this change of attitude. Husbands were less likely to object to their wives working outside the home if they were in a 'safe' environment.

Like other types of business entered by Turkish Cypriots later on, the long hours and poor conditions in the clothing industry were initially offset by two factors. First, the possibility existed for earning 'reasonable' money, and secondly, self-employment was an attainable goal. Although official wage levels in the industry were and continue to be low, the informal economy is well developed. The fact that employers are able to sell off extra or imperfect garments for cash means that the 'official' pay rates of employees can be supplemented informally by their employers. The difference between declared earnings, on which tax and insurance stamps have been paid, and eventual actual earnings is often considerable. Although the employer is the main beneficiary in this arrangement, employees feel they benefit too, and argue that their employer could not afford to pay them as much if these informal practices were not in operation.

As for self-employment, although very many more Greek than Turkish Cypriots have become self-employed – due to their greater numbers and, some would have it, their greater business acumen – the possibility is there for both groups.[9] (It has diminished only recently, due to the disastrous slump in the industry.) The fact that the units of production are small, and that relatively little basic equipment is initially required to start a business, means that the cutter or even the machinist can see him/herself as a potential employer.

(ii) The service sector

Employment in the clothing industry differs in a number of respects from employment in the service sector. In the former, Turkish Cypriots, like their Greek Cypriot counterparts, filled a niche which already existed. In the service sector, however, it was usually a case of providing services for the immediate Cypriot community and, at the same time, trying to create a demand for the service amongst the non-Cypriot general public. There were no 'vacancies' as such. This was not strictly true of catering; like the Italians (see chapter 6), Cypriots quickly responded to the English demand for inexpensive eating-places in the 1950s – even though they had no previous experience of the catering industry. But as the number of Cypriots looking for work increased, they were forced to look outside catering. Cypriot economic activities consequently diversified.

· Some of the occupations entered by Cypriots in the 1960s were traditional ones such as hairdressing and tailoring. The preponderance of Cypriots in retail shopkeeping or mini-cabbing, however, is a result of the readiness of both Greeks and Turks to fill perceived employment niches and to anticipate demand. The preparedness of Cypriots to enter businesses in which they have no experience is partly due to their awareness of the lack of realistic alternatives, but it is also the case that, in most areas of work, a limited market was assured as the patronage of fellow Cypriots could be expected. Thus the service sector, like the clothing industry, offered the aspiring immigrant entrepreneur the possibility of self-employment.

This self-employment potential undoubtedly continues to be an attractive – if compensatory – feature of the work in both industries from a purely cultural point of view, and the Turkish Cypriots themselves frequently refer to it. Perhaps because the opportunities for economic advancement are greater in Britain than in Cyprus, all first generation migrants did – and to some extent still do – see themselves as potentially reaching the apex of the main area of employment open to them, small business. As self-employed business people they are also potentially respected members of the community, as the tie between wealth and status is a close one. A man or woman who is wealthy has only to display the financial rewards of their business acumen in a culturally prescribed way (a Jaguar car, a house in a pleasant residential district of London, possibly a home in Cyprus) and to be seen to use their wealth wisely and generously (by giving assistance to kin and affines, by being generous to employees, or setting up children in business), to be referred to with respect. Status accrues to individuals in Cyprus in the same way: the difference in London is that the greater economic opportunities here give everyone, in theory, the chance to realise these economic and status aspirations.

What emerges from the above discussion is that there is no single factor which can account for Turkish Cypriot involvement with the clothing industry and service sector. Political and economic factors have undoubtedly been of paramount significance for Turkish Cypriots, as they have for all immigrant populations; they have presented opportunities on the one hand, and severely limited choices on the other. Certain cultural aspirations (to become self-employed, for example) and expectations of Turkish Cypriots – modified over time to take these externally imposed constraints into account – have been important too.

I now want to consider how these constraints present themselves to the individual. I have focussed so far on the reasons why a Turkish Cypriot might become involved in a business activity which is peripheral to the labour market. Now I want to look at opportunities and constraints operating in the labour market itself, and focus both on who has found employment outside the ethnic business sphere, and on how their work environment and status aspirations differ (if, indeed, they do) as a result.

Ethnic business vs. the open labour market

In this paper, participants in the 'open labour market' are defined as those whose ethnic identity was irrelevant as a qualification for their present job, and who work outside the 'ethnic' environment discussed above. Thus, to be recruited, they had, in theory at least, to compete with non-Turks for the position. For some, this inevitably meant that they got the job despite rather than because they were Turkish.

The hypotheses advanced in this section are based on my own investigations into the employment history of a sample of Turkish Cypriots in North London (Ladbury 1979a: 234ff), on extensive enquiries in two North London factories where Turkish Cypriots were employed along with members of other ethnic minority groups (Ladbury 1979b: 29ff) and on recent interviews with Turkish Cypriots in jobs or professions outside the ethnic business sphere. Most of those interviewed were men, and all were between the ages of 30 and 60. The employment history – and future – of those who have left school more recently, both men and women, will be considered in the final section.

Investigations revealed that, broadly speaking, there are two categories of people employed on the open labour market. On the one hand, there are those whose educational qualifications have given them access to it. I refer here to a small group of qualified men and women and students in higher education who are, or will be, employed either in welfare, management or business capacities, or in the professions as doctors, lawyers, teachers and so on. On the other hand, there are the 'ordinary' immigrants who have also found employment outside the ethnic business sphere but for quite different reasons when compared to the above group. The distinction between the 'educated' and the 'ordinary' immigrant is, of course, not clear cut. Some ordinary migrants from the villages had very little capital when they first arrived but have since done extraordinarily well in business and now associate socially both with the educated Turkish professional group and with the English middle class. However, for the majority, it is a justifiable distinction and a useful one in the context of this discussion.

(i) The open labour market: middle class participation

What is particularly interesting about members of the first group is that, although they participate in the labour market in a very real sense, they often continue to have very close links with the lower income groups, to whom they may provide a professional service.[10] In this way, they resemble the small ethnic business which receives the patronage of an ethnic clientele while providing a service for the wider community. Whatever the professional service offered – legal advice, medical help, experience in export and shipping – a Turkish Cypriot will seek out the assistance of another Turkish Cypriot qualified in these spheres if advice or help of a particular nature is needed. Thus, although most Turkish Cypriots will visit their local GP for routine medical help, if there is a problem involving, say, virginity, then a Turkish Cypriot doctor may well be contacted. One Turkish Cypriot doctor told me he had many older Turkish Cypriot private patients who had come to him because they did not feel confident about the treatment they had been receiving from the NHS. Their local GPs would apparently prescribe them tablets, whereas they knew injections were more effective (this being the traditional way of administering medicine in Cyprus). Thus, they would come to see him because they knew that he, as a Turk, would appreciate their anxieties and give them 'proper' treatment. Similarly, Turkish Cypriots may contact a Turkish solicitor if they have a problem which they feel might be dealt with more sympathetically by a Turk – a divorce, for example, or a matter concerning immigration. This is not to suggest the Turkish Cypriots in professional or welfare capacities have a specifically ethnic clientele, but rather that their services are sometimes sought, and their positions most definitely respected, by members of their ethnic group. This undoubtedly is one reason why members of this group continue to provide an ethnic service. The prestige which accrues to the Turkish Cypriot doctor in a Turkish area of North London, who can be contacted in moments of crisis, may well be greater than that which would accrue to someone who, though a well known surgeon in the medical profession, could not be called on to provide an everyday service in the community.

Significantly, some of those interviewed, whose present job did not involve providing a service or having any contact with the local Turkish community, saw themselves as failures. This was even the case when the position held was neither poorly paid nor low in status by English middle class standards – a sales manager in a department store, for example. The fact that the job was 'just a job' and did not have either a social or service aspect, in the sense of the Turkish Cypriot lawyer or travel agent, was an important factor here. The fact that it involved employment in a large organisation, the hierarchy of which, like the individual's role within it, was not clear, and therefore could not be easily evaluated, was also significant. Although doctors, teachers and the like also work as part of larger collectives, this is not the paradox it might seem, as these jobs are familiar to Turks and can be immediately identified by them. This is not the case with a job like a sales manager.

I would suggest then that many of those in this middle class group, employed in professional or business capacities, derived prestige from the same source as the lower income group who have gone into business: community acknowledgement. Both are able to build up a reputation in their respective capacities for being 'good' at their jobs. The more the contact they have with the Cypriot public, and the more geographically widespread their sphere of influence, the greater the prestige which can accrue to them.

(ii) The open labour market: participation of lower income groups

So much for the small group of Turkish Cypriots whose training allows them to participate in the labour market at managerial and professional levels. The continuing economic and social contact with the ethnic community that many have has been noted; the fact that community acknowledgement of their positions is still important has been particularly emphasised. I want to turn now to consider those employed in the labour market in the lower income group. How do Turkish Cypriots who work in English-run factories differ from those who work in the clothing industry in terms of their ethnic networks and the nature of their status aspirations?

Settlement patterns would seem to be of a primary importance, as all those interviewed in the two North London factories mentioned above lived in the immediate area. Thus, those who now live in areas close to the industrial fringe on the outskirts of Inner London are more likely to be employed in local industry than those who live in an inner city area, where the clothing and catering trades have provided greater employment opportunities. One of the two North London factories, where both English management and Turkish Cypriot operators were interviewed, was a dairy; the other factory manufactured light metal goods. In the dairy, under the supervision of seven (English) foremen, there were 114 operators working in six different departments. Of these, 42 (37 per cent) were either Greek or Turkish Cypriot, and they worked together in every department but one. In the other factory, there were some 800 employees, 50 per cent of whom were classified as immigrant. Although there were only 62 Cypriots (36 Turkish, 26 Greek), they were all concentrated in the printing department where they constituted 80 per cent of the workforce. Again, all the supervisors in the department were English.

This ethnic clustering is easily explained. Both workplaces had informal recruitment procedures: employees would know in advance if someone were leaving, and if they had friends or relatives who wanted the job they would approach the management on their behalf. This is exactly how Turkish and Greek Cypriots recruit labour for their own workplaces and it is, therefore, how they expect to find employment. That the English, West Indians, African and East African Asians (the other major ethnic groups represented in both workplaces) operated in the same manner was not doubted, but management maintained that the Cypriots were actually 'better at getting their own people in' than the other groups (cf. Dhooge 1981). The point is that, given a well-articulated network of kin and acquaintances in London, an ethnic minority is likely to become concentrated in those workplaces which recruit labour on an informal basis. In this respect, then, the work environment of those Turkish Cypriots employed in the open labour market is similar to that of their counterparts within the ethnic business sphere. Many, if not most, of their immediate work acquaintances are Turkish or Greek Cypriots.

In another respect, however, the work environment they experience is quite different. Unlike the small Cypriot-owned factory, the management here is English, as is generally the supervisory staff. Although contact between operators and supervisors is frequent and personal, the ordinary operator is likely to have little contact with middle management and none with higher management in a large company. The Turkish Cypriots interviewed found this lack of contact both disconcerting and frustrating. The employer–employee relationship in a Turkish-Greek-run firm is, by contrast, extremely close. In a clothing factory, for example, the manager's office is usually a small room directly off the main work area. He or she is directly involved with the production process, and many even join the machinists on the production-line if there is an urgent order to be despatched. In any case, he or she knows the workforce well, and will attend family weddings and other celebrations. Wages and hours may be worked out by negotiation with each individual and, as noted above, employer and employee are bound together by their joint understanding of, and participation in, the informal economy. On top of this, the employer may extend personal favours and gifts to deserving employees – a firm's car, a loan for a mortgage or simply free samples of what is being manufactured. In short, the economic relationship between employer and employee has a social dimension. This is intended to work for the benefit of both parties, though in fact it often imposes constraints on the decision-making power of employees. Working until 9 pm every work day in a busy week, for example, is more or less obligatory if, as an employee, you are in receipt of a firm's car or a loan.

This social relationship is typical of that in any Cypriot-owned business and it is one reason why Turkish employees in such workplaces do not join unions.[11] It is interesting, however, that where Turkish Cypriots are part of a large multi-ethnic workforce, where there is no possibility of personalising the economic relationship, union participation may be strong. In the metal goods factory, the deputy convenor for the Transport and General Workers' Union was a Turkish Cypriot. He acted as spokesman

and representative for all the Cypriot employees who saw union participation as the only way to balance the otherwise arbitrary – and discriminatory – actions of the management, while granting them a sphere of
influence within the union itself in the form of an ethnic voice. In other
words, an attempt was being made through union participation to exert
some control over their own labour and over their employers. This might
be compared to the 'control' an employee in a small Cypriot factory
ideally exerts over his employer as a result of the social relationship established with him or her.

To sum up, so far as the work environment is concerned, Turkish
Cypriots participating in the open labour market often work alongside
other Turkish and Greek Cypriots; the social composition of their
immediate work acquaintances is therefore similar to that in a Turkish
Cypriot-owned business. What is different is the typical lack of communication between Cypriots in the labour market and their employers.
Interestingly, active participation in unions, which is almost totally lacking in the ethnic business sphere, is often strong among Turks in an
English-owned business. Here it functions partly as a compensatory
'control' strategy.

(iii) The open labour market: compensatory strategies

The second question with which we are concerned is the work
and status aspiration of Turkish Cypriots in the open labour market.
Here, it is necessary to reiterate that the focus in this section is the older
generation – those who migrated as adults or teenagers, not those born
here. For this older group, it is probably safe to say that, whatever their
status aspirations in Britain, most have not been able to realise them
through rising to a position of importance in the open labour market. Of
course, there are exceptions: the man or woman who received even some
secondary education in Cyprus, and who came to England able to read
and write a little English may well have started as an operator and been
promoted to charge-hand or supervisor. For most, however, the oral and
literacy skills deemed necessary to fulfil the supervisory role may have
militated against their promotion – or at least been used by management
as the excuse for not promoting more Turks, or any other non-English-
speaker, to a supervisory position. Although in the metal goods factory
the management insisted there were equal opportunities for promotion
for everyone on the shop floor, Turkish Cypriots denied there were any
opportunities for job advancement unless you were English. Since they
did not believe it was realistic to expect promotion within the system,
many were directing their energies into work efforts outside it. Thus, the
'leisure' activities of those interviewed included helping out a brother

with a clothing business, assisting another family member with a fish and chip shop and, significantly, negotiating for premises to open a shop which one man planned to run with a relative in the near future. For the more energetic and entrepreneurial, therefore, the factory job was a source of income, but it did not provide job or status satisfaction; thus, alternative economic ventures were under way or were being planned. Inevitably, these involved the ethnic business sphere with its promise of self-employment if not instant, or even eventual, wealth. It was in this direction that those with some ambition saw their economic activities as eventually leading. Denied the chance to prove themselves in the open labour market, and do a job they considered commensurate with their abilities, the only alternative was to set up their own independent business. Thus, although formally participating in the labour market, they were, in a sense, only nominally part of it, as their future plans and aspirations, as well as much of their present energy, were directed into the ethnic business sphere.

That this should be the case for the first generation of Turkish Cypriots, whatever their income group, is not too surprising. What is interesting, however, is whether the same applies to those born and educated here, those who have, at least in theory, the qualifications which would enable them to compete on equal terms in the open job market. It is to this younger generation of Turkish Cypriots, both men and women, that I now turn.

The second generation: redefining success

So far in this paper, the concern has been primarily with the first generation of Turkish Cypriot migrants, those who were born in Cyprus and who spent at least their first 16 years there. This is a relevant age division in at least one sense: those who were over 16 when they arrived in Britain did not attend school here. Those who came earlier had to attend school until they were 16; this usually meant that they had some form of special language tuition. It also gave them an impression of how the English examination/educational system worked. In this section, the focus is the young generation – those who were born here or received all or most of their schooling in Britain.

As noted above, the first generation migrated primarily for economic reasons: to secure a job – or a better job – and to raise their standard of living. Thus, for the first generation, the successful entrepreneurs were those who responded astutely to existing opportunities and who made enough money to set up on their own and to provide their families with an acceptable standard of living. One effect or function of this achievement was that it exonerated them from the 'guilt' of migration; it allowed them to tell themselves and, more significantly, their kin in Cyprus that this was why they had come to Britain and settled here.

It is important to remember when discussing the so-called 'second generation' that they have grown up in this atmosphere of struggle, with great emphasis put on survival first, and then on achievement and success. At the same time, they have experienced the English educational system, where being successful has meant passing exams and going on to further training courses or, at least, getting a job with 'prospects'. Thus, the second generation has been exposed to two quite different 'success' systems. Like other second-language learners, however, they have been disadvantaged in the second system. The relevant questions in this context are: do Turkish Cypriot school-leavers aspire to and aim for jobs on the open labour market, and, if they do, how successful are they?

Unfortunately, there are no statistics available on the achievements of young Turkish Cypriots at school; nor has any study so far focussed on the job choices and eventual employment status of this group. The following statements and hypotheses are therefore made on the basis of interviews carried out by the author with parents and children from the 14 Turkish households mentioned previously (Ladbury 1979a: 234–6). Interviews were also carried out in the four North London schools with the greatest number of Turkish Cypriot pupils (*ibid.*: 33). All those interviewed were from ordinary working class families; the minority middle class professional group was not represented. On the basis of the information thus obtained, the following points emerged.

(i) Job aspirations of young Turkish Cypriots in schools

The awareness of Turkish Cypriot children of how the English generally, and the schools particularly, classify jobs has undoubtedly affected their own job aspirations. All the girls interviewed rejected machining as a possible form of employment. Boys also saw jobs in the clothing industry as low quality work. The work mentioned most frequently by girls as a desirable alternative to machining was secretarial or personnel work, preferably in an English firm. The two areas in which boys showed most interest were accounting (or, at least, something involving maths) and becoming a car mechanic. These two types of male employment were often presented as straight alternatives, as if failure in the one would involve an immediate consideration of the other. Although boys saw both types of work as involving things at which they were, or might be, good (maths, practical mechanics), the differing qualifications required for each had obviously not been thought out.

Indeed, one overwhelming impression gained from the interviews was that both sexes had received little careers advice in school. Most were unaware of the job opportunities open to them in their immediate area or outside. More importantly, they were ill-informed about the qualifications and further training required for the jobs they desired. Their parents' unfamiliarity with the system meant that they were unable to help or advise about this. Ironically, the only work about which the parents *were* well informed – that which has been discussed under the 'ethnic business' rubric – was not what their children were interested in. Their aspirations were on the whole directed towards the open labour market.

(ii) Turkish Cypriot parents' aspirations for their children

Parents' aspirations have also been influenced by their experiences in this country. Mothers aspired for their daughters to find 'better' jobs than they had themselves found. Secretarial work in an English or Turkish firm was seen as a desirable, higher status alternative. Parents were more ambitious, and more vague, about what sort of work they envisaged for their sons. All wanted their school-age sons to go on to college or to have further training, but few specified what they wanted them to do eventually. One mother who ran a clothing factory wanted her son to qualify as an accountant so he could take over the business side of the firm. Indeed, it was only those parents who ran their own business that envisaged their sons taking it over and therefore continuing in the ethnic business sphere. Others expressed no particular preference for them working for or with other Turks, although a few Turkish mothers felt that their daughters would be 'safer' in an all-Turkish environment. The fact that most of these families had very little awareness of the range of jobs open to their children probably accounts for their inability to specify exactly what sort of jobs they thought they should aim for.

(iii) The ethnic business sphere: a last resort?

The occupational choices of those Turkish Cypriots who leave school with few formal qualifications are limited. Although some Turkish Cypriot young people do go on to higher education or specific training courses many attempt to find a job immediately on leaving school. This is probably more often the case with girls than boys. Many parents in the group interviewed thought it was more important for their sons to obtain formal qualifications than their daughters since the boys would be the eventual bread winners whereas the girls would soon be married and would not have 'time' for a career. There is, of course, nothing particularly Turkish Cypriot about these attitudes.

Those who *did* attempt to get jobs in the open labour market were often disappointed. Unlike their English peers, however, unemployment benefit was not automatically considered as an alternative; a more viable alternative as far as they and their families were concerned was to take a job in the ethnic business sphere. This did not inevitably involve machining for girls, although it sometimes did. Those with secretarial skills looked for secretarial opportunities in a Turkish-owned business; others found employment in, say, a Cypriot-run hairdressing business. Boys would look for work in Cypriot-owned clothing factories as pressers or would persuade a relative to take them on as a driver in their mini-cab firm. The point is that ethnic ties were being used by young Turkish Cypriots to find employment, but only after they had failed in their own attempts to find a job independently of their ethnic network.

What implications do these observations have for future Turkish Cypriot employment patterns? Education is obviously of prime importance. While young Turkish Cypriots, girls and boys, leave school without the educational qualifications which would enable them to compete for jobs in the English job market, they will continue to be absorbed into ethnic businesses due to the virtual necessity of finding work through other Turkish Cypriots. Although the 1981 Census is likely to show a trend by the young away from the traditional areas of work associated with Cypriots (the clothing and service industries), it will probably not be until the next generation of school-leavers enters the job market that any real change will be discernible.

In the meantime, it is likely that the ethnic business sphere will continue to provide a safety net for many. In times of acute job shortage it may continue to function as a job absorption mechanism whereby young people can be drawn into work which, because of its peripherality to the open labour market, is less affected by variations in the demand for employment there. This, of course, has not been the case with the clothing industry, where many lost their jobs when business slumped. Indeed, school-leavers who would otherwise have been persuaded to learn machining or pressing after failing to get a job outside the ethnic business environment, have found that the only vacancies are for skilled workers. Thus, one of the traditional escape routes out of unemployment for young Cypriots has now vanished. In its place is unemployment itself or work in the service industries. In the latter case, this usually means working with parental contacts and may involve an even less secure means of livelihood than machining – mini-cabbing for example, or, for women, hairdressing or 'helping' in a relative's shop. Often such jobs are no more than disguised unemployment.

Conclusions

If one is to explain why an ethnic group has developed a particular economic specialisation, it is important to consider the factors which limit their choices, as well as those which encourage members of the group to enter the type of work in question. This is a pertinent consideration in the case of Turkish Cypriots. In most respects, Turkish Cypriots fit the model used by Geertz (1963), Cohen (1969) and others in the 1960s, which sought to explain the association between a section of the population and a particular business activity or entrepreneurial skills.[12] Clark summarises the explanations they used as one where attention was focussed:

> on the dynamics of advancement within the wider society and on the social and political aspirations of particular individuals. Such individuals were either previously on the margins of society or of the power structure and sought novel means to advance their status and wealth and to gain social recognition which was more in line with their social aspirations. Or such individuals could belong to an elite whose power base was being threatened by recent events and who sought to maintain their position by rechannelling their resources towards more profitable business enterprises. (Clark 1979: 175–6)

In many respects, Turkish Cypriots fall into the former of these two categories since, as immigrants, they were marginal to the power structure and to the avenues for economic advancement open to the indigenous population. According to this model the exaggerated emphasis in London on owning a business can be explained as a compensatory strategy. Certainly the first generation of Turkish Cypriot migrants were blocked from higher status jobs in the labour market because they lacked the educational qualifications, and often the language, to compete effectively in these spheres. To some extent this has been the experience of the second and third generations also, but, since the criteria for success have changed for them, the relevance of the model has also decreased. As we have seen, the continuing association of Turkish Cypriot young people with traditional ethnic occupations is not due to their desire to become small business owners (let alone small business employees) like their parents, but due to the fact that there are often no alternatives. They are simply trapped, mainly by developments in the wider economic and political context which are beyond their control, but also by their parents and by ethnic group norms, which state that any job is better than no job and if it is within the ethnic business sphere, then at least it is 'safe' and familiar.

The irony is that the Conservative government's call in *Small Business, Big Future* would have been greeted enthusiastically by first generation Turkish Cypriots twenty years ago if only it had been made then. But today, for the second and third generation, many of whom are thoroughly familiar with the reality of the world of small business on the margins of the economy, it does not appeal. Despite the initiative and hard work of their parents small businesses have not been found to lead to 'big futures'. In times of economic depression, there is nothing to suggest they will start to do so.

8

West Indian business in Britain

FRANK REEVES and ROBIN WARD

The encouragement of black people to secure a real stake in their own community, through business and the professions, is in my view of great importance
if future social stability is to be secured . . . I do urge the necessity for speedy
action if we are to avoid the perpetuation in this country of an economically dis-
possessed black population. A weakness in British society is that there are too few
people of West Indian origin in the business, entrepreneurial and professional
class.

(Scarman 1982: 167–8)

Lord Scarman's views on the need to increase the economic prosperity
and social stability of black people in Britain by providing the conditions
to encourage success in business typify the conclusions of official reports
published in the 1980s (see Home Affairs Committee 1981: 88–92).[1] In
this chapter the widespread belief that West Indians are largely absent
from the world of business is examined. In the first section statistical data
on the involvement of West Indians in business is set out. This is followed
by a review of possible causes underlying the present position. Finally,
there is a brief discussion of the interests of government and of the black
community on the question of black business development in Britain.

1 Black business in Britain: some statistical evidence

Some indication of the pattern of business involvement among West
Indians and other ethnic minorities in Britain can be derived from three
sources: the 1971 Census, still at the time of writing the most recent comprehensive available account of the employment position of the British
population, the National Survey of Racial Minorities carried out for PEP
in 1974 (Smith 1976; 1977) and the National Dwelling and Household
Survey (NDHS) carried out by the Department of the Environment in
1977–8 which covers a large national sample of the population. As well as

125

Table 1. *Males: self-employment by country of origin (10 per cent sample)*

	Self-employed with employees	Self-employed without employees	Total self-employed	Total in employment
Irish Republic	870 (3.2)	1,976 (7.3)	2,846 (10.5)	26,957
New Commonwealth America	86 (0.7)	188 (1.6)	274 (2.4)	11,456
India	383 (2.9)	495 (3.8)	878 (6.7)	13,973
Pakistan	171 (2.4)	200 (2.8)	371 (5.1)	7,220
New Commonwealth Europe	414 (11.3)	400 (10.9)	814 (22.2)	3,660
Whole population	57,694 (3.6)	89,486 (5.6)	147,180 (9.3)	1,588,390

Notes: Percentages read across the line. 'New Commonwealth America' refers to Barbados, Guyana, Jamaica, Trinidad and Tobago and other territories in the Americas. 'New Commonwealth Europe' refers principally to Cyprus and Malta but also includes Gibraltar and Gozo. 'Whole population' refers to all economically active males, whether born in or outside UK.
Source: 1971 Census.

providing an account of the position of West Indians in business, the statistical data set out below indicate how far Indians and Pakistanis have penetrated the business sector in Britain (a matter to be taken up in the following chapters) and provide evidence to support the picture of Turkish Cypriot business activity as set out in chapter 7.

(i) The proportion of the ethnic minority population in business

Data from the 1971 Census, as set out in Table 1, allow a comparison between migrants from five geographical areas (the Irish Republic, New Commonwealth America, India, Pakistan and New Commonwealth Europe) and the whole population.

The figure for West Indians in self-employment (2.4 per cent) is less than half that of the Pakistanis (5.1 per cent), slightly more than a third of that for the Indians (6.7 per cent) and a little more than a quarter of the figure for the whole population (9.3 per cent). Migrants from European countries in the New Commonwealth (principally Cyprus and Malta) are

Table 2. *Heads of households: self-employed in specified socio-economic groups by ethnic group for national sample – percentages*

	Employers in		Self-employed professionals (SEG3)	Own account workers (SEG12)	Sum of 1, 2, 3 and 12 (percentages)	(N)
	large firms (SEG1)	small firms (SEG2)				
White	0.3	3.8	1.0	4.9	10.0	1,101,181
West Indian	—	1.0	—	2.6	3.6	4,880
Indian	—	4.6	1.6	5.5	11.6	12,956
Pakistani/ Bangladeshi	—	2.4	0.4	5.1	7.9	4,372
Other non-white	0.8	5.7	0.5	6.0	13.0	23,036
Total	0.3	3.8	1.0	4.8	10.0	1,146,124

Note: Percentages read *across* the line and represent self-employed in designated SEGs as a proportion of all economically active household heads.
Source: 1977/8 National Dwelling and Household Survey, special tabulation.

seen to be very heavily involved in entrepreneurial activity, as noted in the previous chapter, more than one in five males being recorded as self-employed. The New Commonwealth Europeans are the only group with more of their self-employed men having employees than working on their own. Among those from the Caribbean and the Irish Republic the proportion of the self-employed without employees is highest.

Special tabulations on membership of particular socio-economic groups (SEGs)[2] drawn from the 1977/8 NDHS provide more recent information on participation in business by ethnic minorities (see Table 2).

Table 2 reveals that in the late 1970s among the ethnic minorities the number of employers in large firms was minimal but that there were far more in small firms. It also shows considerable variations between minorities, with a higher proportion of Indians being small employers than of whites. Proportionately four times as many whites as West Indians were managing employees in small businesses. Among self-employed professionals, Indians were over-represented in comparison with whites, but no self-employed West Indian professionals were caught in the national sample.[3] The highest numbers of people from all ethnic groups were to be found in the category of own account workers. The figures for Indians and Pakistanis were slightly above the national average, and for West Indians below. If the four categories of self-employed are combined, the percentage for the total population is 10 per cent, as against 3.6 per cent for West Indians.

Table 3. *National trends in self-employment in specified socio-economic groups by ethnic group (1971–8) – percentages*

	Employers in		Self-employed (SEG3)	Own account workers (SEG12)	Sum of 1,2,3 and 12
	large firms (SEG1)	small firms (SEG2)			
West Indian	—	1.0	—	2.6	3.6
	(0.03)	(0.7)	(0.2)	(1.6)	(2.5)
Indian	—	4.6	1.6	5.5	11.6
	(0.04)	(2.0)	(1.6)	(3.3)	(6.9)
Pakistani/	—	2.4	0.4	5.1	7.9
Bangladeshi	(—)	(2.1)	(0.5)	(2.7)	(5.3)
Total population	0.3	3.8	1.0	4.8	10.0

Notes: Percentages read *across* the line and represent self-employed in designated SEGs as a proportion of all economically active. Figures from NDHS refer to household heads. Figures from the 1971 Census are enclosed in brackets and refer to the male economically active population.
Source: 1971 Census, 1977/8 National Dwelling and Household Survey.

A further significant detail emerging from this survey was the considerable variation between urban areas in the level of business involvement (Ward and Reeves 1980: 42–3). By far the greatest variation between areas was found among the Indian and Pakistani population.

A rough indication of national trends in self-employment is provided in Table 3 by a comparison of data from the 1977/8 NDHS and the 1971 Census.[4]

There has been a sharp increase in the proportion of Indians running small businesses with employees, and smaller increases for West Indians and Pakistanis. There appears to have been little change in the number of self-employed professionals. The largest rise has occurred among those working on their account (from 1.6 to 2.6 per cent of the West Indian population). The combined figures for ethnic minority self-employed have doubled between 1971 and 1978, but while West Indian and Asian groups show a similar proportional increase, the actual *extent* of the increase among Asians has been much greater because a larger proportion of their population were already engaged in business in 1971.

Table 4. *Self-employed men and women: type of industry by country of origin – percentages*

	General population	West Indians	Indians	Pakistanis/ Bangladeshis	African Asians
Manufacturing	21	14	10	5	20
Construction	17	46	2	—	3
Distributive trades	26	2	62	74	57
Other service industries	36	30	18	12	20
Not classified	—	8	8	9	—
	100	100	100	100	100
N =		37	46	33	28

Note: The general population figures are from the 1971 Census and relate to Great Britain.
Source: D.J. Smith 1976: 220, Table B43.

(ii) The pattern of West Indian business involvement

Information on the kinds of business in which West indians (and members of other minorities) have been involved is contained in the PEP national survey of racial minorities carried out in 1974.[5] We are concerned here not with the proportions of each minority group in business but with the spread of business people over different sectors of the economy. Details are set out in Table 4.

Although because of the size of the sample some caution needs to be exercised in interpreting the results, Table 4 shows a high level of West Indian self-employment in construction and other service industries. The proportion of West Indian businesses in the miscellaneous services sector of the economy (which includes transport) is higher than for the other ethnic minorities and is similar to the figure for the general population. Those from India, Pakistan and Bangladesh are heavily concentrated in the distributive trades, where West Indians are rarely found.

Interviews with bank managers who had experience of running business accounts for West Indians and a content analysis of two West Indian newspapers provided some further evidence of the kinds of business West Indians were entering. The types most frequently mentioned by bank managers included building and construction, property development, hairdressing, retail sales (especially food and off-licences), second-hand car sales, car repairs, taxi-driving, travel agencies, clubs, record shops and insurance broking.

The newspaper content analysis provided a list of 305 services of which the most frequently mentioned were, in descending order: hairdressing; travel and shipping; groups and bands; clubs, records, and entertainment; help lines and introductions; fashion, beauty and modelling; financial services, insurance and estate agencies; religion, healing and astrology; and driving lessons, car hire, removals and deliveries. West Indians did not own or manage all the firms advertising: subsequent enquiries indicated that about one fifth of the firms were either white-owned or Asian-owned businesses. Caution must be exercised in assuming the list to be representative of West Indian business, not only because of this factor but because some kinds of business may see little point in paying to advertise goods and services in the ethnic press, and, furthermore, because newspapers may recognise a particular clientele or geographical market and direct their strategy for obtaining copy accordingly. However, the pattern of West Indian business derived from interviews in London, where advertisers were concentrated, was not significantly different from that gained elsewhere in the country and accorded with that shown in the content analysis. With the exception of the building industry, the order in which types of business were mentioned was the same both for banks and newspapers, though the latter list also included several additional types of business (help lines, introduction services and astrology, for example) which would not have demanded very much capital. Generally, there was a strong emphasis on the service sector but little evidence of movement into distribution.

2 Explanations for the pattern of West Indian business

Questions about the nature and degree of ethnic minority participation in business in Britain are usually premised on the assumption that there are statistical norms against which the performance of a particular group should be judged. In Britain, there is a tendency to compare the business activity of the West Indians with that of the general population as well as with other minority groups, particularly the Indians, who are seen as successful in laying a sound foundation in business. In the United States, by way of contrast, the entrepreneurial activity of West Indians is frequently judged against that of the Afro-American population to produce entirely different results, explanations and views of their talent for business.

Differences in the level of involvement of minorities in Britain in business are considered below under five headings: (i) the overall context of small business, (ii) ethnic settlement patterns and consumer demand, (iii) business skills, (iv) access to business resources and (v) ethnic community organisation and attitudes. The emphasis is on difficulties in getting established in business rather than on the use of business as a strategy for group advancement – an approach more typical in studies of other minorities. Nevertheless, it enables us to consider some of the main theoretical approaches advanced to explain minority involvement in business: that success derives from occupying a protected ethnic niche (see (ii) below), that cultural factors account for business success (taken up in (v) below) and that success or otherwise in business has essentially nothing to do with ethnic factors (see (iii) below).

(i) The overall context of small business

General changes in the industrial structure and business composition of the British economy have particularly affected racial minority employment prospects. A large majority of black immigrants who came to Britain took up manual work and settled in inner residential areas. Despite being caught in a contracting labour market, Asians and West Indians have, until recently, been able to move to other employment, as whites left declining inner areas to move to other jobs and better quality housing in the suburbs. This provided an opportunity for a replacement entrepreneurial class to take over the businesses that came onto the market, particularly in the retail distributive sector, in areas of racial minority settlement – a role filled mainly by Asians (see chapter 11).

We saw in chapter 2 that the number of self-employed persons has declined as business markets have become enlarged as a result of better communications and transportation, with large organisations becoming dominant in all aspects of economic life. Retail outlets have contracted sharply (p. 21) and, following the argument presented by Auster and Aldrich (chapter 3), the structure of the retail market in Britain, particularly the high degree of centralisation, has made it more difficult to start a small business; if such businesses are to be successful, they must fill niches in the retail trade where multiples are at a disadvantage. Willingness to set up in business springs from spotting an opportunity to make money and from the increasingly restricted opportunities for earning one's living as an employee. Small shopkeeping has the advantage that, while many businesses are inherited, it is open to those with little skill or specialised training (Bechhofer and Elliott 1968). Confronted by restrictions on access to other kinds of employment, some members of ethnic minorities turn to small business, both in the retail sector and elsewhere, as a means of economic improvement (see in particular chapters 7, 9, 11 and 12).

(ii) Ethnic settlement patterns and consumer demand

The structural changes described above have affected West Indians and Asians alike, but the two groups are differently placed to take advantage of any business opportunities that might emerge as a result. Having come to Britain to provide a replacement labour force in declining industrial sectors, both West Indians and Asians have also become a replacement residential population in the inner urban areas. But they differ in their relative size, their pattern of settlement and their housing preferences. Not only are the Asian communities numerically stronger in most places, but they are more densely clustered in the inner areas of old terraced housing. While still unevenly distributed around the city, West Indians are to be found in roughly equal numbers both in the older working class areas of private housing and in council tenancies. Council housing allocation practices, together with the locational preferences of white and black families eligible for council tenancies, have resulted in West Indians being quite widely scattered over most central and inner council estates. Clearly, the extent to which minority populations are concentrated or dispersed has important implications for black entrepreneurship.

The point is reinforced when we consider that the minority entrepreneur may rely on finding a viable niche in the market by catering for the special needs and tastes of an ethnic community. Opportunities for Asian businessmen have been created through Indians and Pakistanis bringing with them to Britain a wide range of distinctly different cultural preferences. The phenomenon of the 'ethnic village' arises from the degree to which these cultural preferences continue to be exercised in areas of residential concentration. The potential for the growth of ethnic minority retailing, then, may depend quite heavily on residential concentration and ethnic consumer demand. Conversely, white shopkeepers or property owners facing declining market conditions as a result of the change in population and the cultural tastes of residents may only be able to retrieve or safeguard their capital by selling or letting (at relatively low prices) to Asians (see chapter 12).

In contrast, entrepreneurs among the West Indian community are likely to experience far greater difficulty in establishing an 'ethnic niche' in retailing, though the most recent studies show that at least in some situations the problems that are faced can be overcome (Lambeth 1982, Wilson 1983a). There are fewer potential West Indian customers overall, they are more diffusely settled and, although there are specific West Indian needs and cultural preferences, they are not so wide-ranging and exclusive as to support business activity on the same scale as among the Asian community.

In the older residential areas there will be competition from a numerically stronger Asian population; on modern council estates competition will be with white retailers. While competition between shopkeepers on council estates is usually small, there is often stiff competition for access to the site. Often rents are high because premises are new and purpose-built, and demand is increased by the prospect of profitable trading. West Indians are likely to find it much more difficult to obtain access to shop premises of this kind, and in the absence of a large captive market of fellow countrymen the prospects of trading are far less attractive. Some Asians have been able to move into shopping areas serving the white community. But frequently it is capital acquired in the course of building up trade in an area of ethnic minority concentration that is used to finance expansion into bigger premises and white shopping areas.

Phillips (1978), reviewing the state of West Indian business in Britain, concluded that it was still largely dependent on the ethnic market. There are some signs that this is changing. For example, while recently published accounts show a majority of black-owned retail and service outlets specialising in ethnic goods and services, one third of black firms in a survey undertaken in Brent (Wilson 1983a: 113) and about half of those in a similar survey in Lambeth (Lambeth 1982: 38) had more than half of their custom from outside the Caribbean community. But despite this, it still seems likely that West Indian business activity, while fostered to a point by its ability to occupy an ethnic niche, is severely restricted by the difficulty of breaking out into the wider market. Successful growth seems to require moving out of dependence on the limited custom of the West Indian minority.

(iii) Business skills

In reviewing the literature on the characteristics of business founders, the Economists Advisory Group describe the distinction made by N.R. Smith (1967), in his study of Michigan, between those founded by 'craftsmen' and those founded by 'opportunists'. 'Craftsmen' founders were from a skilled working class background and had a low level of educational attainment. Lacking alternative means of making a living, they went into business in a modest way, using their own capital or money borrowed from friends. 'Opportunists' were from a middle class background, were more highly educated and had broader work experience, including time spent in a managerial capacity as employees. They set up business on a larger scale, responded more flexibly to changing circumstances, and their businesses grew more rapidly than those of the craftsmen.

Admittedly, people have entered retail business without craft skills, educational qualifications or managerial experience (Stanworth and

Table 5. *Males: occupation groups by country of birth (10 per cent sample)
– percentages*

	Irish Republic	NC America	India	Pakistan	NC Europe	Whole population
Manufacturing	26.8	46.5	38.2	44.8	33.2	30.0
Construction	7.1	1.4	0.9	0.2	1.1	3.5
Transport, communications	8.5	12.6	7.2	5.9	6.6	8.0
Service, sport, recreation	7.0	3.5	2.8	6.2	22.6	5.7
Other manual services	10.8	8.9	6.2	5.4	5.6	6.9
Labourers	18.4	15.0	11.2	23.5	7.0	6.9
Clerical, sales	8.6	4.1	12.0	4.2	10.5	14.2
Administrative, managerial, professional, technical	8.3	4.0	19.0	6.4	9.3	15.9
All other occupations including those inadequately described	4.5	4.0	2.5	3.4	4.1	8.9
	100.0	100.0	100.0	100.0	100.0	100.0
N =	23,963	10,971	12,146	6,799	2,826	1,589,020

Source: 1971 Census.

Curran 1973). But in assessing the success of ethnic minorities in business, it seems important to review their occupational skills as suggested by their employment experience.

Table 5 shows substantial differences in the occupations of different ethnic groups. A little less than half the West Indians and Pakistanis were engaged in manual work in manufacturing in 1971 as compared with under a third of the whole population. The proportion of Indians in manufacturing or labouring was smaller than for the other minority groups, and the Indians were much more highly represented in non-manual occupations, either in clerical jobs or sales or in administrative, managerial, professional or technical work. Overall about one in three Indian men was in a middle class occupation, compared with one in five of the New Commonwealth Europeans, one in six of the Irish, one in ten of the Pakistanis, and one in twelve of the West Indians. Even allowing for the possibility that some of those born in India were white, the contrast between the occupational distribution of Indian-born men and those from Pakistan and the West Indies is marked.

In addition, the qualified manpower tables in the 1971 Census emphasise the differences in educational level between the respective minority groups and the general population: 2.6 per cent of West Indian men, 15.2 per cent of Indian men, and 8.7 per cent of the general male

Table 6. *Males: industry by country of birth (10 per cent sample) – percentages*

	Irish Republic	NC America	India	Pakistan	NC Europe	Whole population
Agriculture/mining	2.1	0.6	0.7	0.3	0.5	6.0
Metal manufacture	2.2	5.9	9.1	9.6	1.2	3.2
Engineering	18.5	25.5	22.9	24.0	11.1	18.8
Textiles	1.1	1.8	6.8	18.8	1.0	2.1
Clothing/footwear	0.5	1.3	1.3	3.4	11.6	0.8
Other manufacturing	10.1	16.7	12.9	16.1	10.7	13.1
Construction	28.2	9.2	4.3	0.9	5.6	10.5
Public utilities	1.5	0.7	0.8	0.2	0.6	2.0
Transport/ communications	8.9	16.8	10.5	6.8	6.7	8.6
Distributive trades	5.7	3.8	6.6	5.2	9.9	9.7
Financial/professional/ scientific/administrative services	13.4	8.8	18.4	6.7	11.6	17.5
Other services	6.7	4.9	4.7	6.4	28.4	7.1
Industry inadequately described	1.0	3.9	0.8	1.5	1.1	0.5
	99.9	99.9	99.8	99.9	100.0	99.9
N =	26,957	11,456	13,073	7,220	3,660	1,502,522

Source: 1971 Census.

population were qualified in the sense of possessing graduate or post-GCE 'A' level professional qualifications, including nursing and teaching. The figure for West Indian women, 10.2 per cent, is marginally higher than for Indian women at 9.5 per cent (Reeves and Chevannes 1981).[6]

While Table 5 gives a broad indication of the proportions of different minority groups with managerial, professional or clerical experience that could in principle be applied in business, figures presented in Table 6 show in which areas of the economy ethnic minorities had experience of manual work.

The data in Table 6 acquire significance if it is assumed that, in order to set up in business, an individual may have to make use of knowledge and skills used in the course of employment. For example, on the evidence that 28.2 per cent of the Irish, but only 0.9 per cent of the

Pakistanis were in construction, while 18.8 per cent of Pakistanis as against 1.1 per cent of the Irish were in textiles, it is plausible to suggest that the Irish are more likely to enter business in the building trades and Pakistanis in the textile industry. Areas in which West Indians were more likely to be employed than Indians or Pakistanis include construction and transport and communications. This suggests that West Indians, in considering options for self-employment, are likely to go for construction, like the Irish, or areas of business involving driving or associated skills, such as taxi-driving, driving instruction, road haulage and car repairs and sales rather than trying to enter the distributive trades.

To conclude, in comparison with Indians and the general population, West Indians are far less likely to possess professional qualifications or to be engaged in white collar work, thus making it less likely that they will be found among 'opportunists' in business. At the same time, since participation in business may be a consequence of constrained access to other kinds of employment, Asians with professional and clerical skills (particularly Indians, who possess a higher educational level nearly twice the national average), when denied white collar employment, may be forced instead to look to the business world. Similarly, in trying to set up as craftsmen, West Indians might find themselves at a disadvantage because of the difficulty encountered in getting employment using their craft skills.

From interviews with West Indian businessmen, it appeared that those setting up in business benefited where a combination of craft and administrative skills was available. By contrast some West Indian firms founded by craftsmen suffered from lack of managerial experience when attempts were made to expand. While only a minority of owners in the sample came from a business background, those that did stressed that the experience of running a business had been of great value in helping them to set up in Britain. But in contrast to Indian businessmen, very few possessed any formal qualifications relevant to the world of business. As well as the possession of knowledge of the production process and of suppliers and markets, the acquisition of expertise in finance and taxation would strengthen the West Indian business community. Again, by drawing a parallel with the Asian community, business activity might be further advanced if it were served by a professional class of black accountants, solicitors and other intermediaries who could offer support and sustenance to the West Indian business population to a greater degree than the white professionals who are called on at present (Wilson 1983a; 1983b). In the absence of a sizeable first generation of West Indian businessmen in Britain, the second generation will be unable to acquire business 'know-how' from their elders.

(iv) Access to business resources
Finance
For starting and maintaining some businesses, only a small amount of capital is required; others are founded partly on personal savings or money borrowed from family or friends. But in many cases external funding is required. About half of the Asian businessmen in the samples interviewed in Brent and Lambeth had made use of bank loans in setting up their businesses. But only about one in five of the black-owned firms in Brent and one in eight of those in Lambeth had received start-up finance from the banks. Indeed, it was quite apparent that the banks exercised a great deal of power in assessing the viability of a business proposition and in the decision to grant a loan. West Indian businessmen are at a substantial disadvantage on account of the greater difficulties they experience in obtaining financial help from the banks (Lambeth 1982: 38). Interviews by Ward and Reeves (1980) with West Indian businessmen revealed they had experienced wide variations between different banks in lending policy (see Home Affairs Committee 1981: 90–1). Interviews with bank managers indicated that the most likely areas of racial disadvantage were when banks did not put the same effort into reshaping a business proposition brought to them by a West Indian, decided against giving a loan on the basis of a negative stereotype of West Indian business capabilities (where banks have no knowledge of a group making good businessmen, there may be a greater insistence on a client having a previous good record before they are prepared to lend to him), and insisted on more security to cover the loan.

Premises
No hard data on the extent of discrimination against ethnic minorities in the purchase, leasing or renting of suitable business property are available (one in five of the black firms in Lambeth claimed to have found racial bias in acquiring premises (Lambeth 1982: 40)). But it is likely that, in line with the recorded levels of discrimination in private housing, West Indians in common with Asians are in many cases denied access altogether, confined to the least desirable and most poorly situated premises, or expected to pay a higher price (for an analysis of access to retail premises by Asians, see chapter 12).

Labour
In the employment of labour, West Indian firms may be divided into four categories: those who have no employees, those who employ a very small number of staff, usually West Indian, those who are trying to expand and encountering recruitment and labour problems as a result,

and those who have successfully expanded to employ twenty-five or more staff. While most new firms trying to expand suffer from lack of experience as employers, some employers complained of the hostility of white employees towards black supervision (in some areas of business, particularly construction, efforts were made to solve problems of management by subcontracting work to self-employed labour). Among the few larger employers, the labour force tended to reflect the racial composition of the geographical areas in which the businesses were located – this shows that, in some cases at least, labour problems could be solved.

The market

Given the limited size of the West Indian market, success in business often requires selling to a wider clientele. The survey revealed examples of outlets for West Indians firms being restricted because of racial bias on the part of the purchasers. Less overtly, suppliers of West Indian products indicated that, even in areas where West Indians and Asians were concentrated, some large retail stores showed little interest in stocking ethnic lines.

Contacts

Having a well-developed network of business contacts from whom supplies can be obtained or contracts secured is clearly advantageous for successful business activity (see chapter 10). The recent entry into the field by West Indians, and the small size of their business community, suggest that they are likely to be disadvantaged in relations with white firms and have fewer compensatory facilities to draw upon from within their own circle. While in the long run the growth of West Indian business and business institutions, such as the United Kingdom Caribbean Chamber of Commerce, may aid the development of business networks, small businessmen, who of necessity have confined their activities to a relatively narrow sector of the West Indian market, both geographically and in terms of their goods and services, may find themselves in more direct competition with fellow West Indians than with other businessmen, thus hindering the growth of intra-ethnic cooperation. In contrast, the greater numerical strength of the Indian commercial and business class, demonstrated for example by the presence of Indian banks, credit companies, accountants and estate agents, and its wider range of activities and skills provide it with far more community resources. Attempts by West Indians to attach themselves to white business networks are further curtailed by the existence of discriminatory practices. As one West Indian greengrocer explained, 'racism means that you don't get the favours other fellows would get. Wholesalers try to con you for another 50p.'

(v) Ethnic community organisation and attitudes

Another kind of explanation advanced to account for the undeveloped state of black business in Britain relates to 'the values, family organisation, voluntary associations and other factors that affect the organising capacity' of the different racial minority groups (Aldrich and Feit 1975: 24). In chapter 3 a contrast was drawn between those ethnic minorities who have occupied a similar position in the social structure throughout the world as 'middlemen trading minorities' (such as the Jews in Europe, the Chinese in South East Asia, Asians in East Africa etc.) and the lack of a corresponding tradition of enterprise among blacks in America. Frazier (1957: 410–11) suggested that this was due to the lack of traditions in the field of business enterprise. Ofari pointed to the alienation of blacks from capitalism and to their 'African communal tradition' which has made them 'little attracted to trade, shopkeeping, buying and selling, or employing labor for the purpose of exploitation' (1970: 10–12). This kind of reasoning leads to the assumption that entrepreneurial values are much greater among Indians and Pakistanis in Britain than among West Indians, a view further supported by reference to a comparative study of Indians and West Indians in Jamaica (Niehoff and Niehoff 1960).

There is a tendency to explain this pattern in terms of cultural factors. But the success of West Indians in the United States in the world of business shows that too much emphasis should not be placed on cultural explanations in interpreting the position of West Indians in business in Britain. Foner (1979: 284) has recently used census data to show that 'West Indians in the United States are occupationally more successful than West Indians in Britain. Three factors may help to explain this situation: the history of West Indian migration to Britain and the United States; the occupational background of the migrants; and the structure of race relations in the two receiving areas.'

Overall, West Indians have been established in the United States much longer, a higher percentage of migrants came from a middle class background and they have found in the market provided by the black American population more opportunities for business development. Evidence supporting this view came from interviews with informants. More than one spoke of West Indians who found it difficult to run a successful business in Britain doing very much better when they migrated to the United States.

If West Indians migrating to the United States can become successful in business, this points to a *structural* explanation of the comparative lack of success so far achieved by West Indian business in Britain (in terms of market opportunities) rather than a *cultural* one (in terms of an alleged 'temperamental' inability to run a business).

3 Business development among minorities: inter-ethnic comparisons

Popular comparisons between the success of Asians and West Indians in business in Britain are probably inevitable. Evidence of Asian banks in the High Street and of other large businesses (many of them long established with headquarters abroad) lend evidence to the popular view. While there is some basis of reality in these comparisons, they are likely to underestimate the growing number of West Indian firms who are achieving real success (Lambeth 1982; Wilson 1983a). It is also far from true that all Asians in business are making a great deal of money, or even as much as they would earn if they were in manual employment (see chapters 11 and 12). Further, as we have seen, the two groups differ substantially in their class composition, educational levels, history and background. There are also internal differences of great significance within each category: between those who have come direct from the Indian subcontinent, for example, and those who came via East Africa, or between immigrants from different islands in the Caribbean.

Indeed it is reasonable to ask whether this is necessarily the best comparison in trying to account for the position of West Indian business in Britain. Asians have over generations occupied a world-wide role as middlemen trading communities, whereas most West Indians have gone into construction or areas of the service sector outside distribution. A closer comparison could be expected between the development of Asian and Jewish business, in line with the view that Indians and Pakistanis are likely to have 'a Jewish future' in Britain.

To find a closer match with the position of West Indians in Britain it is necessary to look for a community which has recently settled in Britain, largely of rural origin (perhaps with some experience of living in a city for a while before emigration), lacking any experience of business except in the form of small independent farming and without a strong extended family system, whose members have come to Britain as individual wage workers in British industry.

It has been suggested that the West Indians may have 'an Irish future' in Britain and certainly this seems a better comparison to make. Despite their long history of migration to England (and this is in itself one of the chief points of contrast, since long established immigrants can set up opportunities for more recent arrivals), the Irish in Britain have been remarkably little researched. Together with the difficulty of isolating in official statistics a broadly similar category of recent arrivals from rural areas, this prevents any systematic comparison. However, a general similarity between the development of business among the Irish in Britain and West Indians was noted by many of our informants. Irish firms are dominant in the building trade and informants spoke of an opportunity structure in the construction industry which provided some scope for movement from being self-employed as a brickie on the 'lump', through developing a small business, building or hiring plant, to the larger firms who gain major building and construction contracts. Outside the building trade, however, there was no sign of a spread into retailing or manufacturing comparable to that shown by Asians in recent years. Indeed the view of many bank managers was that Irish business was certainly no more developed, perhaps less so, than West Indian business. The national figures for 1971, the most recent available, which include long established Irish businessmen, show a much higher overall rate of participation in business, but these figures go back to the time when most West Indians were still establishing themselves in Britain.

The broad similarity between the Irish and West Indians in Britain, together with the finding that, where the market has provided more opportunities for West Indians in business, as in the United States, they have shown themselves well able to take advantage of this, should lead us to question any assumption that West Indians in Britain are exceptional in the underdeveloped nature of their business activity.

4 Black business development: the interests of government and the black community

So far we have been concerned with explanations of the level of involvement in business of West Indians in Britain. In this final section we consider some of the interests that seem to be involved in the justification of interventions to raise the level of business activity (Ward 1983b). This raises moral and political issues relating to a group's responsibility for its existing position and the question of whose interests are served by seeking to alter it. In considering this question, it is instructive to start by examining the political pedigree of the idea of salvation for the oppressed black minority through business.

Nothing endeared the negro leader Booker T. Washington more to the American capitalist class than his Atlanta address of 1895 in which he urged economic cooperation between races, yet made no demand for political and civil rights, for 'no race that has anything to contribute to the markets of the world is long in any degree ostracized' (Washington 1967: 137). W.E.B. Du Bois (1969: 80) described how the Southern radicals received this address as a surrender of the demand for civil and political equality, while the conservatives saw it as a generously conceived working basis for mutual understanding – making Washington popular with both parties.

Du Bois pointed out that Washington's gospel of work and money overshadowed any higher aims of life, and in the context of nineteenth-century economic and industrial developments could hardly have come amiss. Furthermore, it surrendered the demands for political power, civil rights and higher education for blacks (in the case of the latter, in favour of vocational education). Du Bois argued that Booker T. Washington faced a triple paradox:

1. He is striving nobly to make negro artisans business men and property-owners, but it is utterly impossible, under modern competitive methods, for working men and property-owners to defend their rights and exist without the right of suffrage.
2. He insists on thrift and self-respect, but at the same time counsels a silent submission to civic inferiority such as is bound to sap the manhood of any race in the long run.
3. He advocates common school and industrial training and depreciates institutions of higher learning.   (1969: 88)

Apart from winning the support of the white ruling class, the strategy of pursuing black entrepreneurial activity for social advancement was also strongly advocated by the black American bourgeoisie. Frazier (1957) describes the 'social myth' of negro business, which in reality is of little significance within the context of the overall American economy and provides only a very small amount of employment and income for black workers (Urban Institute 1980: 31–4). The black bourgeoisie's feeling of inferiority and quest for status in a white society dominated by business activity have led it to exaggerate the importance of black business in order to sustain a 'make-believe world' that satisfies its craving for recognition in the face of white contempt and amusement. In short, he concludes, the idea of developing a black middle class through business serves an important ideological function for the black community despite its irrelevance in the existing economic context for the black community as a whole; and any movement to form a separate 'black economy' by advocating the purchase of black products would primarily help to sustain the black bourgeoisie at the expense of the black proletariat.

Ofari (1970) continues the analysis with a polemic against the black bourgeoisie, whom he accuses of trying to develop their strength by exploiting the ghetto. 'Buy Black' campaigns, he argues, do not benefit the black community but only the black bourgeoisie, who are unlikely to be able to alter any of the basic economic relationships such as the massive economic hegemony of monopoly corporations that affect the lives of black people.

Obviously, such criticism is directed at the strong support elicited in political circles for the idea of encouraging minority business activity. After the report of the 1967 Commission on Civil Disorders, for example, the United States Federal Government took action to increase the level of minority business ownership (Select Committee on Small Business 1979: 40). Policy to encourage greater participation in business by the black community and other minorities has been shared between the Small Business Administration set up by Congress in 1953 and the Office of Minority Business Enterprise set up within the Department of Commerce in 1969 (now known as the Minority Business Development Agency), the latter concentrating on the provision of management and technical assistance to minority-owned business.

What then of the economic and political context in which discussion of black business has emerged in Britain? Although West Indians have been resident in Britain for 30 years or more, there has until recently been little sociological research into West Indian business activity (Indians and Pakistanis, probably by virtue of their greater visibility in retailing, have inspired far more interest). The Economic and Social Research Council's Research Unit on Ethnic Relations became involved when approached by the Race Relations and Immigration Sub-Committee of the Home Affairs Committee of the House of Commons to undertake a short study to assist the Sub-Committee in its enquiry into racial disadvantage in the area of business activity among West Indians (Ward and Reeves 1980). Whatever the reasons for, and policy implications of, this particular initiative, it seems significant that concern for West Indian business should be expressed during the life of a Conservative government committed to reviving the economy by encouraging private investment and enterprise and nurturing, rhetorically at least, a 'seed bed' of small firms. The 1979 Conservative Election Manifesto asserted that the creation of new jobs depended to a great extent on the success of smaller businesses and contained a pledge to make life easier for them (see pp. 105–6).

Thus the idea of black business as an element of such a policy is likely to prove popular with a Conservative government. Faced with industrial contraction and economic decline, the Conservative government sought to encourage the traditional values of enterprise and self-reliance. Committed to cutting public expenditure, with adverse effects on the social services and the urban aid programmes, but confronted with rising levels of unemployment, it had to seek alternative ways of presenting solutions to urban poverty. Nowhere have the adverse effects of monetarist policies been felt more acutely than among the ethnic minorities. Black youth unemployment at two or three times the average for whites, accompanied by deteriorating relationships with the police, are seen as a grave threat to public order (Scarman 1982). Encouragement of minority owned firms is seen as a constructive response to these trends.

> The development of businesses run by members of ethnic minority groups is a vital element in tackling racial disadvantage in inner areas. They stimulate the creation of local jobs, the acquisition and extension of skills, and the promotion of new products. The potential for future growth thus offered helps increase the confidence and prosperity necessary for sustained improvement.
> (Department of the Environment 1983: 5)

The concept of creating a black business class who could be relied upon to embrace Conservative political values, to generate new wealth in the inner city and to provide work for the black unemployed has instant appeal. The plausibility of the solution is encouraged by the apparently spectacular emergence of Asian businessmen, some of whom have been very vocal in Conservative circles.

Within Conservatism the idea of developing ethnic minority business has two great strengths. First, considered in the context of a capitalist economic system which it in no way challenges, it accords in its entirety with the Conservative petit-bourgeois ideological orthodoxy of economic individualism, the possibility of personal advancement, self-reliance and a minimum of state interference to ensure healthy competition – in short, the ethnic version of the 'property owning democracy'. Secondly, the idea of promoting ethnic minority business as an *alternative policy* for dealing with the problems of poverty, unemployment, squalor and the inadequacy of the social services undermines more direct political demands for greater equality, racial justice and an end to racial discrimination.

The Conservative belief that some slight interference in the market can improve the situation of the ethnic minorities is totally at odds with the socialist view that direct political intervention in the economy and legal safeguards are necessary to guarantee working class and minority rights and living standards. Nevertheless, most of the practical measures devised specifically to support black business have been taken by Labour controlled local councils.

Indeed, for the Labour Party positive encouragement of minority business creates an ideological dilemma. For the party represents the interests of organised labour and tends to pursue economic development through big business or through cooperatively controlled small enterprises. Attitudes to the traditionally constituted small business in which union recognition has to be fought for have been much less positive. Thus the encouragement of black business involves support for enterprises whose owners are typically among the fiercest allies of the Conservatives in terms of their class position. The crucial point to be recognised is that in increasing numbers of local authority areas Labour control is secured through ethnic minority support. It is important to ask, therefore, how far measures to assist business development are favoured within the minority communities.

In fact the idea of ethnic enterprise seems likely to attract widespread support. Existing and aspiring entrepreneurs can be expected to favour measures which will improve their access to business resources. More widely, this seems to avoid the stigma of welfare payments and fits in with the philosophy of self-help which holds out the possibility of black people being able to exercise greater control over their own destiny, without white interference. At a time of large scale unemployment, it offers the prospect of jobs. Furthermore, its implementation contains the promise of salaried posts and social advancement for young educated blacks to whom other avenues of upward mobility in management and industry are often denied. Conveniently, its goals are ideologically ambiguous: would a programme of this kind seek to set up socialist cooperatives or small private companies – sorting out answers to such questions is a stimulating prospect.

It is no surprise, therefore, given the assumption that there is a widespread positive attitude towards minority business within ethnic communities (particularly among those community leaders with whom councillors and officers will be in contact), to find that black business support is seen as an important element of an equal opportunities programme (Lambeth 1982; Brooks 1983). The problem lies in finding a way of encouraging minority entrepreneurs without dissipating the financial support throughout the whole of the small business community. Positive discrimination which takes the form of grant aid to particular ethnic cultural and recreational projects is broadly seen as acceptable. But a general policy of directing resources to one sector of small business without providing equivalent support across the board is much more politically adventurous.

What seems to be emerging is that ideological positions on the left can respond flexibly to changes in the base of political support. In contrast, black business promotion policies which rely for their existence on ideological consistency with Conservative orthodoxy face a hazardous future. Where they persist, it is pertinent to examine what other functions they perform. In this context, Du Bois's criticism of the Atlanta address takes on new significance: to emphasise the importance of black economic advancement through new capitalist initiatives, if this is done at the expense of demands for the social justice and equality denied at present, might be seen as political opportunism of the Atlanta variety.

PART THREE

The Asian experience

9

Snakes and ladders: Asian business in Britain

SUSAN NOWIKOWSKI

It has been suggested that ethnic business may provide the ladder by which, over the years, Asians in Britain might climb to socio-economic equality (see chapter 11). Deliberation of these prospects stems from analysis of the experience of other minorities such as Japanese, Jews and Chinese in the USA as reviewed in chapter 3, for whom the ownership and control of small businesses has been a vital instrument of social mobility. Such groups are seen as 'middlemen minorities' who sell goods and services to the host population. Their success is held to lie in the positive advantages of features of their minority status. As we have seen, the 'cultural model' attempts to account for the emergence and role of ethnic business by identifying cultural characteristics internal to ethnic minorities that confer positions advantageous for entrepreneurial activity. With time, the success of such economic activity may be the basis of ethnic socio-economic mobility in Britain. American Chinese have been successful in exploiting the middleman minority role and achieving parity with the majority society (see chapter 3). However, although the Chinese case supports the view that ethnic capitalism may act as a social ladder, it would be ill-advised to imagine that this principle operates for all minorities in all circumstances.[1]

Indeed, in this chapter I will argue for a less sanguine view of the emergence and opportunities of the ethnic small business sector amongst Asians in Britain. I will propose an alternative framework for the analysis of Asian business development using empirical data collected in Manchester in the early 1970s.[2]

Structural disadvantage in core and periphery: white racism and the black minority

My basic proposition is that the analysis of the patterns and potential of ethnic business in postwar Britain cannot be approached from a model

149

which starts with the assumption of the specificity of ethnic enterprise and the internal characteristics of an ethnic minority. Instead, I argue that ethnic business activity can only be understood as part of the wider structure of the British political economy. The starting point for the analysis of business activities amongst racial minorities must be the structures and processes of the wider society and essentially the prevailing relationships of power.

If we are to understand the dynamics of race relations situations, we need to relate race and ethnicity to the wider social structure and investigate the relationships of domination and power between groups (Rex 1970: 50). To understand Asian business development in Britain, we must proceed from analysis of its location in the British social formation and the relationship of racial minorities to the dominant white society. But while the analysis of racial and ethnic relations must be related to the structures of power in the society, power is not nationally bounded. Structures of power are global. The uneven development of the global economy is dominated by the forces of Western imperialism. It is this imbalanced development that creates ethnicity as a structuring force. We see the racial minority in Britain in a position of structured inequality as part of this imbalanced development.

From the sixteenth century onwards, through the penetration of the forces of Western colonialism and neocolonialism, Third World societies have been incorporated into the world capitalist system in positions of structured inequality. This system can be conceptualised as polarised into a dominant core and subordinate periphery. Before and after the political independence of the colonies, Western imperialism shaped, subordinated and exploited the peripheral economies and societies to complement the structural demand of capitalist expansion at the core (Amin 1974; Alavi 1975). The internal development of the post-colonial developing countries – a dependent capitalist development[3] – complements the structural demands of advanced capitalism in the developed countries. It may provide materials, markets, investment opportunities or cheap labour to meet the demands of capitalism in the developed countries. International migration can be seen as one strand of the post-war exploitative dependency relationship between the West and the developing countries (Castles and Kosack, 1973, especially 374–429).

Britain and the Indian subcontinent have been historically locked in such global relationships of interdependence and inequality. Their modern relationship was conditioned by the nature of British colonialism, which in India was basic to the development of British capital 'at home' and it was basic to the development of the internal structure of the subcontinent. It set in process the specific distorted development in South

Asia which, in the postwar years, has reinforced her subordination and exploitation by the West in the international division of labour.

It is in this context of interdependent development that South Asian migration to Britain has taken place. From the start, the global penetration of capitalism from the centre was uneven in its impact on the pre-existing economies and societies in the periphery. While imbalances have emerged at the global level between the developed capitalist economies and the underdeveloped periphery, imbalances and structural tensions have emerged internally in the development of the economies and societies of the peripheries. Such tensions arising from the uneven internal development in the Indian subcontinent have generated distinctive flows of migration to the West in the postwar years. We will discuss structural tensions in three sections of South Asian society that have subsequently been the source of migrant flows. These are the sectors of the Asian business bourgeoisie, and in particular the commercially orientated textile bourgeoisie; the Western educated professional class; and the sector of the urban lower middle class and the middle strata of the countryside.

British colonialism in the subcontinent was oriented to the promotion of trade with the metropolis. There emerged an indigenous Indian bourgeoisie which was essentially a commercial bourgeoisie from the west coast of the subcontinent. On the east coast, commerce remained largely in European hands. Indians entered business there as colonial employees and found their opportunities for entrepreneurship and economic mobility severely blocked by the racist policies of the European establishment (Bagchi 1970: 225–6). On the west coast, however, there were business castes and communities which had been relatively independent and commercially highly successful in pre-British India. They were closely integrated ethnic communities which drew on their historically accumulated resources of business skills, wealth and communal networks to emerge as successful commercial collaborators with the colonial power. There were especially strong links with the textile trade centring in north-west England and Manchester in particular.

Throughout the colonial period, industry and technology were only weakly developed in India. Traditional craft industries such as textiles were devastated by the policies of the colonial power. Industrial development was only encouraged for the processing of goods for export. However, despite the restrictiveness of the colonial regime, in the late nineteenth century there was evidence of an emergent indigenous industrial bourgeoisie, particularly from the west coast. Industrialists arose from the closely-knit ethnic business communities and were active especially in textiles (see Spodek 1965).

This indigenous bourgeoisie was a significant force in the twentieth-century struggles for political independence. The immediate postwar years witnessed attempts to break economic dependence on the metropolitan powers and establish a pattern of self-reliant growth. However, the subsequent development of industry in India made clear the imbalances and contradictions of dependent capitalist development. The backwardness of Indian technology implied dependence on the West for industrial development. The weak internal market was insufficient to sustain domestic industrial expansion and the textile industry was one of the first sectors to experience this restrictiveness. The Indian bourgeoisie pressed for a reorientation towards integration in the international division of labour, a return to export oriented growth, and the strengthening of financial and technological interdependence with the West. Subsequently they have expanded their capitalist activity internationally, seeking commercial and manufacturing opportunities abroad, and strengthening links with the metropolis.

But this is not the only class which has manifested the tensions of dependent capitalist development and responded with an orientation towards the metropolis. The Western-educated professional and administrative class has also experienced frustration in the subcontinent since Independence. This class was a child of British policies in India which were designed to educate a loyal indigenous stratum of professionals, such as lawyers, doctors and administrators, to carry out the tasks of the colonial regime. Especially after 1860, employment opportunities and educational reforms instituted by the British encouraged a Western literary education or a training in the liberal Westernised professions. A class emerged that was ideologically and economically dependent on the colonial power and unevenly recruited from Indian society. It was drawn largely from the Hindu, rather than Muslim, population and from the middle and upper castes of the traditional social order. Furthermore, education and employment opportunities were concentrated in the urban areas, particularly in Calcutta and Bombay. However, members of this urban middle class found their own access to power and status severely restricted. They faced a colonial policy which discriminated by race in employment and gave Indians unequal access to the higher positions in the Civil Service and the professions (Misra 1961: 181, 212–31). The expansion of educational opportunities outstripped the opportunities for employment and achievement in the colonial regime.

With the frustration of their aspirations, the urban middle class supported the early twentieth-century nationalist struggle along with the indigenous business bourgeoisie. However, the uneven development of the South Asian economy that has characterised the post-Independence era has sharpened their frustrations. Popular pressure led to the expansion of education opportunities, but the content and idiom of education has continued to reinforce the aspirations for white collar and professional employment, alongside Western life style and consumption patterns. There is a manifest disjunction between such training and aspirations, and the economic opportunities and demands of the economy. With sharp competition for the few jobs in the modern urban sector, the 'educated unemployed' have remained more or less a constant proportion of a rapidly growing stock of educated labour (Blaugh, Layard and Woodhall 1969: 85). The severity of competition for employment is a motivation for further education to improve one's competitiveness. In response to such pressure and frustration, many highly skilled Asians migrate to the educational and employment opportunities in the West.

The third set of structural tensions that have motivated postwar migration from South Asia to the West are those associated with class developments in the urban lower middle class of non-agricultural and non-industrial workers, and in the middle strata of the large rural sector. Again we can trace the contradictions of contemporary South Asian development to the uneven impact of British colonialism. While the Indian business bourgeoisie and the Western educated middle class made substantial gains in collaboration with the colonial regime, the rural sector and the peasantry experienced increasing impoverishment. British colonialism had little impact on the structures of production in the countryside. Cash crops were merely skimmed off the surface of an immobilised agrarian society (Stokes 1978). There were, however, radical changes in the rights to land subsequent to the British organisation of tax and revenue systems in the countryside. Traditional land rights were redefined: land became private property – a commodity to be bought and sold. The poor found themselves forced from their former traditional rights and status. Proprietors found their land-holdings increasingly fragmented in areas where there was no primogeniture and their status was gradually reduced. However, some gains were made by the middle sectors. A class of moneylenders, traders and shopkeepers arose out of the exploitation of the peasantry. A new class of absentee landlords also emerged. But indigenous investment in the land remained low since the peasantry were often deep in debt while absentee landlords looked to the urban sector for self-advancement.

Conditions in the countryside were further reduced by the demands of trade with the metropolis. Local craft industries were destroyed and hereditary caste occupations declined with the competition of imported industrial goods. Pauperised artisans swelled the numbers of the landless labourers. Income earning opportunities in the village were shrinking.

In the postwar years some regions have witnessed the application of the new technology of the Green Revolution. This has benefited the rich peasantry and an emerging rural bourgeoisie, but it has effectively impoverished the mass in these agricultural areas (Ahmad 1973; Sharma 1973). Indeed for the majority of the rural population the postwar years have meant increased impoverishment in a restrictive village economy, essentially in subsistence agriculture and sharecropping activities. The pressure of rising prices and increasing numbers has further strained scarce land resources and limited incomes. The middle strata of the peasantry are in a particularly contradictory situation, aspiring to social and economic improvement, but constrained by the limited economic opportunities in the rural sector (Ahmad 1973: 213–19).

The pressures of the rural sector have encouraged some of the population to migrate to the city in search of earning opportunities to supplement rural incomes, to provide resources for the purchase of land or agricultural inputs and to raise the family's status in the village. However, the urban sector itself also manifests the distortion of dependent capitalist development, and has offered few income earning opportunities for such migrants.

In the urban sector there have been increasing class disparities. The rapid growth of the cities has been characterised by the expansion of the large tertiary sector of non-agricultural and non-industrial workers, continuing the pattern established before Independence. This sector includes the middle class of administrative and professional workers, but also a vast pool of the urban lower middle class – white collar workers, the educated unemployed, small businessmen, craftsmen, traders and those engaged in other urban services, private and public, such as clerk in the ubiquitous urban bureaucracies, transport workers and those employed in education, restaurants, 'leisure' and the vast array of services that characterise the Asian city (McGee 1976). It is this urban lower middle class that has been particularly vulnerable to downward pressure on their standard of living and security in the postwar years. The price of food has risen, unemployment levels are high and competition for work is fierce. Education is a prerequisite to gain access to industrial and white collar employment. Few employment opportunities are generated by the new capital intensive industrialisation, while the white collar sector has been flooded by educated applicants. In the swollen tertiary sector of small traders, businessmen and craftsmen, competition is likewise fierce for the limited urban markets.

These tensions of postwar development in the rural and urban sectors have generated flows of migration both within the subcontinent and internationally towards metropolitan centres of power. Migration has not generally drawn on the poorest regions or the poorest sectors of the population, but on the rural middle strata and the urban lower middle class.[4] It has selected those with vital resources such as finance, education, bureaucratic 'know how' and interpersonal links with others established abroad.

We have seen the pressure for migration resulting from the contradictions of class developments in three major sectors of South Asian society. Postwar migrants from these three sectors are clearly distinctive in their access to class resources and in the constraints accumulated at the South Asian end of the power structures of the world capitalist system. Further, these three types of migration have complemented specific structural demands of British capitalism in its postwar adjustment and development. Recruitment to these specific structural niches in Britain has further defined the constraints and opportunities facing South Asians, given their global and national class location. The location of the racial minority in the metropolis is largely one of structural disadvantage. The instrument of its subordination and exploitation is the racism of the dominant white society. Racism divides the national minorities from other class members in Britain and gives them a specific position of disadvantage and isolation. In the postwar years the West European and British economies have relied extensively on the exploitation of foreign labour and skills to sustain their capitalist development. Britain recruited readily from sources of New Commonwealth labour, especially from the West Indies and South Asia. Advantages accrue to Western capital from the flexibility and super-exploitability of the migrant labour force, accomplished by nationality laws, labour contract systems and racial and ethnic discrimination. In Britain before the 1960s New Commonwealth immigrants could enter freely and had rights of settlement. At this time, in place of nationality laws and contract labour systems, racial discrimination was the instrument ensuring the subordination of the migrant labour force (Sivanandan 1976). But the postwar years have been a period of rising racial tension. From the early 1960s state intervention to control 'the problem' of coloured immigration through immigration and nationality legislation has institutionalised discrimination against coloured workers and settlers (Sivanandan 1976). Subsequent legislation, culminating in the 1971 and 1981 Nationality Acts has reduced the position of New Commonwealth labour towards that of contract labour on the West European model, and has undermined the security of the settled coloured population (Manchester Law Centre 1981).

However, British capital has not recruited a homogeneous flow of immigrants to this position of structured inequality. Industry demanded cheap and flexible unskilled labour supplies as the basis of postwar reconstruction. It was also necessary to fill the structural gaps vacated as the indigenous white population moved horizontally into new technology industries and vertically into better paid, more secure and desirable positions. Coloured immigrants were recruited as unskilled and semi-skilled labour to poorly paid and undesirable posts in the declining, labour intensive traditional industries and the new technological and highly automated industries (Nikolinakos 1975) and in the rapidly expanding service sector in postwar Britain. Asian unskilled migrants were particularly important as replacement labour in declining traditional industries such as the textile industry in Manchester and the north-west region, and as recruits in metal manufacturing, engineering, transport and communications and the service sector.

The expanding service sector made further demands on the New Commonwealth, this time for skilled labour to fill the less popular and poorly paid skilled service posts. For example, the skills of Asians have been especially vital to the growth of the British medical services but have tended to be concentrated on the lower rungs of the middle class career structure, and in the less popular specialisms (Gish 1971; Allen and Smith 1974).

In the structural adjustments of British capitalism during these years, the decline of the textile sector was especially pertinent to changes in the economy of the north-west region. The export markets of the textile trade declined with the postwar competition in manufactured goods from the developing countries and, moreover, the industry had lost much of its home market to foreign competition. To deal with the problems of the declining industry there were attempts to re-equip, rationalise and restructure (Miles 1968). This decline, and subsequent transformation, underlies the 'pull' of a third flow of Asian migrants to Britain, i.e. the migration of businessmen from the textile communities of South Asia. Despite restrictive trade policies and pressures from the British textile interests, traders from overseas, including South Asians, have established themselves in Britain and promoted textile imports alongside the expanding trade in other manufactured goods from the developing countries. Asian textiles have become a vital part of the manufacturing processes of the British textile industry and the British consumer market. Certain sectors of manufacturing industry have been developed in the hands of Asian entrepreneurs while Asian businessmen have also engaged in the more diversified import/export trade in manufactured goods between Britain and the developing countries.

So far we have seen that in postwar Britain the Asian minority has been located in a position of structural disadvantage effected and maintained through the politico-ideological instrument of racism. The inferior position of the racial minorities is manifest throughout life in Britain – in the institutions of the state and in informal social relationships, in the law, housing, education, the mass media, leisure and at work. We have seen that black unskilled labour has been recruited to the less desirable positions in declining or new industries, and in services, while black skilled labour has been funnelled into the low rungs of the rapidly expanding service sector. Since the mid 1960s, in the face of economic recession, the racial minorities have borne the brunt of contraction, unemployment and declining living standards in these sectors (Smith 1981).

Finally we have seen one dimension of the ethnic business sector that has been manifest in postwar Britain. The entrepreneurial ability of the Asian bourgeoisie has been drawn in with the structural readjustments of the declining British textile trade, and the speedy postwar integration of cheap Third World manufactures into the metropolitan economy. But it is clear that the business sector that has emerged amongst Asians settled in Britain is not confined to the large scale commercial economy of import/export merchants and manufacturers. We will also discuss below the development of small business among the other two groups of the Asian minority – from the Western educated middle class, and more particularly from the unskilled and semi-skilled workers from rural and urban backgrounds. There is clearly an important distinction to be drawn between the dynamics of large and small scale business enterprise. But neither appears in isolation from the wider political and economic setting of racial minorities in Britain. The genesis of the ethnic business sector is part of the structural dynamics of the British postwar society in the global capitalist system. It is conditioned by the wider structural constraints of the capitalist system and its dominant racial and class forces.

Action and ethnic survival strategies: the emergence of an ethnic business sector

So far we have only considered how the ethnic business sector may be seen as shaped by economic forces and political–ideological relations of domination-subordination in the global capitalist system and the British social formation.[5] However, I am not proposing an analytical framework that rests on structural determinism. Structural analysis needs to be accompanied by the analysis of action.[6] Individuals and collectivities are not mere passive agents carrying out the tasks determined by the structural forces of production and politico-ideological relations. They acquire resources and face constraints in the context of their inherited structural location such as we have seen characterising the three distinct groups of Asian migrants to Britain. However, action is relatively autonomous and can usefully be seen as a series of choices reflecting strategies put into practice by individuals and collectivities in the light of the constraints and resources of their historically conditioned location. We will analyse the emergence of businesses amongst Asians in Britain as one such strategy. In short, it is a strategy of survival made from the inherited position of structural disadvantage experienced by the Asian minority. For this analysis we will move to the micro-level and investigate the patterns of action we found amongst Asians living in Manchester. The study took place in the residential middle class commuting belt of 'South Manchester'.[7] The respondents were a representative sample of Asian heads of households in this area.[8] Their occupations placed the large majority of our respondents in the middle class,[9] nearly half being employed in 'new middle class' occupations.[10] A minority (13.3 per cent of the survey sample) were in working class employment.[11] The rest (39.9 per cent) were self-employed (those employing others are included here as self-employed). But it was clear that those in business did not form a homogeneous sector. In this paper we are concerned with the diverse careers of this substantial group of the self-employed.[12]

Almost half of the self-employed respondents described themselves as owners or directors, engaged in import/export or the wholesale trade. Some also had retailing or manufacturing interests. Nearly all had business interests in textiles. The rest of the self-employed were engaged in small business concerns – typically market trading (24.5 per cent), retail shops (7.5 per cent), restaurants or other services. Finally there were professionals engaged in their own practices.[13]

We have discussed earlier how the racial and class location of the Asian minority can be seen as part of the structures and processes not merely of British capitalism, but of the wider global capitalist system. It is this contextualisation of the Asians' role in global structural developments that can help us understand the emergence and diversity of ethnic business patterns in Britain. For all the Asians, self-employment strategies emerged in the context of structural racial disadvantage in the metropolis. However, self-employment as a choice or strategy of management of resources and constraints has a very different meaning depending upon the particular class context in which it arises. We have seen how three macro-class developments have linked Britain and South Asia in the post-war years. The uneven internal development of South Asia has generated migration from three major sectors of the society and each of these migrant flows has complemented specific structural developments of British post-war capital. On the basis of their individual background characteristics and migration career patterns, we located each of the Asian respondents in the Manchester study in one of these three macro-class developments.[14] Businessmen had emerged from amongst each of the three migrant groups, but the nature of the business patterns was quite different, given the distinctive structural constraints and resources that the migrants experienced.

The Western-educated and professional class

The largest group of respondents were from the Western-educated and professional class. Most were male heads of households with nuclear families, though there was a minority of single female and male respondents. They came from professional or small business family backgrounds in urban areas in the subcontinent or in a few cases from East Africa. They were predominantly drawn from the *Indian* middle class, and the largest religious group were Hindus. Generally they had achieved a high level of education before migrating, having university qualifications (typically postgraduate qualifications) and/or professional qualifications. Most had been working in a professional (often medical) or administrative position in their country of origin, or had been studying there.

Their prior class circumstances conditioned their migration and settlement pattern in Britain. Migration had been motivated by the desire to get on further in education or occupational careers. Generally the migrants did not have extensive personal contacts or familiarity with Britain before migrating. Contacts had been established at a distance through a firm or university. The migrants had been drawn into the lower rungs of 'new middle class' career structures and their settlement was essentially defined by available educational or occupational opportunities. The careers were characterised by a very high geographical mobility between urban areas along with some socio-economic mobility.

Of the three groups of Asian migrants we distinguished, this class was the least significant for the emergence of strategies of self-employment. At the time of the study most respondents were competing with varied success in 'new middle class' careers. But about one quarter had moved into some kind of self-employment.[15] A few had joined the business community in Manchester, either by entering the ethnic textile sector (see below) or by establishing property or other commercial businesses. Some had set up their own professional practices (e.g. in accountancy or design).

The career strategies of the Western-educated professionals were forged within the structured constraints and resources of their race and class. In their occupation, housing, education and social life the migrants were competing *in* white society for access to positions dominated by the white society. A small minority had felt no personal experience of racial discrimination and even denied its existence in Britain. But most had felt discrimination and many voiced complaints specifically related to their occupational careers. They had experienced the constraints of their race once they tried to advance themselves out of the less desirable and the poorly paid rungs of their occupational hierarchies. To overcome the problems of career advancement respondents in the medical profession, for example, had adopted the strategy of moving into less popular specialisms or out of hospital work and into general practice.

The business bourgeoisie

The business bourgeoisie was the smallest group of respondents (18). All were male heads of households, typically living in nuclear families. They contrasted strongly with the professionals discussed above. The business bourgeoisie were characterised by their access to a very different set of resources and by very different class constraints in their country of origin and in Britain. Their experience and actions during settlement in Britain were quite distinctive. Most were active in the business sector from the time of their arrival and were engaged in the textile import/export trade as owners, directors or partners. Some also traded in other manufactured goods, and a few had extended their business interests into retailing, manufacture or property.

These business activities were typically an extension of business interests originating in South Asia. The migrants came from business family backgrounds, generally in textiles, on the west coast of India. They were from urban areas and predominantly from Hindu trading castes. Many had achieved college or university qualifications in their country of origin. Some were students prior to migration, but most were working in the business community, often in family firms. It was these business links, finance and expertise that characterised their resources. The family or community business interests stretched overseas (e.g. firms had branches in India, East Africa, Hong Kong and Britain) and the individual's migration might have been preceded by other business trips abroad. The move to Britain was generally directly associated with establishing a branch or new firm. The migrants used their prior knowledge of the country, established ethnic business contacts and their own access to wealth and business skills to set up businesses here.

The timing of their migration was quite distinctive. Over half had entered prior to 1962, and several had come in the immediate postwar years. The very early migrants had often worked as Indian merchants or agents buying British textiles to export abroad. However, in the postwar atmosphere of the decline of the British textile industry, their businesses were reoriented towards the import of Asian and Third World manufactured goods. More recent migrants had entered directly into such import concerns.

Respondents in this career type were well integrated socially, not just economically, into the ethnic business community in Manchester. Most of their daily lives was spent amongst the networks of the Asian textile and trading community. There was frequent social entertaining and community support in times of need. However, they also drew on ethnic links that stretched throughout Britain and overseas. They went overseas for frequent social and business trips.

The business bourgeoisie lived an affluent and urbane life in Manchester. However, unlike the professionals, they were not constantly competing in individualised careers in white society. Few had sought further education in Britain, and socio-economic mobility had been in the opportunities and constraints of the business sector. Many were extremely successful businessmen. Their access to wealth, education and the resources of the ethnic community gave some shield in the face of white racism. These businessmen were not unaware of the salience of their racial group in Britain, but typically their personal experiences of discrimination were limited. They often expressed satisfaction with life in Britain, though their plans for the future would depend on business opportunities. Several expected eventually to retire to their country of origin, where their family and community were established.

The urban lower middle class and the rural middle strata

The third migrant flow was that of respondents (60) from the rural middle strata and the urban lower middle class. Most were males living with their wives and children in Manchester. However, there were a few single males, and a minority whose families were abroad.

Half of this group were now businessmen in Manchester. However, their business activities were quite distinct from those of the business bourgeoisie described above. They were either self-employed in the retail distributive sector (4 shopkeepers, 12 market traders, 1 door-to-door salesman), in the restaurant trade or hotel catering (3) or in the taxi business (1). In addition, there was a small group who were in larger scale businesses and who can be seen as the 'nouveau riche' of this career type.[16]

The 'nouveau riche' manufactured clothing (e.g. crimplene trousers) or were textile and fancy goods wholesalers (a fuller account of this group is given in the following chapter). Some also had interests in property, retailing and restaurants.

The other half of the respondents from this third migrant flow, who were not in business activities, were employees in manual work or in lower middle class white collar work. However, most of those engaged in business at the time of the study had also been in manual or white collar work in Britain before establishing their businesses. Their move *into* the small business sector contrasts clearly with the longstanding entrepreneurial activities of the business bourgeoisie. The Asians in the Manchester suburbs clearly perceived the status distinction between the business bourgeoisie and the small business sector. The 'nouveau riche' were wealthy in the locality and maintained an affluent life style. Their success was acknowledged, but so too was their distinctiveness. For example, the business bourgeoisie might stress, with some disdain, how the 'nouveau riche' had made their money 'standing at a market stall in Manchester!'.

The differences between the business bourgeoisie and the small businessmen lay in their socio-economic background in the country of origin, in their pattern of migration and in their role in Britain. They experienced very different sets of racial and class constraints and resources. Respondents in the small business sector were typically living, working or studying in urban areas prior to their migration to Britain. A minority (17) were born in a rural area, but most of these had moved to live in the city during their childhood or youth. In the rural areas most had been farming. In the urban areas their fathers were typically petty entrepreneurs or lower middle class white collar workers, while most of the respondents had been in white collar employment (e.g. as clerks or railway employees) or students. A few were petty entrepreneurs or unskilled workers. Others described themselves as unemployed.

These respondents typically had a lower level of education in the country of origin than either the business bourgeoisie or the professionals. Most of those who had worked in the white collar sector or were students were educated to secondary level, college or university (intermediate or Bachelor degree). The rest had much lower levels of educational attainment. This was especially true of those from the rural sector.

There was a larger proportion of Pakistanis and Muslims in this career group than amongst either the business bourgeoisie or the professionals. Just over half came from Pakistan and nearly 60 per cent from the Punjab. A few came from East Africa or Bangladesh.

The migrants of this career group had typically come to Britain earlier than the mass of Asian migrants (Smith 1976: 24–8). Their migration was virtually ended by 1968, but it was not concentrated in the years from 1962–8. Only 37.8 per cent entered Britain in these years, whereas 57.9 per cent entered before 1962. They clearly represented an early cohort of the unskilled Asian labour migration. They had been motivated to seek out opportunities in the West to improve their own or their family's situation. Some migrated 'for further education', but most gave the more general reasons 'to make money' or 'for a better future'. Unlike the professionals, they did not draw on their education and occupational resources to migrate to individualised positions in professional or educational career structures. Rather like the business bourgeoisie they tended to move to established ethnic networks. However, the business bourgeoisie had moved to contacts in bourgeois ethnic niches, and to suburban residence with their nuclear family near friends or kin. In contrast these respondents generally migrated as single males and joined ethnic contacts living in the inner city.

Ethnic contacts were an important resource that the migrant could manipulate to survive in Britain. Frequently he used them to find work and/or housing and typically they were the basis of his social group in Manchester. A few respondents had been dependent on ethnic contacts for direct entry into the small business sector, having come to Britain to join people already established in small businesses (see chapter 10). Most of these were restaurant workers, some were traders.

However, this type of occupational career was not typical of the group as a whole. Generally migrants had first found work in Britain in low status and undesirable positions in industry or the service sector. Few had access to white collar work. Most had been recruited as unskilled labour to fill the structural gap that could not be filled with the indigenous white labour force. In Manchester they had worked in the textile, engineering, asbestos, concrete, chemicals, food processing and rubber industries.

Typically the self-employed had been amongst those who had started work in Britain in such positions. They had worked long hours, under difficult conditions, and had experienced white racism both in and outside work. Many reported their inability to get promotion or more rewarding jobs because of their race. They had changed jobs often, moving from one factory to another, or between services and industry, because of redundancies and closures, bad pay, bad working conditions, effects on their health and the lack of opportunities to improve themselves.

There had been two paths of mobility out of this restrictive manual sector. Some migrants tried to advance themselves through gaining educational qualifications and moving into white collar work. A few had succeeded (12.2 per cent of those first employed in manual work).

However, within the white collar sector self-improvement was often problematic and some of those who were originally employed there joined the popular path out of manual work – that of self-employment. This route was followed by 41.5 per cent of those first employed in manual work, and by 33.0 per cent of those employed in lower middle class white collar work. Only in self-employment did the migrants feel themselves more free of the constraints of racial discrimination in employment, though the experience of discrimination clearly varied according to the type of self-employment in which the respondent was engaged and the extent to which he was dependent on the host society (e.g. for customers, supplies or premises). Generally the experience of racism was reduced since daily contact with the white society was confined to the trading or service relationship. Employment did not rest on the insecurity of recruitment, promotion and definition of work conditions by the dominant white society. Market traders and shopkeepers worked alone or often employed the labour of family and kin. Restaurateurs worked in ethnic work situations where employees might be family or kin. The nature of the work itself reduced vulnerability to racial discrimination if the migrant was engaged in servicing the ethnic community (e.g. ethnic food or clothing shops, or restaurants).

Most of those who followed this path of mobility were still petty entrepreneurs at the time of the study. A few, however, had established themselves in the small group of the 'nouveau riche'. Occasionally members of this group had moved directly from manual employment into the larger scale business activities. Most, however, had first set themselves up in small businesses in Manchester, often market trading, and had expanded their businesses over the years, eventually moving into manufacturing or wholesaling. Many respondents who were still employed in poor working conditions in industry or the service sector expressed their hopes that one day they would be able to set up their own business to provide a better future for themselves and their families.

Conclusions: the integration of the ethnic business sector

We have seen that the Asian minority in Britain is in a class location which reflects the experience of racial disadvantage. This structural position is part of the interdependent development of Britain and South Asia in an unevenly developed global capitalist system, dominated by the racial and class forces of Western imperialism. The Asian migration was generated by the historically conditioned distortions of the South Asian economy, and it complemented the structural demands of British capitalism in the metropolis. We have distinguished the different structural constraints and resources of three groups: the business bourgeoisie, the Western-educated professional class and the urban and rural lower middle strata. Business patterns in Britain are varied in the Asian middle class, and their distinctions derive from the particular resources and constraints which historically influenced an individual's career. Self-employment in the three migrant groups emerged as a strategy used by the individual in the active management of the constraints and resources that accrue to his/her particular racial class location. The business bourgeoisie migrated to the relatively advantaged positions of established textile entrepreneurs. They used ethnic and class resources to achieve some degree of economic success in the context of racial subordination in the metropolis. Skilled workers from the Western-educated professional class, and more particularly, unskilled workers of the lower strata, competed in employment in the metropolitan society. Often they found their mobility and success severely limited and many have adopted strategies of self-employment in the small business sector in response. The careers of the business bourgeoisie, active in the faltering textile trade in Britain, are quite distinct from the survival strategies of the small entrepreneur from the lower strata, running shops, market trading or engaged in other service activities. The rewards and opportunities for expansion in this sector are meagre (Aldrich, Cater, Jones and McEvoy 1982), and a very small minority of our respondents had achieved economic success at all resembling that of the business bourgeoisie.

We have argued that Asian business strategies have emerged as part of the structures and processes of the development of metropolitan capitalism. The implication of this analysis is that ethnic enterprise cannot be seen as a feature of a marginal sector, on the fringes of the core society, and characterised by the specificity of isolated ethnic, traditional and cultural tendencies. It is not shaped by ethnic processes that are external to and visited upon British society. Rather the development of the business sector has been conditioned by the dominant racial class forces of British capitalism in the context of the wider development of the global capitalist system. It is an integral part of the British social formation – integrated in a structural position of disadvantage.

This alternative framework that we are suggesting has implications for future research. We have recognised that the emergence of the Asian business sector is part of the structures and processes of the wider political economy and that it is rooted in racial and class inequality. This suggests the urgency of a better understanding of the very nature of the ties of the ethnic business sector with core capitalism if we wish to speak about its role in shaping the future of the ethnic minority in Britain. Finally, our analysis has suggested that the ethnic business sector is a survival strategy initiated from a location of disadvantage, and manipulating the limited resources of this position. It cannot then be meaningful to ask ourselves if the ethnic business sector marks the minority's move towards social and economic equality in Britain.

10

Business on trust: Pakistani entrepreneurship in the Manchester garment trade[1]

PNINA WERBNER

A poorly stocked corner shop or a windswept market stall are often the most visible signs of immigrant entrepreneurship. Frequently under-capitalized and unprofitable, such ventures may be doomed from the start to fail, or to continue at the same low level of profitability. An exclusive focus on them may lead to a completely mistaken assessment of an immigrant group's entrepreneurial skills, and hence of its competitive potential and future success. Part of the mistake is to overemphasize the importance of gains that are specific for individuals. The present paper seeks to show that such retail outlets are merely the tip of what may be conceived of as an economic and cultural iceberg. The 'individual gains' approach which examines only the pounds and pence profitability of such outlets misses the wider organizational context of a trade or economic niche in which the outlets are inevitably embedded. An assessment of immigrant entrepreneurship must necessarily examine the full network of connected businesses and jobs generated within a niche: the importers, wholesalers and manufacturers, the salesmen, transporters, accountants, travel agents, insurance agents and lawyers, as well as the shopkeepers and pedlars, workers and labourers, who all intermesh in the organization of the trade.

I Immigrant enterprise

Large numbers of undercapitalized retail enterprises may nevertheless support this vast structure of economic relations, bringing real economic growth. Moreover, as the organization of the trade or niche develops, it generates far-reaching changes in the structure of the immigrant community and its internal relations. It also creates the basis for what I would call a 'culture of entrepreneurship'. I use the term 'culture' advisedly, for

166

it informs the ambitions, know-how and expertise of larger and larger sections of the community. Failure in business then becomes merely a spur to further, and more carefully planned, business attempts. At the same time specific relations of trust, credit and mutual help also develop within the immigrant community. As the network of jobs and businesses develops further, some families make large fortunes, whilst many begin to probe into economic fields hitherto controlled by the host society or previous immigrant groups. This process takes time – the beginnings are often unimpressive, and may easily be mistaken as leading only towards a dead end.

The extent to which cultural and organizational factors determine the ability, or inability, of immigrant groups and minorities to succeed in business has been extensively discussed in the literature (Glazer and Moynihan 1963: 30; Light 1972). This chapter outlines the strategies of immigrants, initially lacking capital or skills, who nevertheless become successful entrepreneurs. I argue that such immigrants, despite their lack of familiarity with the host culture, may draw on cultural resources which are, perhaps, unavailable to longer established minorities or the host society. Being in the society but – as strangers – not of it, they are freed from the constraints of their hosts' frame of reference, and thus able to pursue a way of living which is, in the Pakistani case, particularly supportive of entrepreneurs (Werbner 1981).[2] They develop, as I suggested, a 'culture of entrepreneurship' which settled minorities often lack. Once established, such a culture may be passed on from one generation to the next, coming to be associated with the very image of the group (Tambs-Lyche 1980).

Immigrants usually start businesses with small capital sums acquired through personal savings and loans, often from friends and relatives. They also rely on the experience and know-how of fellow immigrants. This leads to a concentration in certain economic niches, a concentration which stems also from the entrepreneurial nature of immigrant business activities: they discover new needs, unfulfilled or incipient demands.[3] Hence Pakistanis in Manchester have utilized a potential demand for cheap clothing in British markets. Their astute understanding of trading has been transferred from the bazaars of South Asia to the markets of England, Scotland and Wales.

The rag trade is a typical immigrant niche, being inherently labour intensive and requiring little initial capital or expertise.[4] Immigrants have a pool of cheap labour on which they can draw. Moreover, the tendency towards 'vertical disintegration or fragmentation' of the trade means that each stage in the production of clothing is usually mediated through agents, subcontractors and homeworkers. Hence, entrepreneurs and small firms tend to deal on a personal basis with each other, supplying a number of different firms with small orders and thus minimizing the risks of complete failure. The small size of firms also allows greater flexibility in responding to changes in fashions or to market fluctuations.

In pragmatic terms, immigrants' competitive success has been attributed by informants partly to their tolerance of low profit margins, their reliance on family labour and their willingness to work long and difficult hours (cf. also Shah 1975 and Aldrich 1980 and, for a different view, chapter 11). A hypothesis put forward by Cohen (1969) suggests, however, that this success must be understood in more general terms: a competitive success in business may be acquired, he argues, where relations of *trust* exist. Trust facilitates the extension of credit, the reliance on 'gentlemen's agreements' and the speedy flow of needed information (Cohen 1974a). In place of formal contracts, trust is generated through ritual and kinship ties; in other words, through the evocation of moral bonds specific to members of the group and excluding outsiders. The present paper locates the meaning and significance of trust for migrants at different levels of interaction. How do immigrant entrepreneurs retain, simultaneously, bonds of ritual and kinship, and business relations which are inherently competitive? In other words, how do they resolve the potential contradiction between moral and contractual relations?

II Ethos and ethnicity

Entrepreneurial behaviour is essentially risk-taking behaviour. In attempting to understand why Pakistanis are willing to take economic risks, it is illuminating to examine what Geertz (1973: 123) has called their 'model of and for action'. It is in the nature of such a model that many of its aspects are explicitly referred to by Pakistanis themselves. Thus, the fact that men repeatedly talked of ingenious time-saving innovations they had made in their factory jobs was indicative of the value placed on the workplace. Even a menial job could be a source of pride.[5] By the same token, the 'English' workers were universally condemned for their laziness.[6]

Pakistanis say, however, that they prefer independence to being employed by others. Being subordinated, an employee, whatever the salary and however safe the position, is inferior to being one's own boss (Werbner 1980b: 44).

Moreover, Pakistanis conceive of their immediate family, usually members of a single household, as constituting a joint enterprise having corporate aims and strategies. Each member of the household or joint family is expected to make a contribution, in accordance with his ability, to what are perceived to be shared objectives. Absolute 'trust', if it can be found, is primarily located within this unit, functioning jointly for common goals. Teenage boys and girls, wives, mothers, unmarried cousins or siblings living in the household or still attached to it, contribute their earnings to a common pool. Although each may earn very little, the sum total of accumulated earnings can be quite substantial. Children may be encouraged to save part or all of their income for specific goals (a dowry, going to college, buying a house, setting up a business), but they must first hand their earnings over to the head of the family who, together with his wife, often decides on the priorities for the family. Once a business is started, members of the family are expected to provide labour and other forms of assistance to ensure its success.

Self-sacrifice, self-denial and an emphasis on hard work and saving (in brief, a 'Protestant ethic'), also characterize the Pakistani 'ethos'. Parents work hard and defer self-gratification, often for a lifetime. Children, however mobile, remain obligated to their parents for this evident self-sacrifice made for their future. Indeed, the basic orientation is towards the future. Migrants are able to sustain such frugal life styles because they are, typically, *independent* of the host society's opinion of them, and bolstered in their beliefs by fellow immigrants (Werbner 1981).

Real trust does not, however, extend automatically beyond the household or three-generational family, even to other close kinsmen, and is certainly not characteristic of relations between all Pakistanis. 'Ethnicity' does not in itself confer trust. Pakistani strangers and even acquaintances may be viewed with great suspicion. At the communal level, however, men build up reputations over time, and these are then valued and preserved. The notion of honour and reputation is a fundamental cultural concept and, once a man establishes a reputation, he is considered highly trustworthy. He is, in this respect, set apart from non-Pakistanis. Moreover, Pakistanis can be traced and pressure exerted upon them to pay their debts.

'Ethnicity' needs to be seen as a backdrop for the establishment of reputations and the formation of close friendships, often lasting many years. These friendships sustain vulnerable small businesses through mutual help, loans or credit. Where immigrants feel lost and insecure at first, fearing they might stumble in a foreign culture, doing business with fellow migrants provides a sense of familiarity, an understanding of the unstated, a sense of sharing a common 'system of relevancies', a similar way of 'thinking as usual' (Schutz 1944). Being able to speak a language fluently, to joke, to bargain, to act as though angry or sad, makes business relations easier to manage. This is particularly so for newcomers to the trade, and especially if they are non-professionals and first-generation immigrants. For such traders, dealing in broken speech with a fluent English speaker immediately establishes a relationship of dominance between host and immigrant. Inter-ethnic relations take longer to establish themselves. All this leads to a heavy reliance on fellow Pakistanis – and this in itself encourages the growth of the immigrant niche. Once the 'pioneers' have established themselves in a niche, other migrants utilize their experience, moving from the familiar world of the migrant community to the unfamiliar world outside it. This, indeed, is what happened in Britain.

III Entrepreneurship and opportunity in Manchester

The entry of Pakistanis into the garment trade in Manchester has affected both inter-ethnic relations and those between Pakistanis in the city.[7] Indeed, relations between businessmen in the rag trade have had a profound effect on the social organization of the community, its choice of leaders and the structure of its ethnic associations.[8] In particular, the fact that trading involves a reliance on credit and trust has had a far-reaching influence on the continuity of relations between Pakistanis, and the life styles they lead. It has also affected their understanding of, and familiarity with, members of the host society, and the knowledge that the latter have of them.

Special circumstances have combined in Manchester to make for successful Pakistani entrepreneurship. Some of these features have to do with the position of the city within a wider region; others, with the nature of the immigration to the city, the size of its Pakistani population, and the particular structure of the community.

Manchester had traditionally been the business and commercial metropolis of a wide area and, as we saw in the last chapter, the economic structure of the city has provided opportunities for Pakistani enterprise not always found elsewhere. Whilst the smaller Lancashire cotton-mill towns attracted an unskilled and low paid labour force occupied in primary cloth manufacturing, Pakistanis in Manchester followed other immigrants before them into the manufacturing and distribution of ready-made garments. Initially, they arrived in the city either to study in its institutions of higher learning or to seek factory employment, but the nature of the local industry prevented their concentration in low paid jobs, primarily on night shifts, in particular factories (see Anwar (1979) on Pakistanis in Rochdale). Moreover, because there was never a great demand for cheap labour the 'chains' of migration to the city were relatively short, as job vacancies occurred only intermittently. As a result, Pakistanis in Manchester originate from widely separated parts of

Pakistan and form relatively small clusters of kinsmen and friends, based around areas of origin, neighbourhoods and workplaces. The clusters overlap a great deal, resulting in extensive communication across the entire Pakistani population. The relatively small size of the community,[9] coupled with the large proportion of skilled and educated Pakistanis, has also influenced migrants' perceptions of work opportunities. Contacts have been extensive between immigrants who come from different backgrounds, both urban and rural, and who possess different technical and entrepreneurial skills. Such contacts have opened up opportunities for Pakistanis to venture into independent business whereas the same Pakistanis, in other towns, might have chosen to remain factory employees. Their entry into business was also facilitated by the nature of their industrial employment: factory workers are relatively well paid in Manchester, and have worked alongside English workers, enabling them to learn English and to save the capital needed to strike out on their own.

IV Ethnicity, 'ethnic' business, and stereotyping

The rag trade in Manchester is by no means an exclusively 'ethnic' enclave. Unlike corner grocery stores selling ritually slaughtered *halal* meat or restaurants selling distinctive national foods, there is nothing 'ethnic' about the garments manufactured and sold by Pakistanis. Moreover, traders and manufacturers in the industry come from different ethnic and religious backgrounds. All the non-Pakistanis I interviewed had some business relations with Pakistanis, while all the Pakistanis had some dealings with non-Pakistanis.

As they enter the trade, however, their behaviour is often perceived as alien, while their tendency to tolerate low profit margins is highly resented by established traders. This has given rise to a great deal of negative stereotyping, fed on gossip and rumour.

The main complaint among non-Pakistani manufacturers and subcontractors, and even among some Pakistanis, is that newcomers undercut excessively. Competition is said to be so tough that profit margins are continually being eroded. The influx of Pakistanis into the trade is blamed for this undercutting although, as Mr M., one of the biggest Pakistani wholesalers in Manchester, pointed out to me, rather than hurting the industry this has resulted in Manchester's gaining an increased share of the trade.[10]

The city was traditionally a centre for rainwear manufacturing, but it has now moved into fashion wear, and even to a lesser degree into knitwear. Supplied with goods of local manufacture, supplemented by purchases from the Midlands and London, the wholesale centre of Manchester has become a viable alternative to London for market traders operating in the north of England, Scotland and Ireland.

'Ethnic' credit

The main difference between business relations among Pakistanis, and those between Pakistanis and members of other ethnic groups, appears to relate to the amount of credit given. One wholesaler explained about credit:

> Yes, I give credit to all my [Pakistani] customers. It's open-ended credit and involves no discount. It's only in order that they continue trading with me. It works out that people have a balance of about 500 pounds, a sort of floating balance which is never paid off. It's true it means there's a large amount of money tied up in credit, but on the other hand it does mean that they tend to come regularly . . . No, I never give credit to English customers. They don't expect it and don't get it . . . But Asian traders expect credit as a right.

Wholesalers tend to specialize in either knitwear, material-sewn fashions, lingerie, children's clothing or men's shirts. It is the material-sewn fashions which are mainly manufactured in Manchester. Manufacturing is perhaps the most difficult sector of the trade, for it involves dealing with labour as well as with various wholesalers who are competing with one another. Manufacturers are also expected to allow credit to wholesalers. Wholesalers therefore deal mainly in credit – they receive credit from manufacturers and give credit to retailers. Among Pakistanis in Manchester there is a tendency for wholesalers to be old-timers (I describe their social characteristics in detail below).

Many of the manufacturers are of the Tailor caste, and many come from Gujranwala, although there are quite a few migrants from East Punjab in this branch of the trade as well.[11] Most of the manufacturers I interviewed had some previous experience working as tailors and cutters for English firms before starting their own business enterprises. Most of them, but not all, relied on homework for stitching, but had workshops for cutting, pressing and the storage of material and finished products. Their main problem was to establish permanent relations with a number of wholesalers who were *not* in competition with one another. Thus, one manufacturer making terylene trousers supplied four wholesalers in Manchester and six or seven outside Manchester – in Glasgow (an Englishman), in Cardiff (a Welshman), in Newcastle (an Indian), in Belfast (a Pakistani), in Birmingham (an Englishman) and in Congleton (a Pakistani). He also supplied small market traders directly, but at wholesale prices. He explained that the Manchester wholesalers are in competition with one another and complain if he supplies too many of them. In Manchester three of the wholesalers were Pakistanis, one an Englishman. He said his terms were a strict maximum of two invoices, or two to three weeks' credit. This manufacturer was a qualified chartered accountant who had left his job because he thought there was not much prospect for accountants; the profession had become degraded because so many people were joining it. Other manufacturers did not usually have the option of a salaried job, and most had left wage labour to become manufacturers.

Pakistani manufacturers usually employ young Pakistani men and teenage boys as cutters, pressers and overlockers. Sometimes they are also employed as drivers, going around to the homes of machinists. Their pay is usually lower than the pay in English factories, but the experience and contacts they gain through this type of job are invaluable to them once they become market traders or start their own manufacturing concerns. In many cases the premises they work in are well-lit and clean, but sometimes they can be dark, damp and gloomy. Most machinists, however, are homeworkers, so the conditions in the showrooms do not affect them. The manufacturers all claimed, with notable exceptions (see the case study below) that there was no shortage of machinists – if anything, the demand for work was greater than its availability; they tended to start off with a few machinists who later introduced them to others.[12] Although some manufacturers said they tried out new patterns from time to time, on the whole they preferred to make items to order, as the other method was found to be too risky. Some of the manufacturers were well aware of the reputation Pakistanis had for producing shoddy products. However, one of them pointed out the constraints under which Pakistanis were operating which prevented them, at this stage, from improving the quality of their goods and hence also their 'reputations'. Lack of quality, rather than being due to lack of expertise, is due to the current demand for very cheap clothing and the exclusion of Pakistani firms from higher quality contracts. They are blocked from these mainly because established firms already have their suppliers. Hence the dilemma of immigrants in the trade which must continue as long as they have not established themselves in the higher quality market.

'Joking' relations
Ironic, and often barbed, joking and bantering is the hallmark of relations in the trade, both across ethnic lines and between members of the same ethnic group. Thus, on a visit to one wholesaler, the market trader I was with drove his car directly at the wholesaler and his friend,

forcing them to draw back against the wall of the shop. In another wholesaler's place most of the joking was about the exorbitant prices. Thus, the market trader commented on the rise in prices: 'Imagine that just one bag contains goods worth £80', to which the wholesaler replied: 'Of course, I paid half that but that's the right price for it.' Later the wholesaler said he had no hangers. The market trader joked: 'You are a capitalist, and you mean you don't have hangers?' Wholesaler: 'That's why I'm a capitalist, I don't give anything away.' Market trader: 'You should help someone else.' Wholesaler: 'Capitalists are supposed to exploit people.'

Interestingly, traders usually only joke with long-standing business associates with whom they are particularly friendly – not strangers. But the joking seems to express the underlying ambiguities and tensions in the relationship, where competition and profit considerations must be weighed against the achievement of long term trust and the advantages of permanence in trading relations.

The interviews with Pakistani traders all revealed that the majority of business relations between Pakistanis are impersonal and based on strictly financial considerations. But this general truth obscures the fact that usually at least two or three of a man's business relations are transformed into friendships or were initiated in the first place because of a prior relationship of friendship or kinship. Thus, in the case of one market trader I knew, his relations with his wholesale supplier extended well beyond simple business matters. The wholesaler helped his friend's wife while he was away in Pakistan, delivering goods for her to the market which was quite a distance away. When the wholesaler was himself away his warehouse was broken into and his friend was summoned to deal with the police and sort the matter out. The same market trader also helped another of his wholesaler friends to find a solicitor to deal with a legal problem which came up. There was mutual hospitality between the market trader and the two wholesalers and their families. They are often involved in, and always aware of, personal problems affecting the lives of their suppliers and customers, events surrounding marriage and birth, troubles such as illness, and sometimes even family quarrels.

Inter-ethnic competition

Relations between Pakistanis in the trade can be highly competitive. Market traders are always in search of special prices, and usually try to get at least some of their supplies directly from manufacturers, cutting out the middleman. Market traders living in Manchester sometimes travel long distances, selling at stalls in the Midlands, Wales, Scotland and Northern Ireland, and often only returning for weekends. Stalls at

markets are much preferred to shops. This is because overheads on market stalls are clearly much lower than on retail shops, while the turnover
in them appears to be much greater. Of course, working conditions –
especially in the open air markets – are grim, particularly in winter. However, well-located stalls in some of the old central markets fetch high
'goodwill prices', since the turnover in them is very great.

Hence, in the past few years early entrants into the trade have
prospered, while later arrivals to Britain are still trying their luck in the
industry, challenging the old-timers, both Pakistanis and non-Pakistanis.
A distinctive style of life has developed, however, mainly amongst the
old-timers, first to enter the trade.

V The strategies pursued by migrants

There is no single path to success in small business, and immigrants pursue a variety of strategies in their attempts to found viable enterprises.
Very often success in the rag trade is a matter of perseverance despite
repeated failure. This is particularly so where migrants are not sponsored
by established traders or do not begin as highly skilled tailors. The contrast between those with established connections and skills and the others
is striking, as some of the following cases demonstrate.

Case 1: brothers and traders[13]

Ahmad, a second brother in a family of five brothers, was, I was
told, the family black sheep. He had not finished his matricu-
lation examinations as his elder brother had, and when he was
given a shop to run in Karachi, where the family lived, he
neglected the shop, spending most of his time at the (English)
movies. When some people came back from England and
reported that there were good business prospects there, it was
decided to send Ahmad to England. This was in 1952. At first he
shared living quarters in Manchester with friends from Pakistan
(who subsequently became some of the largest wholesalers in the
community). In 1954 he was joined by his older brother Bashir.
At that time most people, I was told, were door-to-door salesmen. However, Ahmad started a stall at Warrington market
very early on, through a connection made by a friend. First the
two brothers had one stall between them, and later they were
joined by Ibrahim, a third brother, who also shared the stall.
They began to expand, each brother with his own stall, and later
to increase the stall space. Ahmad had a three-length stall,

Bashir and Ibrahim two lengths each. Ahmad and Bashir also owned the concession to the market's coffee-shop-cum-restaurant. Although each brother sells somewhat different types of goods (knitwear, children's wear, men's wear) all the stalls bear the name 'Ahmad and Brothers'. In 1975 a fourth younger brother came to study in England and married a local girl. He quickly became involved in the market and soon established several market stalls of his own.

None of the brothers experienced failure. All, with the exception of Ahmad, were well-educated, with two of the brothers giving up possible professional careers to become traders. All were well-connected through caste, kinship and area of origin links with the important traders in the community, and each brother was supported by those already established while he set up his own stall. A second case demonstrates the importance of connections in the trade:

Case 2: a banker turned trader

Latif came to Manchester as a bank manager for one of the Pakistani banks and later worked for an English bank in the city. When he failed to receive a well-deserved promotion, he decided to resign from the bank and become an independent businessman instead. He bought the 'goodwill' of a stall in a very popular covered market in Greater Manchester for £4,000. At first he and his wife also ran stalls in two open markets. Latif's wife would leave their young son with a babyminder and travel by bus and train to the markets, carrying her baby daughter with her. One market, she recalled, had been especially difficult as the child often got cold and cried. Later the couple gave up the two open air market stalls and opened a shop in a new arcade instead, again in a town on the periphery of Manchester. By 1978, however, competition had increased with new traders entering and undercutting prices. Latif decided to give up the arcade shop which was being undercut by competitors opposite. The competitors sold goods from a wholesale warehouse they owned. He sold all his stock to them at a loss and opened his own wholesale warehouse. He became a wholesaler while retaining the still profitable stall in the covered market. By 1980 his wholesale business was prospering as well. During his period as a trader Latif was helped by his extensive links with wholesalers, derived from connections established during his prior work as bank manager and based on shared caste and origin in East Punjab. As a successful market trader he was granted large amounts of credit, but he also relied on friends in the trade to help with his shops in emergencies, and he in turn helped them when they encountered difficulties. Although he experienced financial problems from time to time, he was always able to overcome these and, like the brothers in Case 1, was extremely affluent.

In general, traders with both wholesale and retail outlets have an edge over their competitors. To offset this edge, traders can sometimes buy directly from manufacturers at slightly advantageous prices, as the next case illustrates. The two following cases show too that many of the traders and manufacturers in Manchester have made several attempts to open small businesses before establishing themselves.

Case 3: sons and fathers

Tariq came to Manchester in 1965 after spending many years as a non-commissioned officer in the Pakistan army. He originated from a small village in Jhellum Sub-District. In the early 1970s most men from this area living in Manchester were factory workers. Tariq too spent most of his early years in Manchester as a factory worker, although he did try to start a business several times – in one case he opened a 'Fish-n-Chips' shop which failed, he claimed, because he lacked experience and was cheated by his workers. He also tried with his friend Yassir to open a shop in Blackpool, and to apply for permanent stalls in various markets. All these attempts failed, costing him over £2,000. In 1976 the factory where he worked shut down and there seemed little prospect of finding a job with equivalent wages and work conditions. By this time Tariq's eldest son had graduated from high school. He gave his son his redundancy pay – several hundred pounds – in order to start a market stall. Tariq's son, although only 17 at the time, succeeded where Tariq and his best friend Yassir had always failed. The son had worked on weekends and holidays in various manufacturing concerns and several of his school friends came from families owning small factories. He was able therefore to obtain 'lines' at a discount directly from the factory and this gave him an edge in starting his market stalls. After a short period he succeeded in obtaining permanent stalls in several markets. Before long Tariq had brought his father into the trade and despite the growing recession their enterprise was thriving. The son's connections had been crucial in enabling the family to succeed in the fierce competition in the trade. By 1982 the family had established a knitwear 'factory'. A younger son and two sons-in-law had also become market traders, and bought their supplies directly from the factory.

During the early period as traders, the family lived off Tariq's social security and his wife and daughters' sewing efforts.

It was usual in the 1970s for fathers to give their sons a start as traders with a capital grant, while they retained their factory jobs. The sons continued to live at home and thus could persist with trading despite low profits and a small turnover in the early stages, until they established themselves.

This case points to a historically significant social process taking place within the community: the breakdown, in the second generation, of the sometimes exclusive immigrant clusters of the first generation of immigrants. These clusters, based on area of origin, kinship or a shared period in 'bachelor housing', tended to reflect entrepreneurial success, with most businessmen concentrating in certain recognizable 'sets'. The teenage peer groups of sons, in particular, cut across these sets, generating friendships between previously separated sections of the community. Tariq, of the Jhellum District and a recent immigrant, was thus able, through his son, to reach Pakistanis of the Jullundur and Gujranwala District who controlled much of the Pakistani part of the rag trade. Women and teenage girls working as machinists in manufacturing concerns often make similarly valuable connections. Among the manufacturers, many of the most successful were of the Tailor or Arain castes, the former benefiting from their special skills, the latter from their extensive connections in the trade. For others, manufacturing was a difficult challenge as the following case illustrates:

Case 4: a partnership that succeeded

Moh, although a member of the Arain caste, had few relatives or connections with members of the trader 'set' in Manchester. He had started his entrepreneurial career by selling clothes from door to door to West Indians. The venture was not a success because many of his clients did not honour their debts to him. Later, he bought two pick-up trucks. This venture too failed. After each failure, he returned to factory work. He began manufacturing fashion clothes but found the machinists unable to cope with the changes in pattern, he claimed. That venture too failed. A shop he opened at the far end of a busy street proved another costly failure. It was during this period that he met Rifat, also struggling as an unsuccessful manufacturer.

Rifat, a Karachi migrant of upper middle class origins, had

come to Manchester to join his brother-in-law. In Manchester, they were part of a small and select Urdu-speaking group from Karachi, with only superficial connections to the various traders and manufacturers in the city. At first Rifat worked as an overseer in his brother-in-law's road-building firm. He then ventured on his own into manufacturing, assisted by his wife who had studied dress design. His manufacturing effort hinged to a high degree on the willingness of his friends' wives to work for him as machinists, although they claimed he paid far less than his competitors. One machinist even gave up a much better paid job to help him out. He himself complained that his failures were due to the fact that machinists were slow to follow new patterns, and that wholesalers did not pay their debts on time but demanded credit. Despite the allegedly low pay he provided, all his manufacturing ventures failed. At one point he was reduced to selling some of the clothes he had manufactured in a market stall – again, without much success. During this period he was propped up with loans from his brother-in-law.

It was at this point, at the end of 1974, that he and Moh met Bourdon, an agent in the trade for many years, who offered them a contract and to whom they offered a deal. Bourdon was a Frenchman who had lived in Britain since his youth. He was trying to place a subcontract to manufacture continental quilt covers for a large factory supplying Marks and Spencer. Two firms had already turned down the contract when he met Rifat and Moh. They accepted the contract and offered him a partnership. Rifat and Moh would provide the capital and sewing expertise, Bourdon the business management skills and contacts needed.

In the early days the factory they set up encountered far more problems than Pakistani manufacturing concerns usually do. High standards of stitching were demanded, and 'rejects' returned to the machinists – who were mainly inexperienced – for resewing. The high standard precluded home sewing, much preferred by many Pakistani women with young children. The combination of high stitching standards and piece work pay meant that machinists were able to earn far less than if working for some of the other manufacturing concerns. At first, there was a high turnover of machinists and several abortive 'strikes' took place in the factory (the ring-leaders were always fired). Once again, Moh and Rifat relied heavily on underpaid kinswomen to stand by them and sustain the production, despite, in Rifat's

case, the unsuitability of his kinswomen, who were highly educated townswomen, for this type of work. As the months went
by, however, the factory did succeed in recruiting machinists. A
nearby factory closed down and Bourdon contacted its personnel
department and offered work to the redundant machinists.
Some Pakistani and Indian 'regulars' were also found over time,
in addition to Rifat and Moh's kinswomen.

The workforce, like the partnership, was multi-ethnic from
the start. In later months, there were, in addition to Pakistani
machinists, also Indians, Bengalis, English, West Indian,
African and Spanish machinists and checkers. The factory survived its first year, with the contract renewed twice despite the
difficulties experienced. This was chiefly due to Bourdon's continuous insistence on high quality control and efficient delivery.
By the end of the year, in which the partners had had little profit,
the factory was a viable enterprise. It had a relatively permanent
workforce of some 25 machinists (with about 35 on the books)
and had established routines. The English machinists brought
friends and placed greater emphasis on sociability than on earnings, while those of the Asian machinists who remained were
content with low pay in return for relatively slow sewing.

What was remarkable in this case was the inability of Rifat in particular
to recruit suitable machinists, with the exception of kinswomen under
personal obligation to him. Moh, an isolate in many respects, was only
slightly more successful, recruiting some machinists through a former factory workmate and some through his parents-in-law. The two partners
encountered these recruitment difficulties at a time when machinist work
was greatly in demand in the Pakistani community. None of the other
manufacturers I interviewed experienced recruitment difficulties, and
this is a measure of Rifat and Moh's lack of extensive contacts with poorer
migrants within the community, as well as their lack of experience which
meant they always paid below the going-rate.

Nevertheless, the efforts of the three partners, and Bourdon's contacts, initiative and supervision, paid off. An educated Karachi gentle-
man, a relatively uneducated self-made village entrepreneur and a
Frenchman-turned-Englishman combined to succeed where previously
the two Pakistanis had encountered only failure. Indeed, in a sense their
inadequate contacts had propelled them to find a valuable contract and
thus to break into a wider and more lucrative part of the textile industry
than most Pakistani manufacturers have succeeded in penetrating.
Whereas most of the other manufacturers employ small numbers of

machinists, the partners employed some 25 machinists on a permanent basis: and the factory had great potential for expansion. Rifat was able to pay back his debts, and in 1979 the partnership was still prospering.

VI The life style in the business community

The life styles of families involved in the rag trade vary a great deal, since people in the trade come from different backgrounds, are resident in different neighbourhoods and have lived in Britain for longer or shorter periods. There is, however, a group of old-time traders who form a 'set'.[14] Members of the 'set' tend to be 'quite exclusive' in the words of one of the manufacturers of the Tailor caste whom I interviewed. The 'set' has also incorporated some later arrivals to Manchester, usually also Arain of East Punjab origin, or current neighbours who have been successful in the trade. Many members of the 'set' have become wholesalers, since they were the first to start off as market traders. The 'core members' of the set live in Chorlton-cum-Hardy and Whalley Range, two adjacent suburbs, although many of the members live scattered in other suburbs of the city. Most, however, live no more than a ten minute drive away from Chorlton (Werbner 1980a).

Most of the families in the set are wealthy, some very wealthy. Consequently, their wives do not usually work, although the wives of market traders and wholesalers sometimes help their husbands on an irregular basis. Despite the fact that they live in the midst of the English middle class, women maintain relations mostly with other Pakistani women and have little communication with neighbours beyond polite exchanges. In a sense, the life style of the women is not unlike that of women in the central residential cluster (Werbner 1979a, ch. 6). Indeed, most families had moved out of the central cluster a few years previously. Like women in the central cluster they spend their days, while their husbands are absent at work, in the company of other women. The husbands, by contrast, mix with other people at work, in the mosque, and in voluntary activities. The wives of wholesalers, in particular, have to rely a great deal on the company and mutual aid of other women, for their husbands work long hours, often not arriving home until late at night. Second cars and telephones serve to shorten distances between the houses of friends in the suburbs, and most women can drive.

Conjugal roles

In most businessmen's families, women are extremely influential in the domestic sphere, and sex roles are to some extent segregated, while relations between men and women – as far as family friends are concerned – are informal and easy. Men dominate more, however, in the choice of friends, for these business families have to withstand the disruptive pressures of competition, a factor which does not enter relations in other sections of the community. Men are very often competitors not only in business but also in central Pakistani voluntary associations,[15] where they rival each other for positions of power. In addition, their wealth and status mean that reputations are under greater scrutiny, there is more at stake.

If, in their business relations, the families in the set are strictly concerned with the maximization of profit, and are hence both calculating and thrifty, in their social relations they veer to the opposite extreme, distributing their wealth with a prodigality more exaggerated and ostentatious than that displayed by anyone else. Weddings, in particular, are extremely expensive events to which all members of the set are invariably invited. Indeed, it is wealth that enables members of the set to maintain its viability despite residential dispersion – through large feasting events, as well as through the use of cars and telephones.

Friendship and competition

The position of women and of the older generation in maintaining the viability of the set is crucial. It is not merely that women's relations complement those of men, but that friendship between families depends ultimately on women's ability to counterbalance their husbands' business and political relations, although they can do so only with the men's agreement. As many wholesalers and manufacturers pointed out to me, women are the ones who maintain friendly relations through day-to-day sociability. If they wish to, men can break off family friendships, so that the exigencies of business relations in which husbands are involved pose a constant threat to the continuity of relations between wives.

The fragility of friendship between businessmen stems from the differing expectations surrounding friendship and business relations. Among Pakistanis, friendship generally tends to be a 'multiplex' relationship, in the sense that friends draw one another into their domestic rituals and into political activities, they are often distant kinsmen and they may come from the same area of origin or belong to the same caste category.[16] The moral bonds evoked through these shared activities and sentimental attachments define the relationship as being one based on mutual aid, generosity and trust. By contrast, businessmen must base their mutual transactions on considerations of profit and loss. The two sets of expectations, those of friends and those of businessmen, are therefore often incompatible. Commenting ironically on this incompatibility, one market trader, a member of the set, said to me rather enigmatically that 'Friends are like business.' When I asked what he meant, he said: 'When business goes down, the friendship goes down as well.'

The problem is especially acute when market traders, long term and regular customers of established wholesalers, open wholesale businesses themselves, thus entering into competition with their former suppliers. Perhaps what is remarkable is not that the stresses of competition some-times drive a wedge between friends, but that, despite the rivalry, members of the set continue to maintain an appearance of friendliness and solidarity, as expressed on major ceremonial and ritual occasions. Hence, at one *khatam koran* I attended, my companion was surprised to note that the convenor had invited the wife of his son's most avowed competitor. (Both the host and his son's rival in the trade were Arain, originally from Jullundur. The two men had warehouses on the same street and at work they were so jealous of each other that my companion's husband, a cus-tomer of both, had to park his car around the corner to hide the fact that he was shopping at both places.) My companion even asked the convenor how it was that Mrs X., the wife of the rival, had been invited. The answer she received was that 'even if my son is jealous of them, I am still a good friend of theirs'. Hence, women, and men of the older generation who have passed on their businesses to their sons, as in this case, retain family friendships despite current rivalries, for as long as this is possible. This makes the set extremely powerful politically, in relation to the rest of the community.

Relations of dependency

The other side of the influence of husbands' relations on their wives' friendships concerns cases where relations of business dependency exist among members of the set. In these cases women are careful not to offend. This is especially relevant to relations between market traders and wholesalers. Market traders often need additional credit to tide them over 'quiet' periods, if they are to continue to stock their stalls with the latest fashions. Credit gives them flexibility in this respect. It means they can also pay their mortgages and other regular expenses, despite tempor-ary and seasonal lulls in trading. In short, it allows them to plan their lives without the need for large reserves of cash. This is why the position of the big wholesalers who are able to give large amounts of credit, such as Mr M. mentioned above, is so powerful. Ultimately, he is able to make or break a market trader during a slack trading period, or when the trader overstretches his resources or purchases a bad 'line' and has to off-load it at a loss. Similarly, manufacturers and wholesalers depend on each other for credit and speedy payment during slack periods, although here the direction of dependency is not so clearly established. If a manufacturer becomes over-committed to a single wholesaler he becomes dependent on him, but manufacturers are usually able to avoid this. Nevertheless, big wholesalers are extremely powerful for they buy large quantities and are therefore difficult for a manufacturer to replace.

For Pakistanis, relations between unequals in wealth are viewed as inherently problematic, because they are seen inevitably to reflect superiority and inferiority, especially of power. That wealth is translatable into power is regarded as obvious and almost axiomatic. In this set of business families, certain persons such as Mr M. are so widely accepted as superior and more powerful than anyone else that the other members of the set do not attempt to challenge their position. Between these other members, however, differences in wealth are not so apparent and therefore not usually in themselves a source of strain. Most of them are well off and can afford to buy relatively new cars, colour televisions, expensive wall-to-wall carpeting, various electrical goods, etc. Only the wealthiest migrants – a tiny minority – have moved out of semi-detached suburbia into the more exclusive suburbs, and therefore housing – a potential marker of more subtle differences in wealth – has not yet become a major factor in establishing further discriminations between them. The latest Volvo model, rather than the large detached house, is still the most evident and conspicuous sign of its owner's success in the rag trade. Indeed, to own a flashy car – whether a Volvo, Mercedes or Rolls-Royce – appears to be an occupational expectation in the rag trade among all ethnic groups, constituting a yardstick of credit-worthiness.

Social networks

Most migrants from East Punjab have relatively large extended families living locally, simply because they came to Britain earlier than other migrants and were therefore able to bring over more relatives before the tightening of the immigration laws. Many of the Arain among these migrants can trace distant links to one another, often by a chain of marriages, and many of the Jullundur migrants came from neighbouring villages (that is, before Partition). However, members of a single extended family tend to develop different close friendships, mostly within the set. Such close friends become acquainted over time with the rest of a person's extended family. The combined result of close friendships and acquaintances is a complex network of ties among all members of the 'set'. The high density of the acquaintance network is possibly an important reason why relations between businessmen, even though fraught with contradictions and tensions, do not break down entirely.

Thus, although in their closest friendships these early migrants from the Punjab are divided – with their divisions cutting across extended families – when it comes to mobilization for larger events such as weddings, funerals or large *khatam korans*, they are invariably invited to attend each other's events. When confronting other members of the community, they present a common and united front, and this has enabled them to retain a continuing and decisive influence in community affairs. At the 'core' of the set are some five prominent extended families, each boasting among its members a large wholesaler, except for one family headed by a well-known doctor. Rivalry and friendship pepper relationships between these families whose members have known each other for many years. Around the core families cluster a much larger group of families, between 50 and 100 households, who together form the 'set'. These households attend each other's ceremonial and ritual functions selectively. Only representatives of the 'core' families are almost invariably invited to any function held by one of the households. In a sense, therefore, it is friendships of members of the 'core' families which define the boundaries of the set and confer legitimacy on the acceptance of newcomers into it.

There is no single shared criterion defining the set categorically. Although the majority of its members are of the Arain Moslem caste, other castes are also represented in it. Although many come from East Punjab, there are some from the West, and from Karachi. Although most are businessmen in the textile trade, some are professional, while some are involved in other businesses. Although most live in two adjacent neighbourhoods, many live outside these neighbourhoods. Although the majority are early-comers to the city, a few are later arrivals.

How, then, is the emergence of the set to be explained? It would seem that membership originates from accretions around the core families who were among the earliest settlers in Manchester, and who founded the organizations representing the community. As a result, their shared characteristics dominate the set. These characteristics relate to area of origin, wealth, length of residence in Manchester, caste, occupation and neighbourhood of residence. The most typical member of the set is a Punjabi of Arain caste from Jullundur in East Punjab who has lived in Manchester for some 25 years, resides in Chorlton-cum-Hardy or an adjacent neighbourhood and is a businessman in the rag trade. The closer a person is to this archetypal migrant, the more likely he is to be a member of the set. Even among the core families, only some fulfil all these characteristics.

VII Competition and 'political' ethnicity

To what extent, then, is Cohen's hypothesis (1974a: xvi–xxi) confirmed by the data presented here? Cohen has argued that it is through the assertion of exclusive moral bonds that ethnic interests, such as monopolies in business, are protected. But in the case of Pakistanis in Manchester moral bonds are maintained by the same people who, on the surface, compete most directly with one another, i.e. by the 'wholesalers'. It is they who participate in ritual events together. Some are also linked by ties of kinship, caste and neighbourliness. By contrast, many of the Pakistani market traders who are dependent clients but are newcomers to the trade are often excluded from these ritual events. Even if invited to wedding receptions, they are usually excluded from more intimate and restricted rites and ceremonies.

The clear social divide *within* the Pakistani community is between old-timers and newcomers to the trade. Once established and evidently successful, traders may become socially acceptable as well. But are we then to say that the ritual bonds are evoked in an attempt to prevent the entry of Pakistani newcomers into the trade? In other words, rather than applying Cohen's argument to inter-ethnic relations, should it be applied in this case to *intra*-ethnic relations? This would seem to be an unsatisfactory explanation. As new market traders have entered the trade, established market traders have turned to wholesaling. They rely on the new market traders to provide them with their custom. They compete with each other for this clientele.

Even in matters of credit, ethnic identity is not the dominant consideration traders have. Reliability and a good personal record appear to be more crucial in deciding credit-worthiness. And, although credit is more commonly extended among Pakistanis, only in some cases does this lead to the formation of close personal friendships. However, most traders usually rely in a more personal way on a few traders, to whom they turn for help in emergencies. Moreover, among the earliest wholesalers some have now become importers, and they supply many of the wholesalers. So too, interdependence between manufacturers and wholesalers is an unchanging aspect of the trade. In addition, wholesalers help each other by passing on orders they cannot fulfil themselves (either because they do not stock a certain item, or because they lack the full quantity required). It must be remembered as well that the trade is always precarious, subject to the problems of recessions or 'flooding' of cheap imports, and it is sometimes a very lonely occupation. All these factors weigh in favour of extending social relations between traders outside the work context, while the competition between traders militates against it.

Hence, Pakistani traders' interests are not at all clear cut, but are mixed, ambiguous and contradictory. Nor is it evident that the interests of businessmen in the garment trade of different ethnic origins are more, or less, conflicting. The large Pakistani wholesalers are competing with department stores run by non-Pakistanis as well as with other Pakistani wholesalers. Since interests are mixed, ritual and kinship links cannot be said to be simply a function, a reflection or a 'cementing' of economic interests. Rather, they are superimposed on economic relations replete with rivalry, and only sometimes characterized by mutual aid. And, indeed, this is expressed in the form rituals take: rituals are large scale and ostentatious, potlatch-like events of feasting and display. So too donations to charity and voluntary associations are publicly announced and competitively given, while even trips on *Haj* are part of the competition for merit. Hence, while the entry of Pakistanis into the textile trade has been associated with an 'intensification' in ritualism and religiosity, these are manifested in a competitive form. Nevertheless, the result of such competitiveness is a multiplication of particularistic and exclusive bonds between the more prosperous traders and an assertion of their elite status within the community. It is in order to protect this status that exclusive moral bonds are evoked.

VIII Conclusion

This chapter has traced the entry of Pakistanis into several branches of the Manchester garment trade, and outlined some of the strategies and attitudes that have made this entry possible. In broader, more theoretical, terms, the encroachment into a new economic niche may be said to take the form of an 'entrepreneurial chain', as early successful entrepreneurs provide sponsorship, patronage, credit or advice to relatives and friends. Their focal role then enables them to venture into more ambitious economic enterprises, once again assuming a pioneering role and providing further sponsorship to followers. What follows then is an escalation in the numbers of immigrants within a niche and in the scope of their activities. At the same time, as I have argued, a 'culture of entrepreneurship' develops within the immigrant group, informing the actions and dreams as well as the attitudes and beliefs of increasing numbers of immigrants. The whole process is typical of immigrant entrepreneurship. It is, theoretically, a dynamic process in which more and more members of a community get caught up in the trade network and its sub-culture, either directly or through the provision of services to it.

As more immigrants get caught up in the trade, this has a profound effect on internal social relations within the immigrant group. Like business relations, social relations too assume a highly dynamic and competitive form, reflected in the forms of domestic rituals and ceremonials, and in the process of internal stratification of the community. Moreover, trust, as I showed, is then an achievement, and different levels of trust typify different relationships. Competition within an ethnic group, mostly ignored by social scientists hitherto, is thus a key to understanding these relations. It is counterposed by bonds of kinship, ritual and shared membership in various sub-groups, to create a set of social relations in constant flux, yet always internally focussed. Hence, the study of small businesses, if seen in its wider context, may provide an important key to an understanding of major social transformations in ethnic groups and in their relations with their host societies.

11

Ethnic advantage and minority business development

HOWARD ALDRICH, TREVOR P. JONES
and DAVID McEVOY

The recent emergence of Asian business activity in Britain may be seen as simply the latest event in a fairly long history of commercial involvement by Asian exiles. During the last century or so of British imperial history, Indian communities took root in many British colonies, being particularly strongly represented in East and Southern Africa, Burma and the Caribbean. Although the bulk of the migrants went as indentured labourers, they proved to be a socially mobile group who, on becoming established in their adopted countries, transformed themselves into a business, professional and clerical class: 'wherever, under the umbrella of imperialism, there were commercial opportunities to exploit, Indian traders took them' (Rex and Tomlinson 1979: 288–9).

Historically, the overseas Indians came to perform a distinct function for British imperialism, one which placed them in a highly ambiguous social role and ultimately led to the destruction of their communities in several countries of East Africa. Tinker (1976) attaches the label 'middlemen' to them and suggests that their principal task was to act as broker for the white rulers in dealings with the indigenous masses or 'sons of the soil'. In effect, British political domination and economic exploitation operated at one remove behind a screen of Indian frontmen. As Tinker (1976: 9) remarks, 'The African, Malay, Burmese or Singhalese saw the Indian as the man in authority: they confronted an Indian booking clerk at the railway station or an Indian tally clerk weighing their produce: they could not see the European manager who really controlled their affairs.' Nor could they see the profits being amassed from their labour by firms based in London or Manchester, whereas the success of Indian shopkeepers and merchants was a visible object of envy.

The intermediate position occupied by Indians immediately poses problems of interpretation. It is tempting to emphasize the manner in which the exiles succeeded in elevating themselves to a position in the

189

class structure superior to that of the indigenous population. While it is undeniable that Indians overseas 'acquired a component which could be called middle class' (Tinker 1976: 7), we should not overlook their essentially subordinate and powerless status vis-à-vis the imperial rulers. The typical Indian business was limited in scale and probably more preoccupied with survival than with accumulating vast profits. This is not to deny the existence of immensely wealthy large traders but, as a general rule, Indians were managers of *small* workshops and *petty* traders, rather than members of the bourgeoisie proper.

With the mass migration of Indians and Pakistanis to Britain since the mid 1950s, the Asian diaspora has shifted decisively from colony to mother country herself. Almost inevitably, the conflicting images of prosperity and powerlessness, economic success and social subordination have travelled along with them, to the confusion of British public opinion and scholarly analysis alike. Academic opinion seems torn between two opposed views of the Asian position in British society. One body of writers gives primacy to ethnic solidarity and argues that, as an exclusive self-isolating brotherhood, Asians set themselves goals separate from those of majority society and are largely successful in achieving them (Dahya, 1974). Through self-help and the operation of fraternal networks, they have established a considerable degree of self-determination at the local community level, where their ownership and control of housing, small businesses and community institutions free them from most of the social disorders which classically afflict racial minorities in industrial society. Moreover, the activities of their entrepreneurs and the educational achievements of their children suggest that they possess more than a little capacity for social mobility (Tomlinson 1980).

Opponents of this rather harmonious picture stress racial disadvantage rather than ethnic advantage, exclusion rather than exclusiveness. According to their view, ethnic autonomy in limited and marginal sectors of society is of little consequence in itself, serving only as a smokescreen for the real barriers preventing free access to employment, housing and other social resources.[1] In reality, the structural position of Asians in British society is virtually identical to that of any other colonized group but its symptoms are disguised by a surface gloss of ethnic self-determination (Jones 1979).

The ambiguities of Asian business activity

Asian business activity threatens to provoke a new version of this same intellectual schizophrenia. Over the past two decades, Asian participation in business of many kinds (but mainly retailing) has expanded to the point where, as we saw in chapter 8 (p. 128), Asian self-employment is proportionately at least as great as that of the general population (Ward and Reeves 1980). Such entrepreneurial achievement points to a marked capacity for upward mobility, with business presenting many group members with the means for escaping minority status and gaining entry to the bourgeoisie. Their business development has been so rapid, so much against the odds and such a stimulating contrast to the doom-laden inner city environment which surrounds it, that it is difficult to disagree with the commentator (Forester 1978) who claimed: 'Asian businesses are run by ambitious and optimistic people, people (refreshingly) with hopes and aspirations. They provide a stark contrast to the withering apathy, resignation and cynicism of large sections of the white population, who have witnessed the steady decline of British capitalism.' Nevertheless, the implied judgement that decadent British capitalism can be rejuvenated by an injection of minority group enterprise is, to say the least, sweeping and, in any case, the success of Asian enterprise is questionable on much more specific grounds.[2]

Our own research (Aldrich, Cater, Jones and McEvoy 1981; 1982), based on interviews with 580 small shopkeepers (Asian and white) in three urban areas, finds that a sharp rise in the number of entrepreneurs is not necessarily to be equated with increased socio-economic benefits, whether to the participants themselves, to the Asian community as a whole, or to the inner city neighbourhoods in which they are mostly located. Asian business activity has so far been incapable either of absorbing significant numbers into self-employment or of providing an economic return for more than a minority of participants. Although numerous cases of highly successful small firms may be cited, more typical is the marginal firm whose proprietor earns less than the wage he would command by selling his labour in the open market. This proprietor is representative of all small shopkeepers, regardless of race or ethnic origins, since marginality is one of the keynotes of the small retail sector. What is nevertheless germane to this discussion is that, at least in some areas, shopkeeping forms almost the only substantial outlet for Asian entrepreneurial aspirations. Where this is so, business ownership can hardly be presented as an avenue of social mobility. While it may provide some minority members with an alternative to wage employment in the white dominated labour market, the opportunities so presented do not usually represent a qualitative improvement. Rather, they represent a sideways shift from lumpenproletariat to lumpenbourgeoisie.[3]

Any attempt to discover the economic rationale and social significance of Asian business is inevitably confronted by two apparently irreconcilable images. Are we to view the growth of enterprise as a positive initiative, a successful form of self-help, a testimony to the capacity of ethnic solidarity to overcome racial handicaps? Is there perhaps some special feature of the culture and social organization of Asian exiles which prompts them towards entrepreneurship and enhances their chances of commercial survival? Or must we present their commercial behaviour as a negative adaptation to racial disadvantage, a hardy weed clinging precariously to a crack in a wall? These two antithetical themes of cultural advantage and structural disadvantage run throughout the literature on minority business and are crucial to an understanding of the Asian businessman in Britain.

Middleman minorities: a theory of ethnic advantage

Ethnic distinctiveness is normally treated as a disadvantage, a bar to equal participation in the larger society. A large number of historical precedents, however, suggest that entrepreneurs may actually benefit from membership of an ethnic collectivity.

The role of ethnicity as a force for entrepreneurial development has been systematically examined by Bonacich (1973), who used the term 'middleman minority' to describe immigrant groups whose business ownership is extensive enough to provide a major source of livelihood for group members. Overseas Indians are cited among a lengthy list of exiled groups who have acquired a reputation for middleman activities, a term which embraces a wide range of economic functions in addition to distribution and trade. For Bonacich, European Jews are the epitome of the form (see chapter 5). Bonacich argued that the commercial prowess of such groups is essentially attributable to their position as *non-members* of society. Group members are characterized by a 'sojourner cast of mind', a sense of non-identity with the receiving society and a belief in an eventual return to the homeland. Even in cases where return migration is unlikely, the sojourner mentality continues to influence the actions of group members, who persist in a stance of aloofness from mainstream society, retain the customs and institutions of the homeland and behave in many ways as if they were transients rather than permanent settlers. Many studies of Asian immigrants have focussed upon the sojourner mentality as a key determinant of the response to British society (Lawrence 1974; Anwar 1979).

The successful and highly competitive practices of ethnic entrepreneurs may be attributed to the sojourner mentality. Thrift, diligence and willingness to endure punishing hours of work are all consistent with the goals of a migrant group prepared to make short term sacrifices in a foreign country in order to enjoy the spoils on return to the homeland.[4]

Furthermore, the will to succeed in business is reinforced by exclusion from other possible outlets for talent and energy. Discrimination by majority society restricts minority access to political power and social status, so group members turn to the business sphere as a means of furthering personal ambitions. In these circumstances, enterprise appears as a form of displacement activity.[5]

In addition to personal motivation, ethnic entrepreneurs benefit from a supportive business environment, enjoying certain advantages denied to non-ethnic competitors. Internal solidarity – the strengthening of communal bonds of loyalty and mutual aid – is a common feature of any immigrant group strongly differentiated by culture from the host society and subject to exclusion from that society. For the ethnic businessman, this solidarity makes it possible for essential commercial resources to be readily and cheaply mobilized from within the group. One competitive advantage frequently enjoyed by minority firms is their use of informal channels to obtain free credit from co-ethnics, a practice attaining a high degree of sophistication in the rotating credit associations of the overseas Chinese (Light 1972). Another advantage is their use of members of the extended family as unpaid labour. Yet another trading asset is the customer support which they enjoy from fellow ethnics; as one writer remarked of immigrant entrepreneurs in the USA, 'ethnicity . . . served to provide protected niches for entrepreneurs . . . in that non-members have been more or less disadvantaged in competing for the same customers' (Hannerz 1974: 54). In effect, ethnicity creates a tariff barrier shielding businesses from outside competition.

At this point we should emphasize that the protected market is vital only in the initial stages of business development. Indeed, the definitive attribute of any fully fledged middleman group is its 'export' orientation, its function as a seller of goods and services to the general population rather than to an exclusively minority market.[6] As the name itself suggests, a middleman group is usually one which gains its principal livelihood by trading in the majority market. Successful middleman activity ultimately depends on an ability to compete with majority-owned firms in their own markets, and even to oust them from certain sectors of the economy.

Light's (1972) work on Chinese and Japanese business in California confirms the suggestion that, with increasing maturity, the ethnic subeconomy tends to achieve progressively greater penetration of external markets. Prior to the First World War, Oriental business in California was primarily inward looking, consisting mainly of a small retailing sector which relied on an Oriental clientele for 63 per cent of its trade (1910). By 1929, Orientals retailed no less than 41 per cent of the food consumed in the entire state. For two groups with only 2½ per cent of the population between them, this represented a high degree of specialization, and export penetration on this scale created the capacity to absorb a large proportion of group members into viable business activities. When enterprise reaches this level of development, it can be regarded as a highly effective avenue of social mobility for the group.[7]

The progressively increasing strength of the Oriental American sub-economy may imply that, under special circumstances, minority business growth is characterized by a self-sustaining quality. With the passage of time, the group is likely to accumulate capital for further investment and to exploit the possibilities for linkages between retailing, wholesaling and manufacturing. Moreover, through experience its members are likely to acquire expertise in various fields of business, an expertise which is transmitted inter-generationally.

British Asians as middlemen   Model

The foregoing discussion has established that any middleman group will display the following attributes:

1) *Superior access to business resources*: The group's entrepreneurs enjoy an advantage over their non-ethnic rivals with respect to capital, labour and business experience. Capital is largely obtained from family, friends and other informal sources within the group on a mutual aid basis. Labour is provided by the extended family and the entrepreneur himself is a member of an established business family.

2) *Superior competitive practices*: Superior access to resources is translated into practice, with the minority entrepreneur able to take advantage of reduced labour costs and so offer a better service than others in the same market segment.

3) *Export orientation*: If the minority proprietor has a competitive edge, then he is well placed to capture custom from majority rivals. Hence middlemen firms are those whose products are aimed at the majority market.

4) *Specialization*: To the extent that the group's livelihood depends on selling to a majority market and on in-group cooperation, it will show a high degree of occupational specialization. Members will concentrate in a few lines of trade where their shared business experience and economies of scale give them a competitive advantage. If successful in penetrating the majority market, their rate of self-employment will exceed the national norm.

We turn now to examining how closely Asians in Britain fit the model, an exercise which should reveal much about relations between the various

Asian ethnic groups and the larger society. Close conformity to the classic middleman form would imply that community solidarity and self-help is a potent force for overcoming the problems of adaptation to a new environment and of the barriers posed by racism. It would raise hopes about business as an area of opportunity where minorities could gain economic equality with the majority. It may even lead to speculation that enterprise will lead in the direction of a genuine form of integration whereby the various Asian groups engage in fuller participation in national life without losing their ethnic identity.[8]

Preliminary investigations

Until very recently, minority business in Britain was a virgin field unturned by systematic analysis. The first major exercise was carried out in 1975 by Aldrich (1980) who interviewed a sample of Asian and white shopkeepers in Wandsworth. The outcome was a partial and far from decisive confirmation of the middleman pattern. Wandsworth Asians comply with proposition three of the model in that 65 per cent of their clientele is non-Asian, a customer mix which accords well with the ethnic composition of the area.[9] With regard to resources, Aldrich's findings were inconclusive, with Asians displaying no significant difference from whites in the use of informal credit sources but making a slightly greater use of family labour, allowing greater labour intensiveness and considerably longer opening hours.

The three-city survey

Our 1978 interview survey of retailers in Bradford, Ealing and Leicester provides more extensive information about small business behaviour (Aldrich, Cater, Jones and McEvoy 1981). Its findings may also be considered more representative in that the bulk of Asian traders in British cities operate in areas where there is a heavy Asian residential concentration, unlike Wandsworth which is somewhat peripheral to London's major Asian settlements. Of the fifteen wards studied, Asian residents were a majority in two, and in six others more than one quarter of the population were Asian.

The first two propositions of the middleman model – that ethnic entrepreneurs benefit from internal resources and practise more rigorous competition – may be tested by comparing our Asian and white shopkeeper samples, as shown in Table 1. Asian–white comparisons are of particular interest in view of the widely held belief that the newcomers are using 'unfair' methods of competition to drive established shops from the mar-

Table 1. *Resources and competitive practices among Asian and white shopkeepers in three English cities, 1978*

	Owner's ethnicity	
	Asian	White
1. Average number of employees	2.14	1.82
2. Average number of family members and relatives employed	1.39	0.60*
3. Per cent married	92	81
4. Married owners only: per cent with spouse employed in the business	56	58
5. Per cent with children	81	75
6. Owners with children: per cent whose children work in the business	30	22
7. Average hours open per day	10.24	9.08*
8. Per cent open on Sundays	52	17*
9. Per cent make deliveries to customers	37	44
10. Per cent sell on credit	37	38
11. Per cent belonging to merchants' cooperative	14	14
12. Average hours owner works per week	61	57**
13. Per cent with self-employed father	51	27*
14. Per cent inherited the shop	2	8*
15. Per cent with relatives who own shop	31	36
16. Per cent raising some start-up capital from banks	64	28*
17. Per cent raising some start-up capital from family	29	15*
18. Per cent raising some start-up capital from friends	31	5*

*Difference between Asians and whites significant at .01 level.
**Difference significant at 0.5 level.
Source: data collected by the authors.

ket. At the extreme, this belief portrays Asians as an over-ambitious, intrusive group using 'sweatshop' methods to gain a 'stranglehold' on the British economy (Billig 1978). Our results show that such beliefs greatly exaggerate the differences between Asian and white shopkeepers.

Asian-owned shops do not differ significantly from white-owned shops in the number of people employed, although Asians tend to employ more full-time employees than white owners. The two groups differ significantly, however, in their employment of family members and relatives, with Asians averaging about 1.4 and whites only 0.6 employees per shop. Closer examination reveals that the difference lies *not* in a higher rate of nuclear family employment – spouse and children – but in the employment of extended family members, especially mothers and fathers. Among the married shopkeepers (92 per cent of the Asians and 81 per cent of the whites), the proportion whose spouses work in the shop is nearly identical in the two groups. About the same proportion of owners in both groups have children, and Asians are only slightly more likely to employ their children than are whites.

If Asian shopkeepers possess any critical advantage, then, over their white competitors, it is in the realm of labour intensiveness. The greater availability of extended family labour, some of it unpaid, enables Asian firms to operate an hour longer per day and to remain open on Sundays. Table 1 also shows that, apart from being open longer hours, Asian shopkeepers make no abnormally strenuous efforts to court custom by making home deliveries, offering credit, or obtaining cheaper merchandise through cooperative purchasing.

As for expertise and capital, two other factors central to business success, we find a mixed picture when comparing Asians with whites. Using commercial experience as a surrogate for expertise, we find that a higher proportion of Asians than whites had self-employed fathers and thus grew up in a business family. The difference, however, is mostly the result of a very high proportion of Gujeratis in Leicester originating from East Africa, where three-quarters had self-employed fathers. A similar result holds true for Ealing, whereas there is no significant difference in Bradford or in the earlier study in Wandsworth (Aldrich 1980).

With regard to capital, white owners were significantly more likely to have relied solely on their personal assets for starting their businesses. As shown in Table 1, a much higher proportion of Asians than whites raised at least a fraction of their capital from banks, family members or friends. These figures are misleading, however, because the proportion of total capital raised through these sources by Asians was quite small in the case of family and friends. Indeed, the actual proportion of total capital raised via these methods is virtually the same for the two groups. Thus, contributions from Asian shopkeepers' families and friends appear to be mostly token amounts (less than 10 per cent of requirements).

Of those shopkeepers relying on banks for some capital, the proportion raised was nearly identical for Asians and whites: 51 per cent vs. 49 per cent. There is no evidence here that Asians have difficulty raising funds via financial institutions – more than twice as many Asians as whites obtained some capital from banks, and of those with access to bank funds, about half of their capital requirements were provided for.

Proposition one of the middleman model is therefore only partially supported. Asian shopkeepers do benefit from drawing upon extended family labour, in contrast to whites who must employ outsiders as well as their spouses and children. As for raising capital, however, Asian shop-keepers actually relied more heavily upon external resources than whites, contrary to expectations.

Proposition two of the middleman model is supported in only one respect – longer hours – and in general Asians do not differ from whites in the other competitive practices we measured.

Market orientation

One characteristic above all others defines the middleman group and that is its role as seller of goods and services to non-members. Prior to inter-viewing, our expectation was that Asian shopkeepers in the three cities would fail to conform to this pattern. Our initial work, a census of shops to establish numbers, type and location, revealed a striking spatial corre-lation between Asian shops and Asian residents. As illustrated by Figure 1, at the ward level, the distribution of shops mirrors that of ethnic poten-tial customers with remarkable precision. Using 500 m^2 areas as units of analysis, the correlation between the proportion of Asian-owned shops

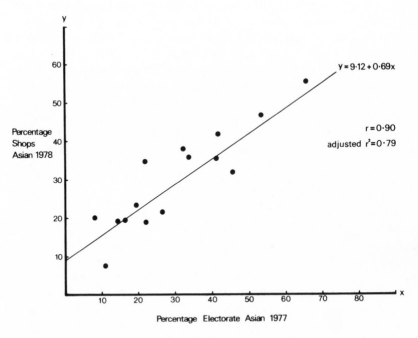

Figure 1 Relationship of Asian share of population to Asian share of shops, by ward

and the proportion of Asian residents is .61 – the higher the proportion of Asians in an area, the larger the proportion of shops owned by Asians. Using regression analysis, we discovered that the form of this relationship was remarkably similar across the three cities studied: every 1 per cent increase in an area's percentage of Asian residents is associated with an increase in the percentage of Asian shops of about three-fifths to three-quarters of 1 per cent (Aldrich, Cater, Jones and McEvoy 1982).

We believe the emergence of Asian shops has occurred in direct response to the rise of Asian population concentrations. The locational characteristics of minority retailers provide us with a reliable and easily obtainable measurement of their market orientation. Since most small shops must be located with regard to convenient customer access, it follows that genuine middleman outlets will be distributed in much the same way as the general population, dispersed throughout the city rather than clustered in close proximity to minority residential concentrations. Conversely, firms depending upon the protected market will exhibit a high level of concentration and will be rigidly confined within territories heavily occupied by minority residents.

On the evidence of their location patterns, Asian retailers in Britain comprise an enclave economy rather than a middleman economy. The supposition that their commercial survival is heavily dependent upon an ethnic clientele is confirmed by the interview results, which attest that on average only 30 per cent of the Asian shopkeeper's customers are white. Most of the respondents explained the ethnic composition of their custom in terms of proximity but significant numbers mentioned carrying special products that appealed mainly to Asians.

When we consider the chronological development of Asian business, we see that its emergence and growth is usually closely tied in with the growth of Asian population in the vicinity. Aldrich and Reiss (1976) represented the rise of minority enterprise as an aspect of the overall process of *ecological succession*, a term customarily used to describe the residential displacement of one ethnic or racial group by another. Their work on neighbourhood racial succession in the USA finds that, in cases where the exodus of white residents leads to the closure of white-owned firms, vacancies are taken up by incoming blacks and hispanics. 'The withdrawal of majority group competition opens up opportunities for minority entrepreneurs and minority businesses eventually occupy the abandoned niches' (Aldrich and Reiss 1976: 848). The dominant theme is one of disadvantaged minorities inheriting discarded premises in unwanted neighbourhoods and surviving only because few white competitors see the inner city market as worth contesting. Just as they acquire mainly filtered housing, so blacks are dependent upon filtered businesses. These remarks are not totally inappropriate to British Asians. Certainly they share with black Americans an over-reliance on a protected market whose purchasing power is too limited to support either widespread business participation or high levels of monetary return.[10]

Middleman specialization

Our information on business as a specialized group function is comparatively scanty. Even so, the available data is sufficient to confirm that self-employment in retailing absorbs only a small fraction of economically active Asians and creates very few additional opportunities for the employment of group members. D.J. Smith (1977: 93) noted that 'self-employed shopkeepers account for only 5 per cent of the total Asian working population'. Using Bradford as an example, we calculated that in 1978 there were a little over 500 Asians self-employed in retailing and allied services, who in turn offered full-time jobs to no more than 700 of their fellows and part-time jobs to a further 250–300. Assuming (very conservatively) that there were 15,000 Asians active in the local job market, we conclude that the Asian-owned retail sector absorbs, at most, 10 per cent: this hardly constitutes a leading source of group livelihood. These rather speculative estimates take no account of non-retailing activities, though this is a rather less serious omission than at first sight. Retailing accounts for the majority of Asian-owned concerns, as pointed out by D.J. Smith (1977: 92–3): 'nearly two-thirds of self-employed Asians (64 per cent) are shopkeepers' (see Table 4 in chapter 8, p. 129).

Controlling for ethnicity

Up to this point we have written as though Asians were a single homogeneous group undifferentiated by religion, language and culture. Nevertheless, we are well aware of ethnic variation and its relevance to business behaviour. Asians in Britain may be differentiated along the lines of religion, language and national/regional origin, three cross-cutting dimensions which produce a proliferation of distinct ethnic groups, each of which provides a focus for communal organization and personal identity. It should be recognized that ethnic heterogeneity is extreme, with three major religions, at least four language groups and three countries of origin all claiming the allegiance of large numbers of Asians in this country. A further dimension is added if we distinguish between migrants originating directly from the subcontinent and those who sojourned in Africa (chiefly Kenya and Uganda) prior to their arrival in Britain. To the extent that the traditions, institutions and historical experiences of each group influence its capacity for entrepreneurial organization, it may well be that not all Asian groups are equally predisposed towards enterprise or as well-equipped to perform successfully.

Somewhat unfortunately, our data do not allow an exhaustive test of these assumptions and expectations. Ideally, we would like to perform a statistical exercise to compare and contrast each of the major Asian ethnicities in order to establish the impact (if any) of cultural background on commercial performance. In practice this is impossible: when the sample is broken down by geographical origin, religion and language, three groups – West Pakistani Muslims, Punjabi Sikhs and Gujerati Hindus from East Africa – predominate to such an extent that all other groups are reduced to statistical insignificance. While this is somewhat limiting, a comparative analysis of these three groups is in itself of considerable value, since Sikhs, Pakistanis and East African Gujeratis represent three of Britain's principal immigrant shopkeeper groups.

Our survey allows us to examine the alleged differences between East African and other Asian groups. The distinction between Asians directly from the subcontinent and those migrating to Britain via East Africa is frequently seen as critical, with the latter being portrayed as the most business-oriented and 'middle class' of all Asian migrants, a picture which is lent some substance by the historic role played by Asians in colonial East Africa. During the pre-Independence period, the Asian population of British East Africa displayed many of the definitive characteristics of a middleman minority – they dominated the distributive trades, acted as a link between the African peasant producer and the world economy and maintained a socio-economic status intermediate between whites and blacks. Above all, they were able to support very high levels of self-employment, so much so that it is no exaggeration to speak of business ownership as a group specialism. With the arrival of large numbers of Kenya and Uganda Asians in Britain (mostly 1968–74), it was politically expedient to promote the newcomers as commercially dynamic with vital skills and experience to feed into the host economy. The possibility of Nairobi being resurrected in Leicester was contemplated as a serious possibility by the more euphoric commentators, although others were careful to point to the economically disruptive effects of what was for many a forced migration (see, for example, Ward 1973).

Evidence suggests, then, that East Africans differ sharply from other immigrant entrepreneurs, both in their expectations and in their ability to draw upon past business experience. The inference is that East African Gujeratis represent a kind of established 'business caste' and as such enjoy many psychological and practical advantages not shared by other Asians.[11] Of the three groups included in this study, it is the West

Pakistanis who stand in sharpest contrast to this, being predominantly rural in origin (whereas the East Africans are almost exclusively from urban backgrounds), comparatively modest in educational achievement and having few members with any kind of previous business experience. In relation to these two extremes, the Sikhs stand in an intermediate position, having historically developed a partial role as commercial middlemen (Ballard and Ballard 1977). We now examine the extent to which Asian businessmen in Britain have succeeded in re-establishing this traditional pecking order.

The three-group comparison

Little more than a cursory glance at Table 2 is necessary to establish that the East African superiority hypothesis is not consistently borne out by the evidence. Of the 16 separate variables used to compare the three groups, only Items 2, 4, 5 and 16 reveal a statistically significant variation in the expected direction. Three of those occur under the heading of resources, a term which is used here to cover all assets, material and non-material, necessary for the launching and operation of a small business enterprise. Table 2 confirms what might generally be expected, namely that the main advantage enjoyed by East Africans takes the form of assets accumulated in that region and subsequently put to work in England. Of particular interest here is *capital assets* and the finding that one in three African Asian respondents was able to transfer wealth into this country, despite the draconian measures against capital export adopted by the Amin government. Although the present sample is certainly dotted with respondents whose businesses have risen phoenix-like from the ashes of destitution, there are surprisingly large numbers of businessmen (including Ugandans) who have been able to finance their English shops wholly or partly from African-acquired capital. In this they have a head start over the Sikhs and Pakistanis, almost all of whom financed their operations through savings or borrowings made after migrating to Britain.

In a sense, of course, the greatest resource available to East African Asians is the non-material asset of *entrepreneurial experience*: the maintenance of continuity between countries of origin and destination, and the smooth transfer of economic function from one region to another. While forced expulsion can rob the refugee of his material possessions, his mental wealth is likely to remain intact – in this case the accumulated knowledge of business practices and other relevant organizational and social skills. Herein lies the greatest distinction between the three groups. Whereas three-quarters of the East African respondents are sons of entrepreneurs, the corresponding figures for Sikhs and Pakistanis are

Table 2. *Relationship between ethnicity and commercial resources, practices and performance*

	Shopkeepers classified by country of origin, language and religion			
	East African Gujerati Hindu	Indian Punjabi Sikh	Pakistani Punjabi Muslim	All
Per cent who:				
Resources				
1. Used bank as one source of starting capital	64.0	71.1	56.9	62.9
2. Brought money to England	35.3	4.1	2.6	12.5*
3. Have relatives who own business	27.5	26.1	33.8	30.1
4. Previously owned business	23.1	4.2	11.7	13.0**
5. Are sons of businessmen	76.5	53.1	26.0	48.0*
Competitive practices				
6. Plough back savings into the business	33.3	45.7	78.9	39.0**
7. Employ 3 or more relatives	19.1	25.9	35.8	28.5**
8. Open 7 days per week	38.5	38.0	60.5	47.8**
9. Make deliveries	23.5	42.0	45.5	38.2**
10. Give credit	84.2	63.1	90.3	81.2**
Performance				
11. Turnover £750 or more per week	38.6	52.7	34.6	40.4
12. Made net profit 1977–8	76.5	80.5	70.3	74.8
13. Expected profit 1978–9	85.4	82.2	82.5	83.2
14. Own another business	17.6	37.5	10.4	19.9**
15. Make savings from business	18.4	25.6	26.7	24.0
16. Average per cent of customers who are white	33.5	30.1	21.6	27.4**

Notes: Statistical significance: the symbol * indicates that the difference between groups is significant at the .01 level. The symbol ** indicates the difference is significant at the .05 level.

53 per cent and 26 per cent (Table 2, Item 5). Moreover, the African family businesses were by far the most substantial, averaging 16.1 employees against 3.4 and 1.9 for the other two groups. In addition, almost a quarter of the East African respondents claim previous personal experience of ownership (Table 2, Item 4). For African Gujeratis, the

shop in England is a means of re-erecting an existing family tradition but for the others it is likely to be a venture into uncharted waters.

Competitive practices

It would be natural to assume that the greater commercial experience of East Africans would be translated into more keenly competitive practices, giving them a definite edge over their ethnic rivals. Yet, according to Table 2 (Items 6–10), it is the Pakistanis who canvass most enthusiastically for custom. This is most noteworthy with respect to opening hours, where they are 50 per cent more likely to open seven days a week than either of the other groups (Item 8), an achievement made possible largely through employing large numbers of family members: as Item 7 suggests, Pakistani shopkeepers tend to achieve greater family labour intensiveness than the others. We should also observe that Pakistanis are more likely to give customer credit, to plough back savings into the business and to make deliveries, although in this last respect they do not differ greatly from Sikhs.

Undoubtedly, the salient discovery here is that East African shopkeepers appear *less competitive than Pakistanis on all five items and less so than Sikhs on three items*. In short, the direction of variance is the opposite to that expected, implying that the greater experience of East Africans is not reflected in action. In all fairness it must be acknowledged that the evidence is not entirely free from ambiguity, since a number of the specified variables are somewhat double-edged in meaning. In the case of Item 8, for example, are we to interpret long opening hours at face value as representing dynamic and aggressive salesmanship? Or should we adopt a view, which the present authors have previously expressed, that long hours reflect a battle for sheer survival in a marginal market (Aldrich, Cater, Jones and McEvoy 1981; Cater and Jones 1978)? Indeed the truth may be neither of these but merely a matter of habit, custom and customer expectation, an absence of any kind of conscious policy at all. Even so, while recognizing the enigmatic nature of much of the data, our feeling remains that the evidence is sufficient to give the lie to the suggestion that an African origin results in any kind of competitive superiority.

Performance

The final section of Table 2 is headed 'Performance' and assesses the retailer sample in respect of turnover (Item 11), profitability (12 and 13), multiple ownership (14), savings (15), and customer ethnicity (16). If ethnic membership is indeed a decisive factor in commercial development, then we should expect inter-group variance to be most conspicuous in these areas. Yet, with the exception of Items 14 and 16 there is a complete absence of significant variation, all three groups displaying traits which may be taken as fairly representative of small retailing in present-day England. It is probably fair to say that the features exhibited here are less a commentary on shopkeeper ethnicity than on the everyday problems shared by most small retailers – black and white, immigrant and native alike. There is very little evidence of a specific Gujerati, Sikh or Pakistani effect and no sign of any particular impact exerted by the East African business heritage.

In the two instances where one of the groups deviates sharply from the common Asian pattern, the Sikhs emerge as the most successful in expanding into multiple business ownership (Item 14) while the Pakistanis appear least successful in attracting non-Asian custom (Item 16). This last finding underlines once more the limited degree to which Asian retailers have been able to develop a function as 'exporters' of goods and services to the majority market (the third requirement of middleman status). Of particular interest is the revelation that Pakistanis are even more than normally disadvantaged in this respect: the immediate temptation is to see this as evidence of the influence of ethnic group traits on business behaviour and to apply the stereotype of Pakistanis as hailing from an unsophisticated Third World background, lacking a group business heritage and hence less able than the more highly organized Sikhs and Gujeratis to compete for custom outside their own group. Yet such a suggestion stands in flat contradiction to the evidence previously examined, which portrays Pakistanis as the most keenly competitive of the three and as highly capable of mobilizing resources to this end.

Ethnic advantage: a null hypothesis

Although the foregoing discussion has indicated that preconceptions about inter-group inequalities in entrepreneurial potential are not entirely without substance, it has produced no evidence that these are in any way decisive determinants of the commercial status of Asian retailers in Britain. As we have suggested elsewhere (Aldrich, Cater, Jones and McEvoy 1981), immigrant business activity is shaped more by external forces than by internal characteristics, i.e. the opportunity structure of the receiving society outweighs any cultural predisposition towards entrepreneurship. This interpretation now seems more than ever the correct one. Among the small shopkeeping fraternity of urban England, similarities between groups are far more striking than differences, a principle which holds good whether one compares Asian with non-Asian or Asian with Asian. The few genuinely consequential inter-group contrasts may be listed as follows:

(1) Asians enjoy greater family labour intensiveness than white retailers but possess no consistent superiority: in particular, the role of informal capital accumulation seems much more muted than expected.

(2) Gujerati East Africans score over other Asians with regard to capital and experience but fail to transform this into any demonstrable operational superiority.

(3) Pakistanis are most reliant on ethnic protection, despite an apparent edge in competitiveness.

(4) Sikhs score most consistently over the range of indicators.

The discovery that resource endowment varies only minimally from group to group and, in any case, plays little part in shopkeeper behaviour or business rewards leads inescapably to the conclusion that ethnic origin is not a good predictor of small business outcomes. Evidently we must look outside the ethnic group itself to explain the failure of Asians to re-establish their traditional middleman role. Irrespective of ethnic background, Asian shopkeepers are faced with a common set of structural constraints which act as a levelling down force, nullifying any slight intergroup differentials and stifling the achievements of many of the more enterprising individuals.

Lack of markets

The most obviously visible expression of structural disadvantage is lack of market outlets, an obstacle which has proved impervious to the efforts of all but a small minority of individual shopkeepers. As noted by Jones (1982), the 'top end' of the Asian shopkeeper range is distinguished by a small number of concerns whose proprietors have found ways to break out of the normal stranglehold of marginality and low rewards. These, however, are of no particular ethnicity and are by no means typical of the genre. As a general rule, selling opportunities are restricted by inability or unwillingness to tap majority markets, while at the same time the pressures of mounting unemployment and racism combine to push increasing numbers of Asians in the direction of self-employment. In bald terms, the ratio of customers to traders is tending to diminish, a trend which has probably been operative since the late 1960s.

In the long term, the Asian retail and service business community may be unable to escape from demographic inevitability. Middleman functions, particularly the exploitation of external markets, can only be developed fully where the group forms a small minority of the total population. In cases of this type, where the ratio of majority customers to minority suppliers is high, trading can form a major group specialization creating plentiful economic opportunities for group members. The Orientals of California in the early part of this century are one group who exemplified the benefits of this kind of situation, but for British Asians any significant developments along these lines would require massive penetration of the white market and more diversification into areas of business other than retailing. Most Asians live in residential areas of high Asian concentration, with a consequent dearth of potential white custom. It is significant that retail market penetration and specialization are greatest in areas like Wandsworth (Aldrich 1980), and Croydon (Mullins 1980), where the ratio of Asians to non-Asians is comparatively low. (Our results do not allow us to generalize to non-retail and service markets.)

The missing component

When we seek to discover the special circumstances which encourage the ethnic middleman to flourish – and which are clearly absent from present-day Britain – we find that demography alone does not hold the key. Once again the economic history of Asian immigrants within the British Empire proves to be a fertile source of instruction. More than any other factor, the Asian traders of colonies in the West Indies and East Africa owed their economic status to an entirely artificial state of affairs created by colonialism. According to Ernst (1980), the expansion of Indian enterprise in East Africa was underwritten by the restrictions placed by the British on the development of African enterprise: 'a socioeconomic barrier was erected artificially by creating a non-African "middle class" consisting of Asians, Greeks and other minority groups in East Africa' (1980: 457). This view is corroborated by other writers such as Lyon (1973), who wrote of African Indians as forming a 'privileged racial estate', and Tinker (1977).

The sense conveyed by these writers is that the Asian middlemen of East Africa benefited from a quite inordinate degree of market protection and from policies which effectively obliged the native African population to play the roles of captive market, cheap labour, and primary product suppliers. Though the Asian response was one of vigour and initiative, it was essentially a response to the privileged opportunities afforded by a virtual racial monopoly.

This brief digression in time and space has served to put the economic role of overseas Asians into perspective and to spell out the basic reasons for our refusal to accept that such a role can be resurrected in Britain at the present time. The position in which Asians find themselves in Britain is not merely dissimilar but, in several senses, antithetical to that experienced in the colonies. Instead of operating in a protected market within an underdeveloped country, Asians now find themselves competing inside the metropolis itself, against an established small business class and against a background of long term decline in small scale trading. Given such circumstances, the odds against Asians achieving middleman status via shopkeeping – or even travelling far along that road – are overwhelming. Even if it were somehow possible to ignore the racist nature of the institutions upon which Asian business depends, one would still be forced to the conclusion that there is simply no vacancy for a major new middleman group in a mature stagnant economy where resources are firmly under the control of established interest groups.

An evolutionary version of the middleman model

Before rejecting the middleman model as inappropriate to British Asians, we should consider a final possibility – that commercial performance is a function of evolutionary stage. Because of its recent emergence, British Asian trading activity may be regarded as being in its infancy: perhaps it is the problems of commercial immaturity (rather than those of being Asian in England) that we have been describing in previous pages. As noted earlier, any immigrant business economy may be expected to undergo change over time, emerging from an initially weak position to achieve breadth and depth. The inter-war development of American Orientals exemplifies this process of maturation and also suggests that the enclave or ghetto economy may be succeeded by a middleman orientation. Light's (1972) work stressed that the enclave stage of Oriental development was fraught with hazards similar to those currently faced by Indians and Pakistanis in England. Far from expressing any 'natural aptitude' for commerce, self-employment was often the sole recourse for workers subject to extreme economic oppression and, as Light (1972: 8) remarked, 'The classic small businesses of prewar Chinese . . . were monuments to the discrimination that had created them.' During this phase, grim survival was possible only by exploiting the ethnic market, yet by the Second World War, Chinese traders were selling over half their produce to non-Orientals.

The question of whether the current enclave structure of Asian activity is likely to be replaced by a similar middleman development is one which is virtually impossible to answer on the basis of the scanty straws in the wind which are available as a substitute for hard information. In particular, there is a dearth of time series data on which future projection could be based. Certainly Asians have been achieving a steady increase in their rate of self-employment over the past two decades (see Table 3 in chapter 8, p. 128) but there is no evidence to show that this has been accompanied either by a growth in market penetration or by improved monetary returns. Our own interview data certainly gives no indication that increasing business maturity leads to greater economic security or better entrepreneurial performance. When Asian firms established in 1967 or earlier are compared with those founded after that date, rates of profit and saving are not significantly different: if there is an inference to be drawn, it is that commercial infancy is not a critical factor in business underdevelopment. Since none of these shreds of evidence is conclusive, we can only reiterate that the future of Asian retailing depends upon market opportunities and that, up to now, the trend has been one of Asian retailers multiplying faster than prospective customers.

Conclusions

Our verdict must be that, except for a minority of firms in areas of sparse Asian settlement, Asian retail and service enterprise in Britain shows most of the characteristics of the enclave – or recluse – economy; and that development in the direction of middleman status will continue to be retarded by the unfavourable opportunity structure of the receiving society. As yet, the commercial advantages customarily ascribed to ethnicity have largely failed to break these barriers. Indeed, in several respects it seems doubtful whether such advantages really exist. To a great extent, therefore, this chapter has been an exercise in deglamorization. While we willingly accept that Asian businessmen have demonstrated great personal initiative in pioneering new ventures in the midst of decay and great resilience in multiplying in the face of adversity, we are nonetheless of the view that Asian business activity represents a truce with racial inequality rather than a victory over it. Despite the façade of self-determination erected by group entrepreneurs, in reality, going into business does little to change the status of group members in relation to majority society: as with members of the majority society, it simply allows a small minority to exchange the role of marginal worker for that of marginal proprietor.

The level of discordance between our findings and the propositions of the middleman model emphasizes the need for an alternative approach to the interpretation of ethnic retailing. It may well be that a realistic assessment will only emerge from the application of models of internal colonialism which lay stress upon the function that non-white colonial groups are compelled to perform for industrial capitalism. Certainly we are inclined to give primacy to racial disadvantage over ethnic advantage as an explanation of Asian commercial development.

12

Acquiring premises: a case study of Asians in Bradford

JOHN CATER

In the last chapter we saw that the prospects for Asian shopkeepers in British cities achieving prosperity through the retail trade were very slight. In this chapter we extend the analysis of the market conditions in which Asian retailers operate through a case study of the acquisition of business premises in Bradford, West Yorkshire, one of the three areas covered in the study of Asian shopkeepers. Much of the analysis is concerned with the question of whether similar processes operate in acquiring shops as in house buying. Studies of Asian owner-occupation have emphasised discriminatory constraints in access to good quality housing and differential pricing for white and Asian purchasers (Duncan 1977; Fenton 1977, 1978; Karn 1969). The payment of a premium in house buying by Asians has been attributed to discrimination by vendors (Duncan 1977; Fenton 1977, 1978), but can be accounted for, according to Robinson (1979b), as the result of Asians putting a greater emphasis on acquiring properties in specific areas of Asian settlement for which demand is correspondingly higher. Information is presented in this chapter on differential pricing in the acquisition of retail premises, and the relevance of these conflicting explanations is assessed. A high degree of market segmentation is shown in both the residential and the commercial sectors and this allows us to focus on another area of minority business, the ethnic estate agency: in what circumstances have Asians come to perform this role and in what ways do they affect the pattern of acquisition of houses and shops?

In the first part of the chapter we consider access to residential premises (how is the pattern of Asian house buying specific in terms of location, type of property and cost of acquisition and how are differentials to be explained). In the second part the same questions are considered with regard to the purchase of shops. The concluding section reviews parallels between residential and commercial sectors and sets out a model incorporating what appear to be the main factors underlying differential pricing, a model which can be applied both to house buying and the purchase of shops.

The development of Asian owner-occupation

The pattern of Asian home ownership has developed particularly rapidly in the last two decades. New Commonwealth immigrants who came to Britain from the Indian subcontinent in the late 1950s and early 1960s were predominantly male, had come to this country as a replacement labour force in certain industries (Peach 1968), saw their stay as short term and were often intent on minimising expenditure in order to facilitate remittances to the homeland. They concentrated initially in lodging houses in the inner city, houses which, in the case of Bradford, were often owned by the previous wave of immigrants, the East Europeans. A similar presence in late Victorian and Edwardian multi-occupied property was graphically illustrated for Birmingham in Rex and Moore's (1967) pioneering study of housing classes.

This pattern was, however, often short lived; many white households were leaving the poor quality pre-First World War terraced property through either local authority relocation schemes or by filtering to better housing in the owner-occupied sector. Demand for old inner city property was low, and movement into this residual sector proceeded apace. Dahya (1974: 90) noted that it was possible to buy a small, unimproved, back-to-back cottage in Bradford for as little as £45–£80 in the early 1960s, and even in the mid 1960s the price range £175–£550 covered most inner city terraces of all types and quality (Dahya 1974: 98). This pattern was repeated elsewhere – for example, Butterworth (1967) noted the availability of a small terrace house in Halifax for 'a few hundred' and a large and improved three-bedroomed terrace with a bathroom and inside toilet was readily accessible to anyone who could afford £1,300. The movement of Asians into owner-occupation continued and by 1977/8 the National Dwelling and Household Survey reported that 70 per cent of Indian, Pakistani and Bangladeshi households in Britain were owner-occupiers (Department of Environment 1979: 33). In manufacturing towns and cities in the North and Midlands the figures are considerably higher (88 per cent in Dudley, for example, 87 per cent in Sandwell and 81 per cent in Bradford).

(i) Segregation

Having established the predominance of house purchase among Asians, particularly in the northern textile towns, we go on to consider certain attributes of the ethnic housing market which may be compared with the retail and service property market later in the paper. The first and most fundamental point is that Asians are strongly segregated residentially.

All the early studies of the residential concentration of Asians in British cities noted the existence of a high degree of residential segregation between black and white.[1] In the case of West Indians it is suggested that this concentration has diminished quite substantially between 1961 and 1971 (Peach, Winchester and Woods 1975). At the same time the segregation of Indians and Pakistanis increased (Peach 1975). However, the spatial expansion of Asian settlement along major roads and some contiguous 'fringing' into adjacent wards have apparently halted increases in ward level residential segregation in Bradford (Cater 1981: 180) and a similar pattern has been identified by Robinson (1981) in Blackburn. But even today, the non-white minorities comprise only a small proportion of the city total – about one in six in the Bradford example – and as such residential concentration is likely to take the form of ethnic predominance in small clusters of streets except in the very heart of the immigrant area. The street or small group of streets is perhaps the most appropriate unit for analysing ethnic segregation, being closest to the scale of a person's everyday experience of 'activity space'. At this scale level, roughly comparable with a 250 square metre grid, the Asian:white Index of Segregation in Bradford is 78.3.[2] Forty-two grid squares of a total of 1,744 (2.4 per cent) have a majority Asian electorate and 62.0 per cent of the Asian voting population in 1977 lived in Asian-dominated environments (Cater, Jones and McEvoy 1977; Cater and Jones 1979: 94).

(ii) Housing quality

Segregation alone does not prove any inferiority in the housing market as Krausz (1972) has illustrated in his work on the Jewish population in the UK. But the key characteristic of Asian segregation in Bradford is that the pattern of ethnic residence mirrors exactly the location of the poorest quality housing environments. The Runnymede Trust (1980), citing a 1976 Department of Environment report, stated that nationally the worst 10 per cent of census enumeration districts in 1971 housed 70 per cent of the black population. These enumeration districts were characterised by the absence of basic amenities such as inside toilets, bathrooms and hot and cold running water, and had three times the national average number of households living at densities above 1.5 persons per room, the statutory overcrowding level. Despite considerable advances in the past decade through local authority improvement schemes, the two main areas of Asian residence in Bradford, Manningham and University, rank among the highest group of wards for the number of properties considered unfit for human habitation and for properties lacking one or more of the basic amenities. This environmental deprivation is further compounded by unemployment rates two and a half times the city norm (itself 16 per cent in the autumn of 1982) and an infant mortality rate far in excess of the urban average. As the local authority states, 'it is clear that many of the obvious indicators of urban deprivation are concentrated here [in Manningham] . . . [this] bears out the rule of thumb that if an area scores badly on one indicator it is likely to score very badly on many other indicators of deprivation' (City of Bradford Metropolitan District Council 1979: 51).

The types of housing bought by Asians in Bradford confirm to the picture set out above. According to the NDHS, 84 per cent of Asian families in Bradford in 1977/8 were living in terraced houses built before 1919 (Ward 1982: 8). Similarly Cater (1981) estimated that about 90 per cent of the Asian population in Bradford live in terraced huses owned by themselves or their immediate family. The NDHS also showed that Asian households were far more likely to live in less attractive residential areas, about two-fifths of Indians and Pakistanis (compared to one sixteenth of white households) being located in districts described as 'industrial, commercial and poor residential' (Ward 1982: 10). In most cases an Asian family will be the last occupiers of this property before a compulsory purchase order and the bulldozer.

Rateable values, while by no means a perfect surrogate for housing quality, offer an alternative method of indicating the status of Asian housing. The NDHS shows that while rateable values are low throughout much of the city, Asian households were more than twice as likely to live in property with a gross valuation of under £100 per annum (76.3 per cent compared with 37.9 per cent). Using median values for the categories used in the NDHS it is possible to estimate the average gross valuation for a white-occupied property at £132 per annum, 45 per cent higher than the average for an Asian-occupied property of £91 per annum. The kind of property represented by these figures is shown by the present author's own survey in Bradford: only five of a total of 177 properties advertised by estate agents for a sample week in April 1975–81 and purchased by Asians were not terraces, cottages, back-to-backs or side-scullieries (Cater 1981).

(iii) House prices
We have already seen that the houses typically bought by Asians in Bradford and other northern towns have been at the bottom end of the

market (see Karn 1969; Robinson 1979a). The prices paid by Asians have been correspondingly low. The present author's study of property trans-actions in Bradford between 1975 and 1980 noted the relatively low value of housing bought by Asians – an average asking price of just £7,954 when adjusted to June 1980 levels. The average house price of £17,222 in June 1980 was well over double that paid by Asian purchasers; even within the inner city the average terraced house was advertised for £10,£125, over £2,000 (21.4 per cent) more than the advertised price of property pur-chased by Asian buyers. This variation by racial group was first quantified by Karn (1969) who noted that Asians paid 28.9 per cent less for their housing in Batley in 1966, and has been further supported in figures pro-duced by Robinson (1979a) for Blackburn, where over three-fifths of Asian households bought property for less than £3,000 in 1975/6 com-pared with less than a quarter of white purchasers; a visual survey further suggested that 96.5 per cent of Asian purchases were of pre-First World War terraced property.

Clearly, if market price is a reasonable indicator of housing size, qual-ity, amenity and environment, Asian buyers are dealing in an inferior commodity. However, this does not mean that they are buying on favour-able terms. We shall return to this point after considering the role of the ethnic estate agents in the purchase of residential property.

(iv) The role of the Asian estate agent in the residential market

Given the highly segregated nature of ethnic housing space in Bradford and the extent of Asian business development, both in this city and elsewhere (Cater and Jones 1978; Mullins 1980; Aldrich, Cater, Jones and McEvoy 1981), it is of no surprise that Asian estate agents have emerged to play a role in the distribution of housing.

The first report of ethnic activity in this aspect of the Bradford housing market can be found in evidence presented to the Select Committee on Race Relations in 1971 and summarised by Duncan (1976: 314–15). In the late 1950s and early 1960s the low price of the majority of houses pur-chased and the lack of interest of formal sources of funding in cheap, unimproved pre-First World War inner city terraces led to the formation of an informal sub-market, with sales often being made on rental pur-chase arrangements. The purchaser would pay perhaps £1 a week to the vendor, his solicitor or, frequently, to a back street financier who would discount the mortgage at a high rate of interest. However an extremely buoyant property market in the early 1970s stimulated a 77 per cent rise in average house prices in two years (Boddy 1980) and helped to reinstate formal methods of exchange to some property sales in the inner city. Building society lending policies were interpreted rather more flexibly (following considerable increases in net assets), local authority mortgage support became more readily available and property turned over rapidly. Several Asian estate agents prospered during the 1972/3 property boom, but only two agencies have survived the rather depressed housing market conditions of the past few years and continue to operate today. Even so, the existence of formal methods of exchange is no guarantee that all Asian housing transactions operate through estate agents, Asian or white, and there is much circumstantial evidence to suggest that a lot of property at the very bottom of the market, particularly that which would not qualify for any kind of mortgage from conventional sources, still changes hands informally.

Within the housing market it is quite evident that even the formal exchanges are concentrated in a spatially segregated sector of the city, with 142 of 143 properties (99.3 per cent) sold by Asian agents being located in the inner ten wards of the old County Borough of Bradford, an area which accounted for 96.2 per cent of the total Asian electorate in 1980. A sample of white estate agents who deal regularly in inner city residential property sold only 175 properties of a city total of 570 in the same area (30.7 per cent), and even within the inner city were more likely to deal in more expensive, better quality property further from the city centre. In particular there were few instances of white agencies being involved in transactions in the main areas of ethnic concentration, University and Manningham; 91 per cent of all residential property sold by white agents in the inner city was in streets with fewer than one Asian family in five, while, by comparison, the Asian estate agents sold only 13 per cent of their advertised property in such white-dominated environments (Cater 1981). Clearly there is little indication of 'blockbusting' – Asian agents pioneering the extension of ethnic residence into previously white areas – in Bradford; rather Asian agents appear to deal largely in the residual spaces long considered as of little interest to the white agency.

The inability to penetrate the wide urban expanses beyond the ethnic core means that the Asian agent is confined to the poorest residential property which characterises this area and really does little more than circulate inferior housing resources within the ethnic community. This statement is not intended to denigrate the agent's importance within the Asian community, however, and there is substantial evidence of a within-group managerial function, defining high status areas within the ethnic enclave (often those with General Improvement Area status) and asking for premium prices for such 'first class residential opportunities' – an example being the Lidget Green area on the south-western fringe of the ethnic heartland. The Asian estate agent may also help to facilitate the sorting of the many sub-groups (each with their own very separate identity) within the Asian community; the location of some of the more prosperous members of the Gujerati community in the same Lidget Green area being an example.

The status of the Asian estate agent within the wider urban economy is, nonetheless, subordinate. Apart from dealing in a spatially segregated housing market, he sells fewer houses at a markedly lower price (only half the city average) and thus generates less commission. 90 per cent of his vendors and 99 per cent of his purchasers are drawn from the Asian community, and 97 per cent of the property he sells is terraced inner city housing of one kind or another.

(v) Explaining ethnic differentials in house buying

We have seen that Asian house prices show some sensitivity to the quality of the commodity, being 21.4 per cent lower than the mean price for an inner city terrace. However, there is some evidence that Asians are paying an inflated price for what is very poor quality housing. The present author (1981: 172–3) has shown that Asian estate agents asked for prices in excess of that asked for a small number of similar properties sold by white agents to Asian households. The size of the sample (36 cases) and a variation of just over £1,000 (12.9 per cent) is insufficient to produce any firm conclusions, particularly as some of the discrepancy may be accounted for by over-ambitious asking prices which may not be reflected in the final selling price of the property.

But the tendency for Asians to pay more for housing of the same quality has been clearly substantiated. Karn (1969) showed in her study of house sales to Indians and Pakistanis in a Yorkshire town that not only did Asians pay significantly more for houses than their current valuation, they also paid substantially more than white households for property given the same valuation. There is no indication of any of the properties being sold through an Asian estate agent. But the premium on house prices paid by Asians applied regardless of whether the vendor was white or Asian – in fact it was significantly higher when Asians were selling to Asians.

We shall return to the question of differential pricing after reviewing the evidence on the acquisition of retail premises. But it is useful to conclude this section on house purchase by sketching out some of the factors likely to underlie the inflated house prices paid by Asians.

It can be argued that Asians pay more for certain kinds of property (whether bought from Asian or white estate agents) because there is more demand for these properties. What is less clear is how far this excess demand reflects the positive value placed on features of the ethnic settlement area (Dahya 1974; Robinson 1979b) and how far the negative effects of discriminatory constraints in access to other properties (Fenton 1977; 1978).

Although the initial purchase of inner city terraces offering cheap and adequate short term residences may have reflected the male immigrants' sojourner orientation, it is important to recognise a wide range of constraining factors influencing access to housing. Hatch (1973) suggested that the choice of housing by ethnic minorities in Bristol may well have been influenced by unofficial racial 'steering' by estate agents; Boddy (1976) and Duncan (1977) have both shown how the structure of mortgage finance has operated against the inner city population in general and the coloured resident in particular, though in Karn's (1969) study Asians had easy access to council mortgages. Similarly, in the public sector Asians have found access to rented property difficult, notwithstanding their evident preference for owner-occupation. Although local authorities have to some extent responded to criticism voiced in the late 1960s (Burney 1967; Rex and Moore 1967; Cullingworth Committee 1969), the existence of 'points' systems of housing allocation, normally incorporating residence requirements, and the latitude given to housing visitors (Gray 1976), have continued to act as constraints on movement into the public sector. However, recent studies have shown a small but increasing number of Asian households in local authority housing (Robinson 1980), though they and other coloured groups have often received properties less desirable than those allocated to whites (Parker and Dugmore 1977; Flett 1979; Skellington 1980). Over the same period the alternative offered by the private rented sector has progressively disappeared, with widespread discrimination by private landlords (Daniel 1968; Smith 1976) combining with the dramatic decline in the number of available properties – from an average of 31.6 per cent of the total housing stock in the 1950s down to 24.1 per cent in 1966 and just 13.0 per cent in 1980 (Central Statistical Office 1981; 1982).

Finally, the presence of Asians in the owner-occupied sector does not necessarily imply that, having paid premium prices, they gain proportionately from owner-occupation. It is widely accepted that property ownership offers the combined benefits of providing a home and creating wealth for its occupants as they live in their appreciating assets (Murie and Forrest 1980). However, as Jones (1980) and Simmons (1981) have pointed out, Asians often own the worst housing with limited amenities and little prospect of rapid capital accumulation. This point has been further supported by Ward (1982) who divides owner-occupation into two basic groups, good quality residential property and cheap, often unimproved terraces, with an increasing gap in the financial attractiveness of the two categories. He argues that in many cities Asians can expect a much lower return on their investment, thus increasing the differential between black and white access to the most profitable elements of this wealth-creating process. Ward cites Bradford, with its low house prices, old housing stock, limited new building, declining industrial base and static population, as a typical example of a city in which the purchase of inner city terraced property is unlikely to provide a rapid or substantial capital gain. Far from gaining from the payment of a premium in buying residential property, the probability is that Asians have paid an inflated price for what is, in relative terms, a deflating asset.

The development of Asian businesses

Closely paralleling the development of Asian residential areas in Bradford has been the progressive emergence of an ethnic sub-economy. The earliest evidence of Asian-owned business in the city dates back to 1959 with Dahya (1974) noting the existence of two grocery shops and three cafes in the Lumb Lane area of Manningham – still one of the main enclaves of ethnic business today. By 1966 this number had increased dramatically to over 130 outlets, half of which were still in low order grocery or restaurant trades. This spectacular growth continued to 1978, with over 400 retail premises and approximately 150 associated services in the city, of which 135 were in Manningham alone – one outlet for every 63 Asian residents (Aldrich, Cater, Jones and McEvoy 1981). Although the period of explosive growth may well be nearing an end, for market saturation has been well and truly achieved, the rate of expansion remains impressive, a survey by the local authority in 1980 noting the existence of 793 Asian-owned firms in Bradford, of which 500 are involved directly in retailing and many more in related services (City of Bradford Metropolitan District Council 1979). This growth must be seen in the light of a general decline in small retail and service business nationally and in inner city outlets in particular, with the total number of all retail units falling from 583,132 in 1950 to 351,187 in 1979, a drop of 38.8 per cent. Although temporal comparisons are not aided by a change in the method of defining small business in the late 1960s, the trend is even more evident in this sector; 503,639 outlets operated by small independent retailers in 1950 have declined to just 231,187 single outlet enterprises in 1976, a fall of 51.4 per cent. Even if all of the 78,674 small multiples enumerated were independently owned, the decline still approaches 40 per cent.

Against this overall trend of small business decline stands the impressive growth of the Asian retail and service sector outlined above, apparently flying in the face of all conventional wisdom about the viability of small independently-owned inner city premises. Many Asian outlets are concentrated in the very sectors which have experienced the most rapid decrease – for example small clothing shops and grocery businesses together accounted for 66 per cent of the Asian retail outlets in Manningham in 1975, yet these are the precise areas which have suffered most from the advances of the large High Street clothing multiples on one hand and the ravages of the high turnover, low margin and very competitive supermarket trade on the other. While the specific consumer demands of Asian women may offer clothing businesses some market protection, this is less so in the food trade. Although some specialist sectors have survived, the number of general grocery stores is little more than a third of those that had existed in 1950 – a decline from 145,709 outlets to just 51,910 in 1979 (Central Statistical Office 1977; 1982). Yet the pattern of business ownership in Manningham is not untypical of inner city wards in other cities. For example, in Wycliffe, Leicester, Asians ran three-quarters of all the grocery shops and over half of the retail clothing outlets in 1978 (Aldrich, Cater, Jones and McEvoy 1981).

Where there has been a growth in the number of small retail enter-

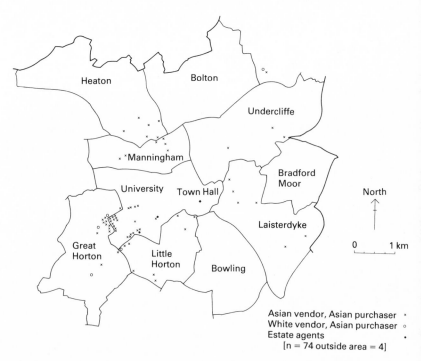

Figure 1 Location of all retail and service premises sold by Asian estate agents in Bradford CB (sample week in April 1975–81 inclusive)

prises in the last two or three decades, it has been in sectors in which Asians have been noticeably absent – antiques and craft and gift shops are good examples. However, in the last five years there is some evidence of an awakening of interest in small business opportunities (see chapter 2), illustrated by the gentlest variation in the long-standing decline in the number of retail and service outlets in 1979, when the number of premises operating rose by 1,419 (0.3 per cent). It is suggested that in many instances this is a response, often involuntary, to the closing of other opportunities in the job market, possibly stimulated by government publicity but difficult to sustain in the climate of economic recession. But even this slight rekindling of interest is unlikely to have an effect on the typical small inner city business, with the majority of the host community well aware of its extremely marginal nature in a city like Bradford.

(i) Segregation

Figures 1 and 2 identify the location of all the advertised properties sold by Asian and white estate agencies in the sample period.

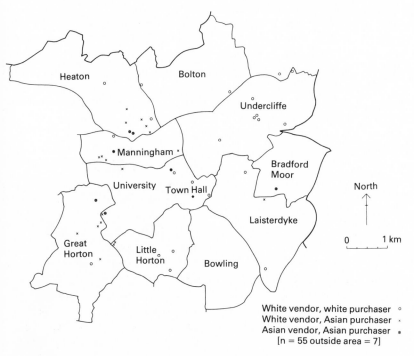

White vendor, white purchaser ○
White vendor, Asian purchaser ×
Asian vendor, Asian purchaser •
[n = 55 outside area = 7]

Figure 2 Location of all retail and service premises sold by white estate agents in Bradford CB (sample week in April 1975–81 inclusive)

Unlike the market for housing opportunities, in which white agents sell only a small proportion of their properties in the inner city, both groups deal predominantly in premises in the inner ten wards; this substantially reflects the geography of small independent retail outlets in the city. Of the total of 129 properties sold 115 are located in this area (89.1 per cent); 92 per cent of properties handled by Asian agencies fit into this category, as do 85 per cent of the white sample. But at the local level there are differences in this pattern. Property exchanges involving white agencies (Figure 2) are quite well spread around the inner city, reflecting the broad distribution of corner shops and small linear shopping areas throughout the inner wards. Sales through Asian estate agents are, by comparison, decidedly concentrated, particularly in the Great Horton area and along the main A647 road. Both areas are in close proximity to the agencies themselves, with 40 of the 74 premises sold within 1 kilometre of the advertising agency, suggesting that the Asian agent is indeed serving a very localised market both spatially and socially, the market also being apparently stratified by ethnic sub-group. This is particularly true in one case, with the majority of transactions through one estate agent involving members of the Gujerati community.

In general terms the Asian estate agents also appear to deal in property which is closer to the city centre, although no agents were involved in selling property in the central business district. The mean distance from City Hall for an exchange involving an Asian agent was 1.95 km, compared with 2.48 km for exchanges through a white agent. In both cases, however, a distance band of between 1.5 and 2.5 km from the city centre contains the majority of properties sold. This property is usually just beyond the area of postwar clearance and renewal and in most cases has a minimum life expectancy of at least 10 to 15 years; it is, however, an area dominated by pre-First World War property, and most of the businesses combine residential functions with retailing.

One of the most evident points about the location of Asian business is how closely it reflects the pattern of ethnic residence, as Aldrich and his colleagues (1981: 180) have shown for Bradford, Leicester and Ealing.[3] Given that most Asian businesses deal in low order goods this strongly supports a 'protected market' hypothesis (see chapter 11), with Asian retailers serving a loyal and local clientele. An interview survey carried out in Bradford among Asian retailers in five inner wards found that their own estimate of the percentage of white customers they served was only 29 per cent (McEvoy 1980), further supporting a protectionist hypothesis. By supporting their own small business sector, a degree of independence from wider society is achieved (Saifullah Khan 1976) and the contribution this makes to a group's 'cultural exclusiveness' helps to limit non-Asian contact (Brooks and Singh 1978/9).

Research in other countries and among other ethnic groups has offered an alternative interpretation of ethnic business operations, suggesting that in many instances they develop to fulfil a 'middleman minority' role, taking over a specific niche within the retail and service industry which has been relinquished by the white majority (Light 1972; Bonacich 1973). Although this approach has been most successfully applied to the Chinese and Japanese in the United States, it is possible to see its application to groups such as the Chinese and the Cypriots in the UK. In some cases this model can be applied to Asian business development in the British city, for example among small businessmen in the Thornton Heath area of Croydon (Mullins 1980). In the Bradford case the Asian retailer serving a predominantly white clientele is the exception rather than the rule, with approximately 85 per cent of Asian-owned business being in wards which account for 96.2 per cent of the Asian population. However exceptions do exist, and there are several examples of Asian retail outlets in almost exclusively white residential areas – for example in local authority premises on council estates. In these examples, however, the Asian retailer is likely to be in one of two trades, either operating as a corner grocery shop or as a newsagency; the conditions under which such businesses operate are outlined in the next section.

(ii) Business quality

Business quality is difficult to quantify. But we have seen that Asians largely reside in relinquished housing territory, and it is possible to make out a plausible case for their parallel concentration in residual economic sectors. While the ethnic business community has apparently blossomed in the past two decades, with a profusion of outlets offering a wide variety of goods and services, there are substantial grounds for doubting its effectiveness as a route to financial security.

The business opportunities offered by the Asian property agents and readily grasped by the Asian community in Bradford are overwhelmingly dependent upon their own ethnic market, and as such are heavily constrained by the limited purchasing power of the community. In most cases the battle is for survival or for an additional income to supplement that earned elsewhere rather than a road to personal enrichment; too many businesses are chasing too limited a market to offer anything other than a marginal return to all but the most successful. Although it would be fair to say that the relatively depressed state of Bradford contributes to this lack of genuine opportunity, the conditions for small business nationally do not promote optimism. The 'average' Asian retailer in inner Bradford is open 6.4 days a week, 11.1 hours a day, some 71 hours each week. Of Asian businesses 66 per cent are open on Sundays, three times the white total, yet only 27 per cent claimed a gross turnover in excess of £750 per week in 1978 and only one in four claimed that the business provided anything more than their weekly living expenses.

This was equally true of Asian retailers serving a white-dominated market, even though this middleman function is the most plausible route to economic success. At present they are concentrated in trades readily relinquished by white retailers such as news and tobacco, characterised by anti-social hours and low margins, and corner grocers, again 'open all hours' and vulnerable to the large supermarkets for all but the most menial day-to-day purchases. A much more extensive penetration of high order, large scale retail services would be necessary to provide a social ladder even remotely adequate for all but a few.

(iii) Business prices

Given the long term trend noted above, it would be realistic to assume that competition for small inner city retail and service outlets would not be high and that the price of such opportunities would reflect the chances of commercial success. In fact, in inner Bradford this is not so, with the mean price of retail premises offered for sale and converted to September 1982 prices standing at £13,523, plus stock as valued. In almost all cases this property is standard inner city terraced housing, usually with the downstairs front room 'converted' for retail uses, yet the price is an average of 30 per cent or £3,000 higher than comparable residential property. In part this may be due to houses which combine this business and residential function being larger than the typical terrace, but there is little evidence to support this assumption with the average premise having no more than two bedrooms and less than half the premises advertising a storeroom or attic. Even along the arterial roads which comprise the main ribbons of ethnic retail development the price for comparable premises varied according to whether they combined a retail function or not. It would seem, therefore, that there is some evidence of a 'goodwill' or 'opportunity' element to be paid when buying a business over and above the basic value of the property as a domestic hereditament.

(iv) Explaining ethnic differentials in the acquisition of commercial property

Significantly, this 'opportunity' element was noticeably higher when Asians bought from Asian estate agents.

Table 1. *The price of retail and service premises advertised and sold by Asian and white estate agents*

Price	Number of properties sold		
	By white agents	By Asian agents	Total
Under £6,000	4 (8.5)	6 (8.1)	10 (8.3)
£6,000–£8,999	8 (17.0)	8 (10.8)	16 (13.2)
£9,000–£11,999	11 (23.4)	10 (13.5)	21 (17.4)
£12,000–£14,999	10 (21.3)	14 (18.9)	24 (19.8)
£15,000–£17,999	8 (17.0)	21 (28.4)	29 (24.0)
£18,000–£20,999	3 (6.4)	6 (8.1)	9 (7.4)
£21,000–£23,999	2 (4.3)	3 (4.1)	5 (4.1)
£24,000–£26,999	—	3 (4.1)	3 (2.5)
£27,000–£29,999	—	2 (2.7)	2 (1.7)
Over £30,000	1 (2.1)	1 (1.4)	2 (1.7)
Sub-totals	47 (100.0)	74 (100.1)	121 (100.1)
Price not traced	8	—	8
Total	55	74	129
Average sale price:			
To all purchasers	£12,540 (55)*	£14,253 (74)	
To white purchasers	£14,353 (22)	—	
To Asian purchasers	£10,630 (23)	£14,253 (74)	

*Of the ten remaining cases, seven did not combine retail and residential functions and were thus not strictly comparable. Prices for the other three properties were not traced.
All prices are adjusted to September 1982 price levels.
Source: Personal fieldwork, April 1975 to April 1981 inclusive.

(a) Sales by Asian and white agents

While the average price of residential property purchased by Asians is over 20 per cent below the inner city average, Asian purchasers paid an average of £14,253 for the 74 commercial properties purchased through Asian agencies, and in 36 cases (48.6 per cent) they paid over £15,000, as Table 1 indicates. This compares with a price of £12,540 for the 55 properties sold (to whites or Asians) through white agencies, of which only 14 (25.5 per cent) were priced at over £15,000.

Reasons for this discrepancy were not evident; for example the number of bedrooms available in both categories of advertised outlet was virtually identical (1.98 compared with 1.91), which suggested that businesses bought from Asian agents were no more likely to combine the business/residence function than their white counterparts. In fact the only objective difference in the nature of the premises advertised is the availability of attics in the Asian-advertised property (an average of 0.67 per property compared with 0.12). Even this may not necessarily reflect any tangible difference in the property, however, but merely the tendency of Asian estate agents to advertise attics as potential living accommodation, a practice not generally followed by their white counterparts.

In a further attempt to try and account for this discrepancy in price between apparently similar properties, a full check on the Gross Rateable Valuation of every property advertised was undertaken. Although the GRV of a property is only an indirect indicator of market value, taking little account of small improvements in a property and virtually no account of changes in an area in the short term, it would be a reasonable general assumption that properties advertised at a higher market price would be likely to have higher gross valuations across a reasonably sized sample. In this instance the opposite is the case, with the average GRV of property sold by Asians being over 10 per cent lower.

Another possibility, that asking prices for Asian-advertised property differ markedly from final selling prices (more so than with white agents), was discussed with one of the Asian estate agents operating in the city. Although he acknowledged that a certain amount of bargaining inevitably takes place, he found that discounting was much more widespread for residential-only premises and could think of few examples in which a retail outlet had been sold for significantly less than its asking price, citing £1,000 as the maximum variation between his valuation and the final selling price. He also claimed that selling business premises was relatively easy, particularly on main road sites. The most likely reason for a potential Asian retailer to be paying a higher price for comparable property when dealing through an Asian estate agency may simply be the effects of supply and demand. Faced with a lack of opportunity in the white-controlled job market, the Asian community is competing for viable small businesses, and a premium has to be paid to realise this possibility in a business which has already been Asian-run.

(b) Sales by white estate agents to Asian and white purchasers

In contrast to this are the 23 cases in which an Asian purchaser, either unable to realise his intent in the Asian market or aware of the cost of doing so, bought businesses from white agencies. In the eighteen instances in which it was possible to ascertain a price the mean figure was just £10,630, compared with £14,353 for the 22 properties which remained in white ownership. It may be reasonable to assume that these represented the inferior end of the market, but it is equally reasonable to suggest that this may be nearer to the true worth of the business opportunities that Asian retailers appear to be paying premium prices for.

Conclusion

We saw earlier a strong suggestion that Asians were paying more for a house of given quality when buying from Asian estate agents rather than white. An earlier study, also carried out in a mill town in Yorkshire (Karn 1969), had shown that Asians paid premium prices for housing compared to white families, with the highest premiums being paid when they bought from other Asians (there was no indication of Asian estate agents at the time). The findings on differential pricing of retail and service premises in Bradford are partly consonant with the results for housing and partly in conflict. In both situations Asians paid more when buying from Asian estate agents. Further, the finding that Asian shopkeepers paid more when buying from Asians than whites did in purchasing shops from white agents is consonant with Karn's results on differential pricing. What is unexpected is to find that Asians buying premises of comparable quality from white estate agents paid the lowest prices of all.

It would be valuable to establish whether this pattern obtains in other places where Asians have moved into shopkeeping and have a choice of acquiring premises from white or Asian estate agents. All that can be done at this stage is to identify some of the factors that seem likely to be responsible for this outcome.

First, there are factors which predispose Asians to look to shopkeeping and self-employment and services as the most appropriate way of making a living in the situation they face. In particular, the lack of satisfactory options in the white-controlled job market, and the status given to small businessmen within the ethnic community, combine to leave the potential Asian businessman looking to self-employment but likely to have to pay a premium price for a marginal economic opportunity, usually serving a poor clientele in an inferior location. Secondly, the type of premises sought and the preferred location are constraining factors.

The wish to combine residential and business uses (often the only way that one can afford to purchase retail premises) narrows acceptable locations to those in which his fellows reside. Further, some of the properties advertised by white estate agents were in the Manningham and Heaton districts, an area largely populated by the very low status Bengali community, and unattractive to the more typical Gujerati businessman who wishes to remain, and is only likely to prosper, within his own subgroup. Thirdly, the outcome may reflect the highly segmented market for retail premises. The property sold by white agents to Asians may be in areas which are perceived to be of very low status by the white agent and outside his normal area of business. In such circumstances it would prove difficult to sell to his typical (white) client; to him the Asian purchaser represents a last resort. Again the properties are likely to be outside the normal information field of the Asian businessman who thus fails to compete for the opportunity; alternatively he is wary of dealing with a white agent, particularly over financial matters.

Each of these factors appears to have an influence on the differential pricing strategy among white and Asian agents, with that adopted by the latter reflecting the high level of demand for business opportunities within the Asian community. The high price levels are apparently a function of the market for small business premises, with little relevance to their economic potential. Although further research into the motives of the people purchasing small businesses is needed, it appears that the potential Asian retailer is only too aware of the limited opportunities available to him in a market not only segregated between black and white but also into the sub-groups which make up the Indian and Pakistani population. Having paid a premium price to establish himself the shopkeeper faces the prospect of an eleven hour day, a six and a half or seven day week throughout the year; the promise, in inner Bradford at least, is rarely more than survival.

PART FOUR

Overview

13

Ethnic minorities in business:
a research agenda

RICHARD JENKINS

The contributors to this book have presented a number of perspectives, some of them conflicting, on the topic of 'ethnic business' in the United Kingdom. Bearing in mind that there are many ethnic groups concerned, and that business activity in a mixed and open economy is a highly variable enterprise, it would have been surprising to find complete agreement among our authors – and all the more so, given that a number of academic disciplines are represented. However, the heterogeneity of topics and findings does not mean that nothing useful can be said in conclusion. In this brief final chapter I shall draw on the other contributions in order to sketch out an outline of some of the courses which research into ethnic minority business activity might usefully follow in the future.

Looking over the other papers, it seems that there are three major explanations being offered for the involvement in business of ethnic minority group members. In the first place, there is the argument based on *economic opportunity*. In this model, ethnic minority business activity is essentially no different from routine capitalist entrepreneurial activity, depending for its success or failure upon the opportunities presented by the market. In this case the opportunity is typically an *ethnic niche* (Barth 1969), although this need not be the case. The second explanatory model rests on the hypothesis that some cultures predispose their members towards the successful pursuit of entrepreneurial goals – very much as in Weber's classic analysis of the relationship between Calvinism and European capitalism (Weber 1968; 1976). This is based on the view that cultural predispositions are a resource in business activity and may be called the *cultural* model. Finally there are those analyses which see self-employment by members of ethnic minority groups as a reaction against racism and blocked avenues of occupational mobility, a survival strategy for coping on the margins of the white-dominated mainstreams of the economy, though access to resources is still required to achieve this. For convenience, I shall characterise this as the *reaction* model. Although these explanations may be seen as sufficient in themselves, there is no intrinsic reason why they should not be combined when brought to bear upon any particular case.

The next obvious step to take is to examine the variation in the participation rate of ethnic minorities in business activity: why do members of some groups set up in business, or survive in business, more frequently than members of other groups? A number of answers to this question have been offered, most of which stem from one or other of the three explanatory models outlined above.

First, drawing upon the economic opportunity model, there are three possible scenarios: (a) that the intrinsic boundaries of the ethnic market being exploited are such as to constrain or limit the potential for expansion (see the chapters by Aldrich *et al.*, Nowikowski or Cater, for example); (b) that conjunctural or historical circumstances, relating to the political situation, the business-cycle or the world economy, for example, are important in determining the scope which particular ethnic groups have for business activity (Pollins, Jenkins, Nowikowski, Boissevain); and (c) that differences in the level of 'Western' business skills, such as accounting or marketing, may be important (Reeves and Ward).

The second set of possible explanations relates more closely to the cultural model of business activity. Under this broad rubric, there are two different answers to our question: (a) that the decisive factor is the strength of the entrepreneurial ethic among the members of a particular ethnic group (Werbner and, to some extent, Boissevain and Palmer); and (b) that some ethnic groups may, by virtue of their own patterns of social organisation, have access to economic institutions, such as 'rotating credit associations' among East Asians, which give them a competitive edge (Auster and Aldrich). This latter is, in a sense, the obverse of the point made earlier concerning 'Western' business skills, which are, after all, no more than culturally specific economic institutions and practices (Gambling 1974; 1978; Gee 1980). The fact that they constitute the dominant 'rules of the game', within which business is conducted globally at this point in time, should not blind us to their essentially arbitrary and culturally defined nature.

This brings us finally to the reaction model of ethnic enterprise. Within this category there are at least two possible explanations for differential patterns of business success: (a) that ethnic groups are discriminated against to different degrees and in different ways, and, as a result, they have differential access to the resources required for business activity (Reeves and Ward, Cater, Aldrich *et al.*, Ladbury); and (b) that historical factors, rooted in the heterogeneity of the Empire and colonialism, have left different ethnic groups in markedly different positions with respect to the resources available to them (Nowikowski, Jenkins). This brief survey, whilst it may do necessary violence to the subtleties of particular chapters, does outline the explanatory options which appear to be available. Furthermore, it is also apparent that, as explanations, these models of ethnic minority business activity are not mutually exclusive.

Several contributors to this volume, including Ladbury and Mars and Ward, have discussed the political significance which has recently been attached to the promotion of the small business sector, and ethnic minority business in particular. The two most important political interpretations of ethnic minority enterprise are worth a brief mention. The first we may call the model of *entrepreneurial social mobility*; in this model business activity is seen as an avenue of social mobility into the middle class and the 'mainstream' of indigenous white society for those ethnic minority group members who 'pull themselves up by their bootstraps'. This is, for example, the argument of the Scarman Report (Scarman 1982). The archetypal examples of this type of mobility are Jewish entrepreneurs such as Sir John Cohen (Tesco) or Simon Marks and Israel Sieff (Marks and Spencer's), although their spectacular success should not draw attention from the large numbers of Jewish businessmen who achieved more modest prosperity in the bourgeoisie. The point has to be made, however, that, regardless of one's views concerning the viability of the entrepreneurial social mobility strategy for English Jewry in the late nineteenth and early twentieth centuries, there are compelling reasons for suggesting that the same opportunities for class mobility and 'integration' do not present themselves at this period in our history to the Asian and Afro-Caribbean communities of the United Kingdom.

Indeed, the more one examines the comparison between, for example, Jews and black ethnic minorities, the more differences become apparent. In the first place, the fact that Asians and Afro-Caribbeans are *ex-colonial* immigrants means that they occupy a very different position within British society, with specific and attendant disadvantages and penalties attached, to that which Jewish immigrants from Europe occupied. Secondly, the historical contexts within which the respective migrations took place differ to a degree which makes comparison less than instructive – the opportunity structure provided by the British economy in decline in the 1970s and 1980s is self-evidently less open than that encountered by nineteenth-century immigrants. Finally, to develop the first point about the importance of the colonial background, the fact that Asians and Afro-Caribbeans are *black* ethnic minorities has, in the context of a society in which racism of one form or another plays a major role in routine decision-making, certain definite consequences for the possibility of 'integration'.

A sub-theme of the social mobility argument, well developed in public statements by politicians in the wake of the 1981 riots, is that a major contribution to the regeneration of the inner city areas of Britain, in the provision of employment and services and the up-grading of the 'quality of life', is expected to come from 'community-based' (i.e. ethnic minority) business enterprises. It is clearly consonant with the political philosophy of the new Conservatism that the state should see the encouragement of enterprises of this nature as one of its major interventions in the inner city (see, for example, speeches by Michael Heseltine, then Secretary of State for the Environment, reported in *The Daily Telegraph*, 23 March 1982, and the *Guardian*, 9 July 1982). Without wishing to suggest that the encouragement of small businesses, from whatever section of the community, is undesirable – it clearly is not – in the light of some of the chapters of this book, in particular those by Aldrich *et al.*, Cater, Ladbury and Nowikowski, it is very hard to discern the conditions under which ethnic minority business activity can play the central role in the rehabilitation of Britain's inner city areas in which it has been cast. Such a view of ethnic minority business seems to depend more on political ideology than the sober consideration of what little substantive research there has been to date.

The second possible political interpretation of the situation is that ethnic minority business, and, in particular, state-sponsored or encouraged ethnic minority business, far from providing a solution to the problems of living in inner city areas and suffering discrimination in employment, merely acts, on the one hand, as a 'safety-valve', and, on the other, a legitimation exercise: 'if some blacks can do it, why can't others?'. Very quickly, by this logic, the problems of ethnic minorities living in inner city areas who are economically unsuccessful come to be seen as 'their own fault'. Given the seductive appeal of arguments of this kind in the present political climate, it is therefore all the more important that the dynamics and difficulties of ethnic minority business activity be more widely understood in the political arena than they are at present.

A research agenda

Given the need for a better understanding of the realities of ethnic minority business activity, the closing section of this chapter will briefly delineate some of the areas about which our knowledge is incomplete and in which research could make a contribution to more informed debate. In so doing, however, it is not my intention to suggest either that these are the only areas in which research might be worthwhile, or that they are necessarily the most desirable. Other commentators would doubtless produce a different list. In making my suggestions I shall first of all discuss general areas for research; following this I shall look at more specific topics upon which research might shed some light.

The first general area in which further research is desirable is, perhaps obviously enough, that of small business in general. In order to understand what, if anything, characterises the 'ethnic' business sector as in any sense different or peculiar we need to know more than we do about that with which we are comparing it. In particular, I would argue, we need to know more about why people set up on their own, the marketing strategies employed by small business owners, their management and accounting methods (including their participation in the 'informal' or 'black' economy – see Mars 1982), their labour relations strategies and the relationship between business life and the domestic domain. Some of these questions have been discussed by Scase and Goffee (1980; 1982); since their study mainly concerns the construction industry, however, wide scope for further research remains.

The need for research of this nature can be well demonstrated if we look at two concrete topics. It has been suggested earlier that ethnic business may be a reaction to disadvantage and discrimination in the labour market. Interestingly enough, however, Scase and Goffee suggest that, 'for many of the people we interviewed, the reason for starting a business was not out of a desire ultimately to become a successful entrepreneur, but as a rejection of working for somebody else' (1980: 33). If they are correct, white small business owners might well be not too dissimilar to their black counterparts in this respect. Furthermore, the same authors are emphatic as to the role of unpaid family labour in underpinning whatever economic viability small businesses may have (*ibid.*: 90ff). Clearly if we are to understand, for example, the role of the Asian extended family, or family labour in ethnic minority business generally, we must be able to bring comparative data for white-owned businesses to bear on the discussion (see chapter 11). What might at first sight appear to be a 'cultural' phenomenon, related to family structure, might in fact be simply a characteristic feature of the organisation of small businesses, dictated not by kinship norms but by the economics of the enterprise.

If there is a need to establish the general 'non-ethnic' features of small business, there is also a corresponding requirement to understand the routine salience of ethnicity in the wider business world. As part of this understanding we need to know more about the informal channels of communication and arenas of sociability within which many important business decisions are effectively taken: the clubs, dining rooms and social networks of the more-or-less influential in the commercial, industrial and financial spheres. There is a danger that, in constituting 'ethnic' business, i.e. the business activity of members of ethnic minorities, as a discrete domain of inquiry in itself, we will lose sight of the 'ethnicity' of mainstream white business.

The third general point to be made concerning future research (and this is implicit in the above) is that we need more *qualitative* studies. If we are to understand and distinguish between 'cultural' and 'structural' factors which go to encourage or inhibit the success of ethnic minority businesses, then this is imperative. We must be in a position to understand the decisions and actions of all those individuals, whether black or white, who are involved. This does not necessarily involve a traditionally anthropological participant-observer methodology; it does, however, point to the need for detailed case studies of particular business and organisations within their local contexts.

The final general point, and this is also implicit in the above, is that there is a need for research into ethnic minority business to be more explicitly comparative than it has been so far. There are a number of different areas in which this might be achieved. In the first place we need more studies which set out to compare the business activity of different ethnic groups within the United Kingdom, including white Britons. Secondly, we need more international comparisons of business activity; what comparative work there has been tends to be heavily oriented towards either small scale petty commodity production in the 'informal sector' (Bryant 1982), or the problems of industrialisation, factory management and industrial relations (Holzberg and Giovannini 1981). Neither of these approaches adequately addresses the topic we are concerned with; if we are to understand Pakistani businessmen in Manchester, for example, we need to know more than we do about the practice of business in Pakistan. If we are to attempt to untangle the relationship between 'culture' and 'structure', as mentioned earlier, such a comparative approach is essential. The third dimension of comparability which requires exploration is the historical, both in the short and the long term. In particular, I would emphasise the potential usefulness of detailed micro-level studies of the development of individual businesses over time, and of particular inner urban areas with respect to their business populations, to the broadening of our understanding of the processes of business growth or failure.

Moving away from general directions which future research might usefully follow, I should like briefly to highlight four specific empirical topics which I consider to be urgent candidates for investigation. The first of these relates to the access which ethnic minority business owners have to various resources. In comparison to the wealth of research which has been done into discrimination in the allocation of employment and public and private housing, we still know very little about the discrimination which members of particular ethnic minorities may (or may not) expect to encounter in the search for finance, credit, business premises, market information and other business opportunities. The chapters in this volume by Cater and Reeves and Ward, in particular, provide us with some indications, but there is clearly much more work to be done concerning the terms of access to business resources.

In the second place, it is readily apparent that in examining existing businesses there is a bias towards looking at those enterprises which, if not necessarily successful, have at least survived. Clearly this ignores those businesses which have failed. It would be particularly useful to have some studies which compared successful and unsuccessful businesses within the 'ethnic' sector, since this is crucial to the production of a relatively comprehensive analysis. This obviously raises problems of method which are common to research on all kinds of business enterprises.

Thirdly, there is an imbalance in existing studies of ethnic minority businesses, inasmuch as the service sector has been very much more the object of academic attention than the manufacturing sector. As Ladbury's paper in this volume demonstrates, this is not simply due to the absence of ethnic minorities from manufacturing. Why there should be this emphasis on service industries is itself intriguing; nonetheless it is an imbalance which requires correction.

Finally, the role of ethnic minority business enterprises as employers, of either black or white labour, is worth investigating. Once again, however, any research of this kind would have to be set alongside comparative material on white-owned small businesses. While research has established the readiness of black workers to join trade unions (Phizacklea and Miles 1980: 90–126; D.J. Smith 1974: 66–77), we know very little about the attitude of ethnic minority business owners to employing union-organised labour. What little information we do have, concerning, for example, the Grunwick dispute in 1976, involving an Anglo-Indian businessman (Rogaly 1977; Ward 1976), merely underlines the need for more vigorous and systematic research into this topic. Given that size of enterprise appears to be a major determinant of union membership (Price and Bain 1976), and that ethnic minority businesses tend to be smaller rather than larger, this is once again an area which calls for a comparative approach to be adopted. If the optimists are correct in suggesting that ethnic businesses will be a substantial source of inner city employment in the future, the arguments for examining this topic become even more compelling.

In summary, therefore, the general tenor of these suggestions is that research into ethnic minority business activity should be both more qualitative in its approach and more explicitly comparative. Given the methodological requirements inherent in these research strategies, this may make such research less immediately responsive to the demands of policy makers, cast as they are within the frenetic time scale of political expediency. Such a programme of research will, however, leave us much better equipped to discuss the matter from an informed standpoint, rather than on the present basis of partial ignorance.

Notes

2. Boissevain: Small entrepreneurs in contemporary Europe

1 This chapter, with minor alterations and the elimination of several statistical tables, is based upon part of Boissevain (1981), and is reproduced with the kind permission of the European Centre for Work and Society, Maastricht.
2 This paper views an entrepreneur as a person in effective control of a commercial undertaking. I am well aware that the term also has a more specialized sense denoting building, innovating and risk-taking in pursuit of profit (Barth 1963: 3f). To what extent and under which conditions an entrepreneur can remain in control of his or her enterprise without building, innovating and taking risks are real and relevant issues but they are not explored here.
3 Although it noted that it could not 'accurately assess the importance of this factor' (Bolton 1971: 81).
4 On the other hand, Scase and Goffee (1980: 24) found that: 'All of the inheritors had been responsible for expanding, often in a dramatic fashion, the enterprises which they inherited.'
5 Unless indicated, the following discussion on Prato is based on Lorenzoni (1979).

3. Auster and Aldrich: Small business vulnerability, ethnic enclaves and ethnic enterprise

1 Ardener (1964: 201) defined a rotating credit association as 'an association formed upon a core of participants who agree to make regular contributions to a fund which is given, in whole or part, to each contributor in rotation'.
2 The extent to which blacks are under-represented in small businesses is a controversial issue. By census definitions, their under-representation is substantial. If quasi- and non-legal small businesses are included, their numbers are larger.
3 Important areas for future research stemming from these findings would be: (1) analyses of intra-ethnic group differences in human capital and ethnic occupational patterns resulting from the different social, economic and political conditions of various time periods; (2) the investigation of whether ethnic enclaves have a life cycle of birth, growth and decline and, if so, how

it differs across ethnic groups and through time; and (3) more cross-cultural comparisons of the different ways in which ethnic groups have responded to similar economic circumstances.

4. Jenkins: Ethnicity and the rise of capitalism in Ulster

1 Liam O'Dowd of the Queen's University of Belfast and Henry Patterson of the Ulster College, Jordanstown, made very detailed comments on a later draft of the paper which I have, where possible, incorporated into the text. I am very grateful to them for their help; the responsibility for any inaccuracies of fact or inadequacies of interpretation remains, however, very much my own.

2 For an analysis of the mobilisation of ethnicity and patronage in a similar situation, see Adam's analysis of (white) South African politics (Adam and Giliomee 1979: 61–82).

3 For other discussions of Jewish business, see the work of Aris (1970) and Kosmin (1979). Another interesting discussion of larger scale ethnic business may be found in Drake and Cayton's classic study of Chicago (1962: 430–69).

4 Although this generalisation is valid enough, there is, of course, considerable variation upon this pattern.

5 For a discussion of the early development of capitalism in England, and the academic controversies attached to the problem, see the work of Alan Macfarlane (1978). A contemporary account of rural England in the late seventeenth century which has a bearing on this topic is Gough's description of the parish of Myddle in Shropshire (Gough 1981).

6 One well established analysis of the development of the Ulster textile industry insists that the 'Ulster custom', the relatively privileged land tenure system discussed above, was the basis of that development (Gill 1925). More recent historical scholarship suggests that 'The prosperity of the linen industry in Ulster was due to English demand for Irish linens . . . and to its duty-free entry into the English market' (Crawford and Trainor 1973: 33).

7 For a critical discussion of the 'labour aristocracy' model of the protestant working class, see Reid (1980).

8 For example, Sir Edward Carson's speech at Finaghy in July 1920: 'these men who come forward posing as the friends of labour care no more about labour than does the man in the moon. Their real object . . . is that they mislead and bring about disunity amongst our own people; and in the end, before we know where we are, we may find ourselves in the same bondage and slavery as is the rest of Ireland in the South and West' (quoted in Farrell 1976: 28).

9 For a discussion of the Northern Ireland Labour Party, see Wright (1973); Rolston's critique of trade unionism in Northern Ireland is also useful (Rolston 1980).

10 The relatively unproblematic nature of industrial relations in the province is illustrated in the Quigley Report (Department of Manpower Services 1974); Bell also makes the point well (1976: 85–93). One of the best discussions of the basis of this harmony, discrimination in employment, is that of Barritt and Carter (1972: 93–108). For the employer, the outcome was the lowest unit labour costs in Europe (Department of Manpower Services 1979: 20–1).

11 It is interesting that the same sort of informal patronage networks appear to characterise politics in Eire (Bax 1976; Sacks 1976).

12 The classic text here is Max Weber's *Protestant Ethic* (Weber 1976). Other important contributions to this debate are the works of Birnbaum (1953), Eisenstadt (1967), Marshall (1980) and Tawney (1938).

5. Pollins: The development of Jewish business in the United Kingdom

1 The main source for much of this paper is Pollins, *Economic History of the Jews in England* (1982).
2 See the work of Kosmin and his colleagues, also Cromer (1974) and Krausz (1969).

6. Palmer: The rise of the Britalian culture entrepreneur

1 Obviously this is an amalgam of 'Briton' and 'Italian'. As a generic it corresponds to Garigue and Firth's 'Italianate' (1956: 67). As with Italianate, 'Britalian' goes beyond 'Italian' to define an ethnic group, all persons of Italian origin in Britain who are not fully assimilated, i.e. the Italian-born, their children and a proportion of their grandchildren. Usually they have dual nationality; the British-born are not, technically, Italians. To describe the whole, therefore, concocted terms are necessary. I did not take up 'Italianate' because it could be offensive, having been derived from a term long used to describe *things* of Italian origin or character. Britalian in its nominative form can only describe *people* of Italian origin. The fieldwork under the aegis of the University of Sussex and financed by the SSRC, occupied eighteen months full time in 1972–4.

7. Ladbury: Choice, chance or no alternative? Turkish Cypriots in business in London

1 Size is a relative variable in the Bolton Report's (Bolton 1971) definition of a 'small' firm. However, all small firms are seen to share three characteristics:
   (a) Economically they have a relatively small share of their market.
   (b) They are managed by owners or part owners in a personalised way, not through the medium of a formalised management structure.
   (c) They are independent in the sense that they do not form part of a larger enterprise and owner managers are free from outside control in taking their principle decisions.
   When the term 'small business' is used in this chapter it is these characteristics which are implicitly referred to.
2 The number of self-employed people in Britain in 1979, the last date from which figures are available, was 1,795,000, a reduction of 80,000 compared to the figure for 1975 (*Employment Gazette*, vol. 90, no. 1: 15–18).
3 Robin Oakley's statistical calculations on Cypriot migration and settlement in Britain between 1945 and 1966 are an invaluable information source and should be referred to for more detailed analysis (1971: 241ff).
4 Sources: 1971 Census (Kohler 1974), Oakley 1971, 1981 Language Census (ILEA Research and Statistics Group 1982). According to this latter survey, there are now more Turkish- than Greek-speaking pupils in ILEA schools (9.8 per cent and 8.6 per cent, respectively). Indeed, Turkish is second only

to Bengali as the first language of pupils whose first language is not English. Thus the proportion of Turkish to Greek speakers, in Inner London at least, has changed considerably over time.

5 Statistical information from the 1971 Census on European New Commonwealth immigrants is contained in Tables 1, 5 and 6 in chapter 8. This category consists largely of Greek and Turkish Cypriots, with which are aggregated much smaller members from Malta, Gozo and Gibraltar. Information relating solely to those born in Cyprus is contained in Draft Table 1240, 10% Sample, 1971 Census.

6 According to George and Millerson (1967) 85 per cent of Cypriot working women were employed in the industry in 1958. This proportion gradually decreased throughout the 1960s and 1970s.

7 The 1971 Census probably underestimated the number of women who were legally self-employed and machined at home. Clough and Quarmby (1978: 74) estimated that 66 per cent of Cypriot women were employed in clothing in 1976.

8 For a more detailed discussion of the reasons why immigrant populations have become associated with the clothing industry see Shah (1975: 8ff). See also chapter 10.

9 In the light of my own investigations, although both Greek and Turkish Cypriots aspire to be self-employed, proportionately more Greeks than Turks managed to become so.

10 Nowikowski (chapter 9) shows that this process operates among immigrant communities from India and Pakistan as well.

11 For a fuller discussion of the relationship between Turkish Cypriot work patterns and trade union membership see Ladbury (1979b: 27–34).

12 Many of the contributors to Cohen's *Urban Ethnicity* (1974b) and Wallman's *Ethnicity at Work* (e.g. Brooks and Singh 1979; Herman 1979; Kosmin 1979; Saifullah Khan 1979) touch on the causes for such a relationship and provide some examples of it in operation.

8. Reeves and Ward: West Indian business in Britain

1 Some of the material reported in this chapter is presented at greater length in a Memorandum submitted to the Race Relations and Immigration Sub-Committee of the Home Affairs Committee of the House of Commons in response to a request to the SSRC Research Unit on Ethnic Relations to review evidence of the performance of West Indians in business in Britain (Ward and Reeves 1980).

2 Table 2 covers those who are self-employed or employers within the specified socio-economic groups. The categories used can be defined as follows: within SEG 1, employers in enterprises employing 25 or more persons; within SEG 2, those employing less than 25 persons; professional workers who are self-employed (SEG 3); own account workers (other than professional) i.e. self-employed people engaging in activities not requiring training of university degree standard and having no employees other than members of the family (SEG 12).

3 Approximately 800,000 interviews were carried out in the NDHS.

4 These two populations are not strictly comparable, since the former deals with household heads and the latter with the male, economically active popu-

lation. But in the absence of a more precise basis for comparison, there is sufficient overlap between these two categories for it to be worthwhile to consider them together.

5   The results of this national survey are representative of approximately 80 per cent of West Indian, Indian, Pakistani and African Asian men and women in Britain. The remaining 20 per cent are outside the scope of the survey because of the prohibitive cost of tracing them in the almost entirely white residential areas where they live (Smith 1976).

6   While the level of qualifications among West Indians as a whole is lower than for all other groups, there is significant variation (over ten percentage points in some instances) between the sexes and between the different islands in the Caribbean.

9. Nowikowski: Snakes and ladders: Asian business in Britain

1   This point is developed further in chapter 11 below.

2   This paper presents some of the material collected and analysed in Nowikowski (1980). The data were collected through participant observation and a survey in South Manchester carried out between 1971 and 1973 in cooperation with the SSRC Research Unit on Ethnic Relations and the Fair Housing Group of Manchester Council for Community Relations. For details of the methodology of the study, see Nowikowski (1980: Appendix 3).

3   Such dependent capitalist development has been described as disarticulated capitalist development (see Amin 1974; Alavi 1964).

4   These post-colonial migration movements can be contrasted with the colonial migration movement described by Jayawardena (1973).

5   Poulantzas (1973) gives an invaluable basis for the discussion of the structural determination of the objective location of agents in the division of labour (i.e. Poulantzas's concept of class place). This location is seen as determined by the relations of production but also by structures on the super-structural level, i.e. politico-ideological relations of domination-subordination.

6   A useful distinction here is Poulantzas's distinction between class place and class position (*ibid.*). Class position is an action or strategy concept. Strategies taken up by individuals or collectivities need not be consistent with class place and strategies can have an impact on relations of production and class place. Poulantzas gives little development of these points in his work, but for discussion of the potentiality of the distinctions see, for example, Mouzelis (1978).

7   The northern boundaries of the study area are marked by Wilbraham/Moseley Road running east to west two miles south of the city centre; the area then extends in a six mile radius stretching into North Cheshire. The following areas were included in the survey: ten wards in Manchester (Baguley, Barlow Moor, Benchill, Burnage, Chorlton-cum-Hardy, Didsbury, Northenden, Old Moat, Withington and Woodhouse Park), two wards in Stockport (Heaton Mersey and Heaton Moor), Altrincham MB, Cheadle and Gatley UD, Hazel Grove and Bramhall UD and Sale MB. South Manchester is a residential area and predominantly one of private owner-occupation where houses are normally bought with the aid of a building society mortgage (see Fenton 1977). The 1971 Census showed that the percentage of professional and managerial household heads in the survey area

varied between 16.8 per cent (South Manchester wards) and 43.4 per cent (Hazel Grove and Bramhall). This contrasts with 10.1 per cent for the city of Manchester (Nowikowski and Ward 1979).

These South Manchester suburbs are predominantly white. The proportion of New Commonwealth-born residents to the total population of the wards in South Manchester varies from just below 0.3 per cent to just over 3.0 per cent. Most areas, however, had a New Commonwealth-born resident population between 0.5 per cent and 2.0 per cent of the total population, consisting largely of South Asians. Source: 1971 Census, 100% Population, Small Ward Statistics, Ward Library (UMRCC).

8   See n2. In the survey the total number of Asian respondents was 135 heads of household.

9   In the survey sample 74 per cent were in professional and managerial posts (Registrar General social classes 1 and 2). A further 8 per cent were in other non-manual occupations, 10 per cent were in skilled manual work and 9 per cent in unskilled and semi-skilled work.

10 Some were in the lower stratum of the new middle classes, working as technicians and laboratory assistants for example. However, a large proportion were in the higher stratum and in white collar and professional work. They were employed in the medical services, education, accountancy and insurance, architecture and design, engineering and management in industry.

11 They worked in factories, transport and communications, the distributive retail sector, construction and catering services.

12 For discussion of the careers of these respondents and respondents with other occupational patterns, see Nowikowski (1980).

13 This includes three doctors who were General Practitioners.

14 This analysis involved the use of the conceptual tools of ideal types and career analysis. For discussion of this methodology see Nowikowski (1980: ch. 7).

15 Eleven out of fifty respondents, or fourteen out of fifty if we include GPs.

16 Eight who were economically active and one who was retired.

10. Werbner: Business on trust: Pakistani entrepreneurship in the Manchester garment trade

1   The research amongst Manchester Pakistanis was conducted between the years 1975–9 with the help of a Project grant from the Social Science Research Council. I wish to thank the Council for its generous assistance. Sections of this paper were published in *New Community*, vol. 8, nos. 1 and 2 (1980) (Werbner 1980b). I am grateful to Mr Ash Lawrence for the invaluable insight he provided into the trade and Drs Tim Ingold and Richard Werbner for their comments on earlier drafts of the paper.

2   For a discussion of the role of the stranger who often turns trader see Alfred Schutz (1944) who, like Fallers (1967) and Shack and Skinner (1979), draws on the ideas of Georg Simmel (1950).

3   For a discussion of this role of the entrepreneur cf. Barth (1966: 17–18).

4   For a discussion of the more technical aspects of the textile trade see Shah (1975).

5   In this respect Pakistanis differ from blacks in the United States studied by

Liebow who scarcely mentioned their low paid jobs outside the work context (Liebow 1967: 56–61).

6 It is therefore not surprising that being unemployed is, for Pakistanis, a terrible blow to their self-esteem. A man I knew was confined to bed with severe weakness for several weeks after his factory closed down, with no apparent medical cause. From a relatively early age, boys were expected to work on weekends and make some contribution to the family economy.

7 In London, Cypriots and Bengalis appear to dominate the trade (see chapter 7). Elsewhere Pakistanis and Sikhs appear more dominant.

8 For discussion of Pakistani voluntary associations in Manchester cf. Pnina Werbner (1979a: ch. 10); and (nd).

9 According to the National Dwelling and Household Survey, the Pakistani/ Bangladeshi population in Manchester in 1977–8 was about 9,000, about 7,000 of whom lived in South Manchester (see chapter 9).

10 For an interview with this wholesaler, cf. Werbner (1980a).

11 For a more detailed discussion of these migrants from Gujranwala, cf. Pnina Werbner (1979a: chs. 2 and 6).

12 Machinists in Manchester earned, in 1979, between £30 and £50 a week for a 40 hour week, if they were reasonably fast.

13 All names are pseudonyms.

14 A 'set' is a 'quasi-group' (cf. Mayer 1966). The term is used in the sense employed here by Richard Werbner (1975).

15 The Mosque Society and the three Welfare Associations in particular. Cf. Pnina Werbner (nd).

16 A detailed case study of the conflicts arising out of the multiplexity of relations between Pakistanis is presented in Pnina Werbner (1979a: ch. 8).

11. Aldrich, Jones and McEvoy: Ethnic advantage and minority business development

1 The first systematic statement of this viewpoint was offered by Rex and Moore (1967), who argued that Asian and West Indian freedom of access to urban resources (in this case, housing) is curbed by the racist nature of the institutions controlling resource allocation (see also Rex 1971; Rex and Tomlinson 1979). In contrast Dahya and his followers (see, for example, Robinson 1979a) give primacy to internal group organization when accounting for the position of Asians in British society.

2 A recent critique of the currently fashionable view of the small businessman as economic redeemer is found in Scase and Goffee (1980).

3 As far as we are aware, the term 'lumpenbourgeoisie' traces its origin to Wright Mills (1951: 28), who states, 'If we may speak of a "lumpen-proletariat" set off from other wage workers, we may also speak of a "lumpenbourgeoisie" set off from other middle class elements. For the bottom of the entrepreneurial world is so different from the top that it is doubtful whether the two should be classified together.' Frazier (1957) uses the term to emphasize the petty scale and marginality of black business in the USA, and Baran (1957) applied it to the petty traders of the typical Third World city, where such activities are often a form of disguised unemployment. All these usages are highly germane to the present discussion.

4 Thrift, self-sacrifice and the wish to accumulate savings are frequently cited

as explanations for Asians' propensity to occupy cheap low quality housing (Dahya 1974; Robinson 1979a).

5   Within the population of Asian shopkeepers, however, sojourner orientation does not differentiate between those using highly competitive practices and other shopkeepers. Indeed, in our 1978 survey of 302 Asian shopkeepers, we found that sojourner orientation made no significant difference in business practices.

6   We use the term 'export' as a convenient shorthand to describe the sale of goods and services outside the ethnic boundary (Aldrich, Cater, Jones and McEvoy 1981).

7   There are few, if any, instances of ethnic groups relying exclusively upon business and trade as a successful means of social mobility. As Bonney (1975) argues, many of the more mobile American minorities (the Jews in particular) have achieved more through entry into the professions than through business ownership. Furthermore, it is noteworthy that among Indians in East Africa professional employment and educational qualifications were at least as important as entrepreneurship as a basis for middle class status (Tribe 1975; Tinker 1977).

8   This view of integration or cultural pluralism conforms with Banton's (1972: 52) model of a society embracing 'self segregation in private life [coexisting] with equality in civil rights'. In effect, groups are permitted to retain their ethnicity while sloughing off their minority status.

9   A similar penetration of the white market in an area of comparatively moderate Asian settlement, Croydon, was reported by Mullins (1980).

10 The underdevelopment of black business in the USA – including the limitations of the protected market – has been extensively analysed. See for example Andreasen (1971), Bonney (1975), Cross (1969), Frazier (1957) and Tabb (1979).

11 One would expect the benefits of East African experience to be reinforced by Gujerati ethnicity itself. For example, Lyon (1973: 9) asserts that Gujerati businessmen are remarkable for their commercial aspirations and for the 'unusual cosmopolitan knowledge and communal means by which they were able to achieve their goals'. This is held to apply to Gujerati traders irrespective of whether or not they have been based in Africa.

12. Cater: Acquiring premises: a case study of Asians in Bradford

1   See, for example, surveys carried out in London (Doherty 1969), Birmingham (Jones 1976), Coventry (Winchester 1974), Glasgow (Kearsley and Srivastava 1974) and Huddersfield (Jones and McEvoy 1978).

2   The Index of Segregation is an indication of the number of members of one sub-group who would have to cross boundaries at the given scale to produce an even distribution when compared with the total white population. In this instance about four-fifths of Asians would have to relocate to produce such a distribution.

3   A regression test was undertaken and shown to be significant at the 0.1 level.

References

Adam, H., and Giliomee, H. (1979), *Ethnic Power Mobilised: Can South Africa Change?*, Yale University Press, New Haven.

Ahmad, S. (1973), 'Peasant Classes in Pakistan', in Gough, K., and Sharma, H.P. (eds.), *Imperialism and Revolution in South Asia*, Monthly Review Press, New York.

Alavi, H. (1964), 'Imperialism Old and New', in Miliband, R., and Saville, J. (eds.), *The Socialist Register 1964*, Merlin Press, London.

(1975), 'India and the Colonial Mode of Production', in Miliband, R., and Saville, J. (eds.), *The Socialist Register 1975*, Merlin Press, London.

Aldrich, H. (1973), 'Employment Opportunities for Blacks in the Black Ghetto: The Role of White-Owned Businesses', *American Journal of Sociology*, vol. 78, pp. 1403–25.

(1979), *Organisations and Environments*, Prentice Hall, Englewood Cliffs.

(1980), 'Asian Shopkeepers as a Middleman Minority', in Evans, A., and Eversley, D. (eds.), *The Inner City: Employment and Industry*, Heinemann, London.

Aldrich, H., Cater, J., Jones, T., and McEvoy, D. (1981), 'Business Development and Self-Segregation: Asian Enterprise in Three British Cities', in Peach, C., Robinson, V., and Smith, S. (eds.), *Ethnic Segregation in Cities*, Croom Helm, London.

(1982), 'From Periphery to Peripheral: The South Asian Petite Bourgeoisie in England', in Simpson, I.H. and Simpson, R. (eds.), *Research in the Sociology of Work*, vol. 2, JAI Press, Greenwich, Ct.

Aldrich, H., Cater, J., Jones, T., McEvoy, D., and Velleman, P. (1982), 'Residential Concentration and the Protected Market Hypothesis', unpublished paper, University of North Carolina, Chapel Hill.

Aldrich, H., Cater, J.C., and McEvoy, D. (1979), *Retail and Service Businesses and the Immigrant Community*, Final Report, Grant HR5520, Social Science Research Council, London.

Aldrich, H., and Feit, S. (1975), 'Black Entrepreneurs in England: A Summary of the Literature and Some Suggestions for Further Research', unpublished Ms.

Aldrich, H., and Fish, D. (1981), 'Origins of Organizational Forms: Births, Deaths and Transformations', unpublished paper, Cornell University.

Aldrich, H., and McEvoy, D. (1983), 'Ethnic Succession in Business Ownership in Three British Cities, 1978–1980–1982: The Impact of Economic Recession', paper presented to the annual conference of British Geographers, December.

Aldrich, H., and Reiss, A. (1976), 'Continuities in the Study of Ecological Succession: Changes in the Race Composition of Neighbourhoods and Their Businesses', *American Journal of Sociology*, vol. 81, pp. 846–66.

Allen, S., and Smith, C. (1974), 'Race and Ethnicity in Class Formation', in Parkin, F. (ed.), *The Social Analysis of Class Structure*, Tavistock, London.

Amin, S. (1974), *Accumulation on a World Scale*, Monthly Review Press, New York.

Andreasen, A.R. (1971), *Inner City Business*, Praeger, New York.

Anwar, M. (1979), *The Myth of Return: Pakistanis in Britain*, Heinemann, London.

Ardener, S. (1964), 'The Comparative Study of Rotating Credit Associations', *Journal of the Royal Anthropological Institute*, vol. 94, pp. 201–29.

Aris, S. (1970), *The Jews in Business*, Jonathan Cape, London.

Aunger, E.A. (1975), 'Religion and Occupational Class in Northern Ireland', *Economic and Social Review*, vol. 7, pp. 1–18.

Bagchi, A.K. (1970), 'European and Indian Entrepreneurship in India, 1900–1930', in Leach, E., and Mukherjee, S.N. (eds.), *Elites in South Asia*, Cambridge University Press, Cambridge.

Bailey, T., and Freedman, M. (1981), *Immigrant and Non-Immigrant Workers in the Restaurant Industry*, Conservation of Human Resources, New York.

Baker, S.E. (1973), 'Orange and Green: Belfast, 1832–1912', in Dyos, H.J., and Wolff, M. (eds.), *The Victorian City: Images and Realities*, Routledge and Kegan Paul, London.

Ballard, R., and Ballard, C. (1977), 'The Sikhs: The Development of South Asian Settlement in Britain', in Watson, J.L. (ed.), *Between Two Cultures*, Basil Blackwell, Oxford.

Banton, M. (1972), *Racial Minorities*, Fontana, London.

Baran, P. (1957), *The Political Economy of Growth*, Monthly Review Press, New York.

Barritt, D.P., and Carter, C.F. (1972), *The Northern Ireland Problem: A Study in Group Relations*, Oxford University Press, London.

Barth, F. (1963), 'Introduction', in Barth, F. (ed.), *The Role of the Entrepreneur in Social Change in Northern Norway*, Universitetsforlaget, Bergen.

(1966), 'Models of Social Organisation', *Occasional Paper*, no. 23, Royal Anthropological Institute, London.

(ed.) (1969), *Ethnic Groups and Boundaries*, Universitetsforlaget, Bergen.

Bax, M. (1976), *Harpstrings and Confessions: Machine-Style Politics in the Irish Republic*, van Gorcum, Assen.

Bechhofer, F., and Elliott, B. (1968), 'An Approach to a Study of Small Shopkeepers and the Class Structure', *European Journal of Sociology*, vol. 9, pp. 180–202.

Bechhofer, F., Elliott, B., Rushforth, M., and Bland, R. (1974), 'The Petits Bourgeois in the Class Structure', in Parkin, F. (ed.), *The Social Analysis of Class Structure*, Tavistock, London.

Beckett, J.C. (1966), *The Making of Modern Ireland, 1603–1923*, Faber and Faber, London.

(1973), 'Introduction', in Crawford, W.H., and Trainor, B., *Aspects of Irish Social History, 1750–1800*, HMSO, Belfast.

Bell, G. (1976), *The Protestants of Ulster*, Pluto Press, London.

Belshaw, C. (1955), 'The Cultural Milieu of the Entrepreneur: A Critical Essay', *Explorations in Entrepreneurial History*, vol. 7, pp. 144–6.

Berger, S. (1981), 'The Uses of the Traditional Sector in Italy: Why Declining Classes Survive', in Bechhofer, F., and Elliott, B. (eds.), *The Petite Bourgeoisie*, Macmillan, London.

Berk, F. (1972), 'A Study of the Turkish Cypriot Community of Haringey with Particular Reference to its Background, Structure, and Changes Taking Place Within It', unpublished MPhil dissertation, University of York.

Bew, P., Gibbon, P., and Patterson, H. (1979), *The State in Northern Ireland, 1921–1972*, Manchester University Press, Manchester.

Billig, M. (1978), 'Patterns of Racism: Interviews with National Front Members', *Race and Class*, vol. 20, pp. 583–94.

Birch, D. (1979), *The Job Generation Process*, MIT Program on Neighborhood and Regional Change, Cambridge, Mass.

Birnbaum, N. (1953), 'Conflicting Interpretations of the Rise of Capitalism: Marx and Weber', *British Journal of Sociology*, vol. 4, pp. 125–41.

Bland, R., Elliott, B., and Bechhofer, F. (1978), 'Social Mobility in the Petite Bourgeoisie', *Acta Sociologica*, vol. 21, pp. 229–48.

Blaugh, M., Layard, P.R.G., and Woodhall, M. (1969), *The Causes of Graduate Unemployment in India*, LSE Studies on Education, Penguin Press, London.

Blok, A. (1974), *The Mafia of a Sicilian Village, 1860–1960*, Basil Blackwell, Oxford.

Boddy, M.J. (1976), 'The Structure of Mortgage Finance: Building Societies and the British Social Formation', *Transactions, Institute of British Geographers* (NS), vol. 1, pp. 58–71.

(1980), *The Building Societies*, Macmillan, London.

Boissevain, J. (1970), *The Italians of Montreal*, Royal Commission on Bilingualism and Biculturalism, Ottawa.

(1974), *Friends of Friends*, Basil Blackwell, Oxford.

(1981), *Small Entrepreneurs in Changing Europe: Towards a Research Agenda*, European Centre for Work and Society, Maastricht.

Bolton, J.E. (1971), *Report of the Committee of Inquiry on Small Firms*, Cmnd 4811, HMSO, London.

Bonacich, E. (1972), 'A Theory of Ethnic Antagonism: The Split Labour Market', *American Sociological Review*, vol. 37, pp. 547–59.

(1973), 'A Theory of Middleman Minorities', *American Sociological Review*, vol. 38, pp. 583–94.

(nd), 'U.S. Capitalism and Korean Immigrant Small Business', unpublished paper, University of California, Riverside.

Bonacich, E., and Modell, J. (1980), *The Economic Basis of Ethnic Solidarity: Small Business in the Japanese American Community*, University of California Press, Berkeley.

Bonney, N. (1975), 'Black Capitalism and the Development of the Ghettos in the USA', *New Community*, vol. 4, pp. 1–10.

Booth, C. (ed.) (1902), *Life and Labour of the People in London*, vol. 3, Macmillan, London.

Boswell, J. (1973), *The Rise and Decline of Small Firms*, George Allen and Unwin, London.

Bovenkerk, F. (1982), 'Op eigen kracht omhoog. Etnisch ondernemerschap en de oogkleppen van het minderheden circuit', *Intermediair*, vol. 18, no. 8.

Brimmer, A., and Terrell, H. (1971), 'The Economic Potential of Black Capitalism', *Public Policy*, vol. 19, Spring.

Brooks, A. (1983), 'Black Businesses in Lambeth: Obstacles to Expansion', *New Community*, vol. 11, pp. 42–54.

Brooks, D., and Singh, K. (1978/9), 'Ethnic Commitment versus Structural Reality: South Asian Immigrant Workers in Britain', *New Community*, vol. 7, pp. 19–30.

(1979), 'Pivots and Presents: Asian Brokers in British Foundries', in Wallman, S. (ed.), *Ethnicity at Work*, Macmillan, London.

Bryant, J. (1982), 'An Introductory Bibliography to Work on the Informal Economy in Third World Literature', in Laite, J. (ed.), *Bibliographies on Local Labour Markets and the Informal Economy*, Social Science Research Council, London.

Buckland, P. (1980), *James Craig*, Gill and Macmillan, Dublin.

Buckman, J. (1983), *Immigrants and the Class Struggle: The Jewish Immigrant in Leeds, 1880–1914*, Manchester University Press, Manchester.

Bunzel, J. (1955), 'The General Ideology of American Small Businessmen', *Political Science Quarterly*, vol. 70, pp. 87–102.

Burney, E. (1967), *Housing on Trial*, Oxford University Press, London.

Burris, V. (1979), *Class Formation and Transformation in Advanced Capitalist Societies: A Comparative Analysis*, Working Paper, University of Oregon.

Butterworth, E. (1967), *Immigrants in West Yorkshire*, Institute of Race Relations, London.

Cable, J.R. (1974), 'Industry and Commerce', in Prest, A.R. and Coppock, D. (eds.), *The UK Economy: A Manual of Applied Economics*, 5th edn, Weidenfeld and Nicolson, pp. 170–222.

Castles, S., and Kosack, G. (1973), *Immigrant Workers and Class Structure in Western Europe*, Oxford University Press, London.

Cater, J.C. (1981), 'The Impact of Asian Estate Agents on Patterns of Ethnic Residence', in Jackson, P., and Smith, S.J. (eds.), *Social Interaction and Ethnic Segregation*, Academic Press, London.

Cater, J.C., and Jones, T.P. (1978), 'Asians in Bradford', *New Society*, no. 810, pp. 81–2.

(1979), 'Ethnic Residential Space: The Case of Asians in Bradford', *Tijdschrift voor Economische en Sociale Geografie*, vol. 70, pp. 86–97.

Cater, J.C., Jones, T.P., and McEvoy, D. (1977), 'Ethnic Segregation in British Cities', *Annals, Association of American Geographers*, vol. 67, pp. 305–6.

Cavalli, C. (1972), *Recordi di un Emigrato, La Voce degli Italiani*, London.

CBI (1980), *Smaller Firms in the Economy*, Confederation of British Industry, London.

Central Statistical Office (1977), *Annual Abstract of Statistics 1977*, HMSO, London.

(1981), *Social Trends 12, 1982*, HMSO, London.

(1982), *Annual Abstract of Statistics 1982*, HMSO, London.

CERC (1980), *Le Revenue des non-salaries: professions artisanales, commerciales et liberales*, CERC no. 53, Centre d'Etude des Revenus et des Coûts, Paris.

City of Bradford Metropolitan District Council (1979), *District Trends*, Policy Unit, Bradford MDC, Bradford.

Clark, D. (1979), 'Politics and Business Enterprise', in Wallman, S. (ed.), *Ethnicity at Work*, Macmillan, London.

Clough, E., and Quarmby, J. (1978), *A Public Library Service for Ethnic Minorities in Great Britain*, The Library Association, London.

Coe, W.E. (1969), *The Engineering Industry in the North of Ireland*, David and Charles, Newton Abbott.

Cohen, A. (1969), *Custom and Politics in Urban Africa*, Routledge and Kegan Paul, London.

—— (1974a), 'Introduction', in Cohen, A. (ed.), *Urban Ethnicity*, Tavistock, London.

—— (ed.) (1974b), *Urban Ethnicity*, Tavistock, London.

Cohen, R. (1978), 'Ethnicity: Problem and Focus in Anthropology', *Annual Review of Anthropology*, vol. 7, pp. 379–403.

Conservative Central Office (1977), *Small Business, Big Future*, Conservative Party, London.

Constantinides, P. (1977), 'The Greek Cypriots: Factors in the Maintenance of Ethnic Identity', in Watson, J.L. (ed.), *Between Two Cultures*, Basil Blackwell, Oxford.

Crace, J. (1978), 'The Bazaar on the Corner', *Sunday Telegraph Magazine*, no. 114, pp. 82–99.

Crawford, W.H. (1972), *Domestic Industry in Ireland: The Experience of the Linen Industry*, Gill and Macmillan, Dublin.

Crawford, W.H., and Trainor, B. (1973), *Aspects of Irish Social History, 1750–1800*, HMSO, Belfast.

Cromer, G. (1974), 'Intermarriage and Communal Survival in a London Suburb', *Jewish Journal of Sociology*, vol. 16, pp. 155–69.

Cross, T. (1969), *Black Capitalism*, Athenaeum, New York.

Crotty, R.D. (1966), *Irish Agricultural Production*, Cork University Press, Cork.

Cullen, L.M. (1969), 'The Irish Economy in the Eighteenth Century', in Cullen, L.M. (ed.), *The Formation of the Irish Economy*, Mercier Press, Cork.

Cullingworth Committee (1969), *Council Housing: Purposes, Procedures and Priorities*, HMSO, London.

Dahya, B. (1974), 'Pakistani Ethnicity in Industrial Cities in England', in Cohen, A. (ed.), *Urban Ethnicity*, Tavistock, London, pp. 77–113.

Daniel, W.W. (1968), *Racial Discrimination in England*, Penguin, Harmondsworth.

Davis, J. (1975), 'Beyond the Hyphen: Some Notes and Documents on Community-State Relations in South Italy', in Boissevain, J., and Friedl, J. (eds.), *Beyond the Community*, Ministry of Education and Science, The Hague.

Davis, W. (1978), *It's No Sin to be Rich*, Sphere, London.

Davison, R.B. (1966), *Black British: Immigrants to England*, Oxford University Press, London.

Dawson, J., and Kirby, D. (1979), *Small Scale Retailing in the UK*, Saxon House, Farnborough.

Day, C., and Thies, G. (1980), *The Situation and Prospects of the European Textile and Clothing Industry*, Directorate-General for Internal Market and Industrial Affairs, III C 2 III F 3, Commission of the European Communities, Brussels.

Department of the Environment (1979), *National Dwelling and Household Survey*, HMSO, London.
(1983), *The Urban Programme: Tackling Racial Disadvantage*, HMSO, London.
Department of Manpower Services (1974), *Industrial Relations in Northern Ireland: Report of a Review Body, 1971–74*, HMSO, Belfast.
(1979), *Northern Ireland Labour Market: A Guide in Graphs and Charts – 1979*, DMS, Belfast.
Dhooge, Y. (1981), 'Ethnic Difference and Industrial Conflicts', *Working Papers on Ethnic Relations*, no. 13, ESRC Research Unit on Ethnic Relations, Birmingham.
Dieten, J. (1980), 'Term midden- en kleinbedrijf verhult uiteenlopende belangen', *Achtergrond*, vol. 6, pp. 138–41.
Doherty, J. (1969), 'The Distribution and Concentration of Immigrants in London', *Race Today*, vol. 1, no. 8, pp. 227–32.
Douglas, M., and Isherwood, B. (1978), *The World of Goods: Towards an Anthropology of Consumption*, Penguin, Harmondsworth.
Drake, St C., and Cayton, H. (1962), *Black Metropolis*, Harper Torchbooks, New York.
Du Bois, W.E.B. (1969), *The Souls of Black Folks*, Signet, New American Library, first published 1903.
Duncan, S.S. (1976), 'Self Help: The Allocation of Mortgages and the Formation of Housing Sub-Markets', *Area*, vol. 8, pp. 307–16.
(1977), 'Housing Disadvantage and Residential Mobility', *Faculty of Urban and Regional Studies Working Papers*, no. 5, University of Sussex, Brighton.
Economists Advisory Group (1978), *Small Firms in Cities: A Review of Recent Research*, Shell UK, London.
Eisenstadt, S.N. (1967), 'The Protestant Ethic Thesis in Analytical and Comparative Perspective', *Diogenes*, vol. 59, pp. 25–46.
Emden, P. (1944), *Jews of Britain: A Series of Biographies*, Sampson, Low, Marston, London.
Endelman, T.M. (1979), *The Jews of Georgian England 1714–1830*, Jewish Publication Society of America, Philadelphia.
Ernst, K. (1980), 'Racialism, Socialist Ideology and Colonialism Past and Present', in *Sociological Theories: Racism and Capitalism*, UNESCO, Paris.
Eurostat (1973), *Social Statistics 1968–72*, Statistical Office of the European Communities, Luxembourg.
(1979), *Employment and Unemployment 1972–1978*, Statistical Office of the European Communities, Luxembourg.
Fair Employment Agency (1978), *An Industrial and Occupational Profile of the Two Sections of the Population in Northern Ireland*, FEA, Belfast.
Fallers, L.A. (1967), 'Introduction', in Fallers, L.A. (ed.), *Immigrants and Associations*, Mouton, The Hague.
Farley, N. (1972), 'Italians in London, 1836–1905', unpublished Cert.Ed. dissertation.
Farrell, M. (1976), *Northern Ireland: The Orange State*, Pluto Press, London.
Fenton, M. (1977), 'Asian Households in Owner Occupation', *Working Papers on Ethnic Relations*, no. 2, RUER, Bristol.
(1978), 'Costs of Discrimination in the Owner-Occupied Sector', *New Community*, vol. 6, pp. 279–82.

Feuchtwanger, L. (1925), *Jew Süss*, Drei Masken Verlag, Munich. English translation by W. and E. Muir (1926), Martin Secker Ltd, London.

Flett, H. (1979), 'Black Council Tenants in Birmingham', *Working Papers on Ethnic Relations*, no. 12, RUER, Birmingham.

Foerster, R. (1919), *The Italian Emigration of Our Times*, Harvard University Press, Cambridge, Mass.

Foner, N. (1979), 'West Indians in New York City and London: A Comparative Analysis', *International Migration Review*, vol. 13, pp. 284–95.

Forester, T. (1978), 'Asians in Business', *New Society*, no. 803, pp. 420–3.

Franklin, S.H. (1969), *The European Peasantry: The Final Phase*, Methuen, London.

Frazier, E.F. (1957), *Black Bourgeoisie*, Free Press, New York.

Gambling, T. (1974), *Societal Accounting*, George Allen and Unwin, London. (1978), *Beyond the Conventions of Accounting*, Macmillan, London.

Ganguly, P. (1982), 'Small Firms Survey: The International Scene', *British Business*, 19 November 1982.

Garigue, P., and Firth, R. (1956), 'Kinship Organisation of Italianates in London', in Firth, R. (ed.), *Two Studies of Kinship in London*, Athlone Press, London.

Gee, K.P. (1980), 'Financial Control', unpublished inaugural lecture, University of Salford.

Geertz, C. (1963), *Pedlars and Princes*, University of Chicago Press, Chicago. (1973), *The Interpretation of Cultures*, Hutchinson, London.

George, V., and Millerson, G. (1967), 'The Cypriot Community in London', *Race*, vol. 8, pp. 277–92.

Gershuny, J.I. (1978), *After Industrial Society: The Emerging Self-Service Economy*, Macmillan, London.

Gibbon, P. (1975), *The Origins of Ulster Unionism*, Manchester University Press, Manchester.

Gill, C. (1925), *The Rise of the Irish Linen Industry*, Oxford University Press, Oxford.

Gish, O. (1971), *Doctor Migration and World Health*, Occasional Papers on Social Administration, no. 43, Bell, London.

Glazer, N., and Moynihan, D.P. (1963), *Beyond the Melting Pot*, MIT Press, Cambridge, Mass.

Goffee, R., and Scase, R. (1980), 'The Problems of Managing Men', *Guardian*, 19 September 1980.

Gough, R. (1981), *The History of Myddle*, ed. Hey, D., Penguin, Harmondsworth.

Gray, F. (1976), 'Selection and Allocation in Council Housing', *Transactions, Institute of British Geographers* (NS), vol. 1, pp. 34–46.

Greenberg, D. (1974), 'Yankee Financiers and the Establishment of the Trans-Atlantic Partnerships: A Re-examination', *Business History*, vol. 16, pp. 17–35.

Grillo, R.D. (1980), 'Introduction', in Grillo, R.D. (ed.), *'Nation' and 'State' in Europe: Anthropological Perspectives*, Academic Press, London.

Gross, N. (ed.) (1975), *Economic History of the Jews*, Keter Publishing House, Jerusalem.

Hannan, M. (1979), 'The Dynamics of Ethnic Boundaries in Modern States', in Hannan, M., and Meyer, J. (eds.), *National Development and the World System*, University of Chicago Press, Chicago.

Hannerz, U. (1974), 'Ethnicity and Opportunity in Urban America', in Cohen, A. (ed.), *Urban Ethnicity*, Tavistock, London.

Harbinson, J.F. (1973), *The Ulster Unionist Party, 1883–1973*, Blackstaff Press, Belfast.

Hart, K. (1973), 'Informal Income Opportunities and Urban Employment in Ghana', in Jolly, R. *et al.* (eds.), *Third World Employment*, Penguin, Harmondsworth.

Hatch, J.C.S. (1973), 'Estate Agents as Urban Gatekeepers', paper presented to the British Sociological Association Meeting, Stirling.

Hechter, M. (1974), *Internal Colonialism: The Celtic Fringe in British National Development*, University of California Press, Berkeley.

Henriques, H.S.Q. (1908), *The Jews and the English Law*, Oxford University Press, Oxford.

Herman, H.V. (1979), 'Dishwashers and Proprietors: Macedonians in Toronto's Restaurant Trade', in Wallman, S. (ed.), *Ethnicity at Work*, Macmillan, London.

Hirschman, C. (1982), 'Immigrants and Minorities: Old Questions for New Directions in Research', unpublished paper, Cornell University.

Holzberg, C.S., and Giovannini, M.J. (1981), 'Anthropology and Industry: Reappraisal and New Directions', *Annual Review of Anthropology*, vol. 10, pp. 317–60.

Home Affairs Committee (1981), *Racial Disadvantage*, HC 424-I, HMSO, London.

Ianni, F.A.J., and Reuss-Ianni, E. (1972), *A Family Business*, Routledge and Kegan Paul, London.

ILEA Research and Statistics Group (1982), *1981 Language Census*, RS 811/12, ILEA, London.

Jacobs, J. (1891), *Studies in Jewish Statistics: Social, Vital and Anthropometric*, D. Nutt, London.

Jamal, V. (1976), 'Asians in Uganda, 1880–1972: Inequality and Expulsion', *Economic History Review*, vol. 29, pp. 602–16.

Jayawardena, C. (1973), 'Migrants, Networks and Identities', *New Community*, vol. 2, pp. 353–7.

Jones, P.N. (1976), 'Coloured Minorities in Birmingham, England', *Annals, Association of American Geographers*, vol. 66, pp. 89–103.

——— (1980), 'Ethnic Segregation, Urban Planning and the Question of Choice: The Birmingham Case', paper presented to the symposium on Ethnic Segregation in Cities, St Antony's College, Oxford.

Jones, T.P. (1979), 'The Third World Within: Asians in Britain', paper presented to the Institute of British Geographers Annual Conference, Manchester.

——— (1982), 'Small Business Development and the Asian Community in Britain', *New Community*, vol. 9, pp. 467–77.

Jones, T.P., and McEvoy, D. (1978), 'Race and Space in Cloud-Cuckoo Land', *Area*, vol. 10, pp. 162–6.

Karn, V. (1969), 'Property Values Amongst Indians and Pakistanis in a Yorkshire Town', *Race*, vol. 10, pp. 269–84.

Kearsley, G., and Srivastava, S.R. (1974), 'The Spatial Evolution of Glasgow's Asian Community', *Scottish Geographical Magazine*, vol. 90, pp. 110–24.

Kim, D., and Choy Wong, C. (1977), 'Business Development in Koreatown, Los Angeles in Hyung', in Kim, C. (ed.), *The Korean Diaspora*, ABC Clio Press, Santa Barbara.

Kohler, D. (ed.) (1974), *Ethnic Minorities in Britain: Statistical Data*, Community Relations Commission, London.

Koo, H. (1976), 'Small Entrepreneurship in a Developing Society: Patterns of Labor Absorption and Social Mobility', *Social Forces*, vol. 54, pp. 775–87.

Kosmin, B. (1979), 'Exclusion and Opportunity: Traditions of Work Among British Jews', in Wallman, S. (ed.), *Ethnicity at Work*, Macmillan, London.

Kosmin, B.A., Bauer, M., and Grizzard, N. (1976), *Steel City Jews*, Research Unit, Board of Deputies of British Jews, London.

Kosmin, B.A., and Grizzard, N. (1975), *Jews in an Inner London Borough*, Research Unit, Board of Deputies of British Jews, London.

Kosmin, B.A., and Levy, C. (1981), *The Work and Employment of Suburban Jews*, Research Unit, Board of Deputies of British Jews, London.

Krausz, E. (1969), 'The Edgware Survey: Occupation and Social Class', *Jewish Journal of Sociology*, vol. 11, pp. 75–95.

(1972), *Ethnic Minorities in Britain*, Paladin, London.

Kuepper, W.G., Lackey, G.L., and Swinerton, E.N. (1975), *Uganda Asians in Britain*, Croom Helm, London.

Ladbury, S. (1977), 'The Turkish Cypriots: Ethnic Relations in London and Cyprus', in Watson, J.L. (ed.), *Between Two Cultures*, Basil Blackwell, London.

(1979a), 'Turkish Cypriots in London: Economy, Society, Culture and Change', unpublished PhD dissertation, University of London.

(1979b), *Cypriots in Britain: A Report on the Social and Working Lives of the Greek and Turkish Cypriot Communities in London*, National Centre for Industrial Language Training, London.

(1980), 'The Family and the System: Influences on the Performance and Aspirations of Turkish Speaking Children in London Schools', paper presented to the Turkish Area Studies Group Conference, SOAS, University of London.

Lambeth, London Borough of (1982), *Black Business in Lambeth: Report of Survey*, RM 20, March.

Lawrence, D. (1974), *Black Migrants, White Natives: A Study of Race Relations in Nottingham*, Cambridge University Press, Cambridge.

Leifer, E. (1981), 'Competing Models of Political Mobilization: The Role of Ethnic Ties', *American Journal of Sociology*, vol. 87, pp. 23–47.

Leoni, P. (1966), *I Shall Die on the Carpet*, Leslie Frewin, London.

Leuwenburg, J. (1979), 'The Cypriots in Haringey', *Research Report No. 1*, School of Librarianship, Polytechnic of North London, London.

Lieberson, S. (1980), *A Piece of the Pie: Black and White Immigrants Since 1880*, University of California Press, Berkeley.

Liebow, E. (1967), *Tally's Corner*, Little Brown and Company, Boston.

Light, I. (1972), *Ethnic Enterprise in America: Business and Welfare among Chinese, Japanese and Blacks*, University of California Press, Berkeley.

(1979), 'Disadvantaged Minorities in Self-Employment', in Petersen, W. (ed.), *The Background to Ethnic Conflict*, E.J. Brill, Leiden.

(1980), 'Asian Enterprise in America', in Cummings, S. (ed.), *Self-Help in Urban America*, Kennikat Press, Port Washington.

Lipset, S.M., and Rokkan, S. (1967), *Party Systems and Voter Alignments*, Free Press, New York.

Lloyd, P. (1980), 'New Manufacturing Enterprises in Greater Manchester and

Merseyside', *Working Paper Series*, no. 10, North West Industry Research Unit, Manchester University.

Lorenzoni, G. (1979), 'A Policy of Innovation in the Small and Medium Sized Firm: An Analysis of Change in the Prato Wool Industry', Ms., unrevised translation by Boissevain.

Lovell-Troy, L. (1980), 'Clan Structure and Economic Activity: The Case of Greeks in Small Business Enterprise', in Cummings, S. (ed.), *Self-Help in Urban America*, Kennikat Press, Port Washington.

Lyon, M.H. (1973), 'Ethnicity in Britain: The Gujerati Tradition', *New Community*, vol. 2, pp. 1–11.

Lyons, F.S.L. (1973), *Ireland Since the Famine*, Fontana, London.

McCutcheon, A. (1977), *Wheel and Spindle: Aspects of Irish Industrial History*, Blackstaff Press, Belfast.

Macdonald, J.S., and Macdonald, L.D. (1972), *The Invisible Immigrants*, Runnymede Trust Industrial Unit, London.

McEvoy, D. (1980), *Retail and Service Business and the Immigrant Community*, Final Report, Project HR5520, Social Science Research Council, London.

Macfarlane, A. (1978), *The Origins of English Individualism*, Basil Blackwell, London.

McGee, T.G. (1976), 'Hawkers and Hookers: Making Out in the Third World City', *Manpower and Unemployment Research*, vol. 9, no. 1, pp. 3–21.

Manchester Law Centre (1981), *The Thin Edge of the White Wedge*, Immigration Handbook No. 5, Manchester Law Centre, Manchester.

Mansergh, N. (1936), *The Government of Northern Ireland*, George Allen and Unwin, London.

Marin, U. (1975), *Italiani in Gran Bretagna*, Centro Studi Emigrazione, Rome.

Mariti, P. (1977), 'On "Disintegration" in Industry: Theoretical Considerations with Empirical Evidence Relating to Italy', paper presented to First Conference of the European Industrial Organisation Association, Newcastle, September 1977.

Markwalder, D. (1981), 'The Potential for Black Business', *Review of Black Political Economy*, vol. 11, pp. 303–12.

Marris, P., and Somerset, A. (1971), *African Businessmen: A Study of Entrepreneurship and Development in Kenya*, Routledge and Kegan Paul, London.

Mars, G. (1982), *Cheats at Work: An Anthropology of Workplace Crime*, George Allen and Unwin, London.

    (1983), 'The Drinking of Dockworkers', in Douglas, M. (ed.), *The Anthropology of Drinking*, Cambridge University Press, Cambridge.

Marshall, G. (1980), *Presbyteries and Profits: Calvinism and the Development of Capitalism in Scotland, 1560–1707*, Clarendon Press, Oxford.

Marx, K. (1964), *Precapitalist Economic Formations*, International Publishers, New York.

Mayer, A. (1975), 'The Lower Middle Class as a Historical Problem', *Journal of Modern History*, vol. 47, pp. 409–36.

Mayer, A.C. (1966), 'The Significance of Quasi-Groups in the Study of Complex Societies', in Banton, M. (ed.), *The Social Anthropology of Complex Societies*, Tavistock, London.

Mendras, H. (1970), *The Vanishing Peasant: Innovation and Change in French Agriculture*, MIT Press, London.

Miles, C. (1968), *Lancashire Textiles: A Case Study of Industrial Change*, Cambridge University Press, Cambridge.

Miller, R. (1978), *Attitudes to Work in Northern Ireland*, Fair Employment Agency, Belfast.

(1979), *Occupational Mobility of Protestants and Roman Catholics in Northern Ireland*, Fair Employment Agency, Belfast.

Mills, C.W. (1951), *White Collar*, Oxford University Press, New York.

Misra, B.B. (1961), *The Indian Middle Classes*, Oxford University Press, London.

Moody, T.W. (1974), *The Ulster Question, 1603–1973*, Mercier Press, Cork.

Mordsley, B.I. (1975), 'Some Problems of the "Lump" ', *Modern Law Review*, vol. 38, pp. 504–17.

Mouzelis, N.P. (1978), *Modern Greece: Facets of Underdevelopment*, Macmillan, London.

Mullins, D. (1979), 'Asian Retailing in Croydon', *New Community*, vol. 7, pp. 403–5.

(1980), 'Race and Retailing: The Asian-Owned Retailing Sector in Croydon', paper presented at the Institute of British Geographers Annual Conference, Lancaster.

Murie, A., and Forrest, R. (1980), 'Housing Market Processes and the Inner City', *Inner City in Context*, Report No. 10, SSRC, London.

NEDO (1972), *Reclaiming the '70s: The Future of the Low Cost Woollen Industry*, National Economic Development Office, London.

New York Times (1981), 'In Praise of Small Business', Magazine Sections, 6 December 1981, pp. 135–52.

Newcomer, M. (1961), 'The Little Businessman: A Study of Business Proprietorships in Poughkeepsie, New York', *Business History Review*, vol. 35, pp. 477–531.

Niehoff, A., and Niehoff, J. (1960), *East Indians in the West Indies*, Milwaukee Public Museum, Milwaukee.

Nielsen, F. (1980), 'The Flemish Movement in Belgium After World War II', *American Sociological Review*, vol. 45, pp. 76–94.

Nikolinakos, M. (1975), 'Towards a General Theory of Migration in Late Capitalism', *Race and Class*, vol. 17, pp. 5–17.

Nowikowski, S.E. (1980), 'The Social Situation of the Asian Community in Manchester', unpublished PhD dissertation, University of Manchester.

Nowikowski, S., and Ward, R. (1979), 'Middle Class and British? An Analysis of South Asians in Suburbia', *New Community*, vol. 7, pp. 1–10.

Nugent, N., and King, R. (1979), 'Ethnic Minorities, Scapegoating and the Extreme Right', in Miles, R., and Phizacklea, A. (eds.), *Racism and Political Action in Britain*, Routledge and Kegan Paul, London.

Oakley, R. (1970), 'The Cypriots in Britain', *Race Today*, no. 2, pp. 99–102.

(1971), 'Cypriot Migration and Settlement in Britain', unpublished DPhil dissertation, University of Oxford.

O'Connor, J. (1973), *The Fiscal Crisis of the State*, St Martin's, New York.

O'Dowd, L., Rolston, B., and Tomlinson, M. (1980), *Northern Ireland: Between Civil Rights and Civil War*, CSE Books, London.

OECD (1980), *Labour Force Statistics 1967–1978*, Organisation for Economic Cooperation and Development, Paris.

Ofari, E. (1970), *The Myth of Black Capitalism*, Monthly Review Press, New York.

Osborne, R.D. (1980), 'Religious Discrimination and Disadvantage in the Northern Irish Labour Market', *International Journal of Social Economics*, vol. 7, pp. 206–23.

Osborne, R.D., and Murray, R.C. (1978), *Educational Qualifications and Religious Affiliation in Northern Ireland*, Fair Employment Agency, Belfast.

Palmer, R. (1972), 'Immigrants Ignored: An Appraisal of the Italians in Britain', unpublished MA dissertation, University of Sussex.

—— (1977), 'The Italians: Patterns of Migration to London', in Watson, J.L. (ed.), *Between Two Cultures*, Basil Blackwell, Oxford.

—— (1981), 'The Britalians: An Anthropological Investigation', unpublished DPhil dissertation, University of Sussex.

Parker, J., and Dugmore, K. (1977), 'Race and the Allocation of Public Housing', *New Community*, vol. 6, pp. 27–40.

Patterson, H. (1980), *Class Conflict and Sectarianism: The Protestant Working Class and the Belfast Labour Movement*, Blackstaff Press, Belfast.

Peach, C. (1968), *West Indian Migration to Britain: A Social Geography*, Oxford University Press, London.

—— (1975), 'Immigrants in the Inner City', *Geographical Journal*, vol. 141, pp. 372–9.

Peach, S., Winchester, S., and Woods, R. (1975), 'The Distribution of Coloured Immigrants in Britain', *Urban Affairs Annual Review*, vol. 9, pp. 395–419.

Pettenati, P. (1979), 'Mutamenti strutturali dell' industria italiana: un quadro d'insieme', in Antonelli, C., Balloni, V., Crivellini, M., and Pettenati, P., *Lo Sviluppo dei fattori imprenditivi dell'industria italiana*, Istituto Adriano Olivetti, Ancona.

Phillips, M. (1978), 'West Indian Businessmen', *New Society*, no. 815, pp. 354–6.

Phizacklea, A., and Miles, R. (1980), *Labour and Racism*, Routledge and Kegan Paul, London.

Piore, M.J., and Sabel, C.F. (1981), *Italian Small Business Development: Lessons for United States Industrial Policy*, Working Paper, MIT, Cambridge, Mass.

Policy for the Inner Cities (1977), Cmnd 6845, HMSO, London.

Pollins, H. (1982), *Economic History of the Jews in England*, Associated University Presses, London and Toronto.

Poulantzas, N. (1973), 'On Social Classes', *New Left Review*, no. 78, pp. 27–54.

Prais, S.J., and Schmool, M. (1967), 'Statistics of Jewish Marriage in Great Britain: 1901–1965', *Jewish Journal of Sociology*, vol. 9, pp. 149–74.

—— (1975), 'The Social-Class Structure of Anglo-Jewry, 1961', *Jewish Journal of Sociology*, vol. 17, pp. 5–15.

Price, C. (1963), *Southern Europeans in Australia*, Oxford University Press, Melbourne.

—— (1969), 'The Study of Assimilation', in Jackson, J.A. (ed.), *Migration*, Cambridge University Press, Cambridge.

Price, R., and Bain, G.S. (1976), 'Union Growth Revisited: 1948–1974 in Perspective', *British Journal of Industrial Relations*, vol. 14, pp. 339–55.

Raban, J. (1974), *Soft City*, Fontana/Collins, London.

Ragin, C. (1979), 'Ethnic Political Mobilization: The Welsh Case', *American Sociological Review*, vol. 44, pp. 619–35.

RCDIW (1979), *Royal Commission on the Distribution of Income and Wealth, Report No 8: Fifth Report on the Standing Reference*, Cmnd 7679, HMSO, London.

Reeves, F., and Chevannes, M. (1981), 'The Underachievement of Rampton', *Multiracial Education*, vol. 10, no. 1, pp. 35–42.

Reid, A. (1980), 'Skilled Workers in the Shipbuilding Industry 1880–1820: A Labour Aristocracy', in Morgan, A., and Purdie, B. (eds.), *Ireland: Divided Nation, Divided Class*, Ink Links, London.

Rex, J. (1970), 'The Concept of Race in Sociological Theory', in Zubaida, S. (ed.), *Race and Racialism*, Tavistock, London.

(1971), 'The Concept of Housing Class and the Sociology of Race Relations', *Race*, vol. 3, pp. 293–301.

Rex, J., and Moore, R. (1967), *Race, Community and Conflict*, Oxford University Press, London.

Rex, J., and Tomlinson, S. (1979), *Colonial Immigrants in a British City*, Routledge and Kegan Paul, London.

Robinson, V. (1979a), 'Contrasts Between Asian and White Housing Choice', *New Community*, vol. 7, pp. 195–201.

(1979b), 'The Segregation of Asians within a British City: Theory and Practice', *Research Paper*, no. 22, School of Geography, Oxford University.

(1980), 'Asians and Council Housing', *Urban Studies*, vol. 17, pp. 323–31.

(1981), 'The Development of South Asian Settlement in Britain and the Myth of Return', in Peach, C. *et al.* (eds.), *Ethnic Segregation in Cities*, Croom Helm, London.

Rogaly, J. (1977), *Grunwick*, Penguin, Harmondsworth.

Rolston, B. (1980), 'Reformism and Class Politics in Northern Ireland', *Insurgent Sociologist*, vol. 10, no. 2, pp. 73–83.

Rosentraub, M.S., and Taebel, D. (1980), 'Jewish Enterprise in Transition', in Cummings, S. (ed.), *Self-Help in Urban America*, Kennikat Press, Port Washington.

Routh, G. (1980), *Occupation and Pay in Great Britain 1906–79*, Macmillan, London.

Runnymede Trust (1980), *Britain's Black Population*, Heinemann, London.

Sacks, P.M. (1976), *The Donegal Mafia*, Yale University Press, New Haven.

Saifullah Khan, V. (1976), 'Pakistanis in Britain: Perceptions of a Population', *New Community*, vol. 5, pp. 222–9.

(1979), 'Work and Network: South Asian Women in South London', in Wallman, S. (ed.), *Ethnicity at Work*, Macmillan, London.

Scarman, Lord (1982), *The Scarman Report: The Brixton Disorders, 10–12 April 1981*, Pelican, Harmondsworth.

Scase, R., and Goffee, R. (1980), *The Real World of the Small Business Owner*, Croom Helm, London.

(1982), *The Entrepreneurial Middle Class*, Croom Helm, London.

Schneider, J., and Schneider, P. (1976), *Culture and Political Economy in Western Sicily*, Academic Press, New York.

Schutz, A. (1944), 'The Stranger: An Essay in Social Psychology', *American Journal of Sociology*, vol. 49, pp. 499–507.

Select Committee on Small Business, US Senate (1979), *Discussion and Comment on the Major Issues Facing Small Business*, Government Printing Office, Washington.

Senior, H. (1966), *Orangeism in Ireland and Britain, 1795–1836*, Routledge and Kegan Paul, London.

Shack, W.A., and Skinner, E.P. (eds.) (1979), *Strangers in African Societies*, University of California Press, Berkeley.

Shah, S. (1975), *Immigrants and Employment in the Clothing Industry: The Rag Trade in London's East End*, Runnymede Trust, London.

Shapiro, E. (1978), 'American Jews and the Business Mentality', *Judaism*, vol. 27, pp. 214–21.

Sharma, H.P. (1973), 'The Green Revolution in India: Prelude to a Red One', in Gough, K., and Sharma, H.P. (eds.), *Imperialism and Revolution in South Asia*, Monthly Review Press, New York.

Shepherd, M.A. (1981), 'How Petticoat Lane became a Jewish Market, 1800–1860', in Newman, A. (ed.), *The Jewish East End, 1840–1939*, Jewish Historical Society of England, London.

Simmel, G. (1950), 'The Stranger', in Wolff, K.H. (ed.), *The Sociology of Georg Simmel*, Free Press, New York.

Simmons, L. (1981), 'Contrasts in Asian Residential Segregation', in Jackson, P. and Smith, S.J. (eds.), *Social Interaction and Ethnic Segregation*, Academic Press, London.

Sivanandan, A. (1976), 'Race, Class and the State: The Black Experience in Britain', *Race and Class*, vol. 17, pp. 347–68.

Skellington, R. (1980), 'Council House Allocation in a Multi-Racial Town', *Urban Research Group Occasional Papers*, no. 2, Open University, Milton Keynes.

Smith, B. (1974), 'Employment Opportunities in the Inner Area Study Part of Small Heath, Birmingham in 1974', *Research Memorandum*, no. 38, Centre for Urban and Regional Studies, Birmingham University.

(1977), 'The Inner City Economic Problem: A Framework for Analysis and Local Authority Policy', *Research Memorandum*, no. 56, Centre for Urban and Regional Studies, Birmingham University.

Smith, D.J. (1974), *Racial Disadvantage in Employment*, Political and Economic Planning, London.

(1976), *The Facts of Racial Disadvantage: A National Survey*, Political and Economic Planning, London.

(1977), *Racial Disadvantage in Britain*, Penguin, Harmondsworth.

(1981), *Unemployment and Racial Minorities*, Policy Studies Institute, London.

Smith, D.M. (1959), *Italy: A Modern History*, University of Michigan Press, Ann Arbor.

Smith, N.R. (1967), *The Entrepreneur and his Firm*, Bureau of Business and Economic Research, University of Michigan, Ann Arbor.

Sontz, A.L. (1978), 'Neighbors and Strangers: Factory and Community in a West German Immigrant Zone', unpublished PhD thesis, Columbia University, New York.

(1980a), 'The Industrial Bases of Ethnic Entrepreneurship: A View from Urban Europe', unpublished Ms.

(1980b), 'The Urban Hispanic Community and Small Business Enterprise', unpublished Ms.

Sowell, T. (1981), *Markets and Minorities*, Basil Blackwell, London.

Spodek, H. (1965), 'The "Manchesterisation" of Ahmedabad', *Economic Weekly*, vol. 17, pp. 483–90.

Stanworth, M.J.K., and Curran, J. (1973), *Management Motivation in the Smaller Business*, Gower, Farnborough.

Stewart, A.T.Q. (1977), *The Narrow Ground: Aspects of Ulster, 1909–1969*, Faber and Faber, London.

Stokes, E. (1978), *The Peasant and the Raj*, Cambridge University Press, Cambridge.

Tabb, W.K. (1979), 'What Happened to Black Economic Development?', *Review of Black Political Economy*, vol. 9, pp. 392–415.

Tambs-Lyche, H. (1980), *London Patidars: A Case Study in Urban Ethnicity*, Routledge and Kegan Paul, London.

Tawney, R.H. (1938), *Religion and the Rise of Capitalism*, Pelican, Harmondsworth.

Thies, G. (1979), *Thoughts About the Industrial System of Prato*, Directorate-General for Internal Market and Industrial Affairs, III C 2, Commission of the European Communities, Brussels.

Thomson, G. (1975), 'The Ismailis in Uganda', in Twaddle, M. (ed.), *Expulsion of a Minority: Essays on Uganda Asians*, Athlone Press, London.

Tinker, H. (1975), 'Indians Abroad: Restriction and Rejection', in Twaddle, M. (ed.), *Expulsion of a Minority: Essays on Uganda Asians*, Athlone Press, London.

(1976), *Separate and Unequal: India and Indians in the British Commonwealth, 1920–1950*, Hurst, London.

(1977), *The Banyan Tree: Overseas Emigrants from India, Pakistan and Bangladesh*, Oxford University Press, London.

Tomlinson, S. (1980), 'The Educational Performance of Ethnic Minority Children', *New Society*, vol. 8, pp. 213–14.

Tribe, M.A. (1975), 'Economic Aspects of the Expulsion of Asians from Uganda', in Twaddle, M. (ed.), *Expulsion of a Minority: Essays on Uganda Asians*, Athlone Press, London.

Trow, M. (1958), 'Small Business, Political Tolerance and Support for McCarthy', *American Journal of Sociology*, vol. 64, pp. 270–81.

Urban Institute (1980), *Trends in Racial Disparities during the 1970s*, Washington.

Van den Tillaart, H.J.M., *et al.* (1981), *Zelfstandig Ondernemen*, Instituut voor Toegepaste Sociologie, Economisch Instituut voor het Midden- en Kleinbedrijf, Nijmegen.

Veblen, T. (1934), *The Theory of the Leisure Class*, Modern Library, New York.

Waldinger, R. (1982), 'Immigrant Enterprise and Labor Market Structure', working paper, Joint Center for Urban Studies, MIT and Harvard University.

Walker, J. (1977), 'An Analysis of Aspects of the Retail Trade in Sparkhill, Birmingham, in the Light of Theories of Economic and Social Dualism', unpublished MPhil dissertation, Birmingham University.

Wallman, S. (1978), 'The Boundaries of "Race": Processes of Ethnicity in England', *Man* (NS), vol. 13, pp. 200–17.
    (1979), 'The Scope for Ethnicity', in Wallman, S. (ed.), *Ethnicity at Work*, Macmillan, London.
Ward, G. (1976), *Fort Grunwick*, Temple Smith, London.
Ward, R. (1973), 'What Future for the Uganda Asians?', *New Community*, vol. 2, pp. 372–8.
    (1982), 'Race, Housing and Wealth', *New Community*, vol. 10, pp. 3–15.
    (1983a), 'Middlemen Minority, Ethnic Niche, Replacement Labour or General Migration? Patterns of South Asian Settlement in Britain', paper presented at the Mid West Sociological Society Conference, Kansas City. To be published in Loveridge, R. (ed.), *The Manufacture of Disadvantage in Employment*, Wiley, Chichester, forthcoming.
    (1983b), 'Ethnic Communities and Ethnic Business', *New Community*, vol. 11, pp. 1–9.
Ward, R., and Reeves, F. (1980), *West Indians in Business in Britain*, Report to the House of Commons Home Affairs Committee (Race Relations and Immigration Sub-Committee), HMSO, London.
Washington, B.T. (1967), *Up From Slavery*, Airmont, New York.
Watkins, D.S. (1976), 'Regional Variations in the Industrial Ecology for New Growth-Oriented Business in the U.K.', unpublished paper, Manchester Business School, Manchester.
Watson, J.L. (1975), *Emigration and the Chinese Lineage: The Mans in Hong Kong and London*, University of California Press, Berkeley.
    (1977), 'The Chinese: Hong Kong Villagers in the British Catering Trade', in Watson, J.L. (ed.), *Between Two Cultures*, Basil Blackwell, London.
Weber, M. (1968), *Economy and Society*, ed. Roth, G., and Wittich, C., Bedminster Press, New York.
    (1976), *The Protestant Ethic and the Spirit of Capitalism*, George Allen and Unwin, London.
Werbner, P. (1979a), 'Ritual and Social Networks: A Study of Pakistani Immigrants in Manchester', unpublished PhD dissertation, Manchester University.
    (1979b), 'Avoiding the Ghetto: Pakistani Migrants and Settlement Shifts in Manchester', *New Community*, vol. 7, pp. 376–89.
    (1980a), 'Rich Man, Poor Man, or a Community of Suffering: Heroic Motifs in Manchester Pakistanis' Life Histories', *Oral History*, vol. 8, pp. 43–8.
    (1980b), 'From Rags to Riches – Manchester Pakistanis in the Textile Trade', *New Community*, vol. 8, pp. 84–95.
    (1981), 'Manchester Pakistanis: Life Styles, Ritual and the Making of Social Distinctions', *New Community*, vol. 9, pp. 216–29.
    (nd), 'The Organization of Giving and Urban Ethnicity', unpublished Ms.
Werbner, R.P. (1975), 'Land, Status and Movement among the Kalanga of Botswana', in Fortes, M., and Patterson, S. (eds.), *Studies in African Social Anthropology*, Academic Press, London.
Whyte, W.F. (1955), *Street Corner Society*, University of Chicago Press, Chicago.
Williams, B. (1976), *The Making of Manchester Jewry, 1740–1875*, Manchester University Press, Manchester.
Wilson, K., and Portes, A. (1980), 'Immigrant Enclaves: An Analysis of the

Labor Market Experiences of Cubans in Miami', *American Journal of Sociology*, vol. 86, pp. 295–315.

Wilson, P. (1983a), *Black Business Enterprise in Britain: A Survey of Afro-Caribbean and Asian Small Businesses in Brent*, Runnymede Trust.

(1983b), 'Black Minority Business and Bank Finance', *New Community*, vol. 11, pp. 63–73.

Wilson, T. (1955), 'Conclusions: Devolution and Partition', in Wilson, T. (ed.), *Ulster Under Home Rule*, Oxford University Press, London.

Winchester, S. (1974), 'Immigrant Areas in Coventry in 1971', *New Community*, vol. 4, pp. 97–104.

Wischnitzer, M. (1965), *A History of Jewish Crafts and Guilds*, Jonathan David, New York.

Wright, E.O. (1979), *Class, Crisis and the State*, Verso, London.

Wright, F. (1973), 'Protestant Ideology and Politics in Ulster', *European Journal of Sociology*, vol. 14, pp. 213–80.

Yancey, W., Erikson, E., and Juliani, R. (1976), 'Emergent Ethnicity: A Review and Reformulation', *American Sociological Review*, vol. 41, pp. 391–403.

Yergin, D. (1982), 'The Last Locomotive', *New Republic*, 20 January 1982, pp. 22–5.

Yogev, G. (1978), *Diamonds and Coral: Anglo-Dutch Jews and Eighteenth Century Trade*, Leicester University Press, Leicester.

Index

Adam, H., 240
Ahmad, S., 154
Alavi, H., 150, 243
Aldrich, H., 6, 7, 8, 40, 43, 47, 50, 131, 139, 165, 168, 191, 195, 197, 199, 204, 205, 207, 219, 220, 222, 232, 234, 246
Allen, S., 156
Amin, S., 150, 243
Andreasen, A.R., 34, 246
antisemitism, 76
Anwar, M., 12, 170, 192
Ardener, S., 239
Aris, S., 86, 240
Ashkenazim (Jewry), 74–6
Asian shopkeepers, 15, 191, 195–210, 219–27
Aunger, E.A., 70
Auster, E., 6, 7, 8, 131, 232

Bagchi, A.K., 151
Bailey, T., 44
Bain, G.S., 237
Baker, S.E., 71
Ballard, C., 202
Ballard, R., 202
Bangladesh, migrant workers from, 10, 127, 128, 129
banking and finance, 78, 80–1, 176–7, 197
Banton, M., 246
Baran, P., 245
Barritt, D.P., 240
Barth, F., 57, 89, 90, 231, 239, 244
Bauer, M., 85
Bax, M., 240
Bechhofer, F., 29, 43, 131
Beckett, J.C., 59, 63
Bell, G., 240
Belshaw, C., 89

Berger, S., 41, 42
Berk, F., 108
Bew, P., 69
Billig, M., 196
Birch, D., 40
Birnbaum, N., 241
black Americans, in business, 44–5, 46, 48, 50, 130
'black capitalism', 45
Bland, R., 29, 43
Blaugh, M., 153
Blok, A., 92
Boddy, M.J., 215, 218
Boissevain, J., 6, 7, 8, 36, 105, 232, 239
Bolton, J.E., 6, 7, 21, 23, 24, 25, 26, 239, 241
Bonacich, E., 11, 44, 45, 46, 47, 48, 49, 50, 192, 223
Bonney, N., 246
Boswell, J., 24, 25, 26
Booth, C., 84
Bovenkerk, F., 28
Brimmer, A., 45
'Britalian' community in United Kingdom, 89–104, 241; see also Italy
Brooks, A., 145
Brooks, D., 223, 242
Bryant, J., 236
Buckland, P., 69
Buckman, J., 83
Bunzel, J., 44
Burney, E., 218
Burris, V., 40, 41, 42
business: births, 6–7, 20–1; deaths, 19, 21–6, 39–43, 50–1; opportunities, for ethnic business, 14–19, 45–6, 76–7, in the 'open market', 16–19, 77–83, 89–104, 138, 193–4, 198–200, 206–7, in

264

the 'ethnic market', 8, 14–16, 49–52, 94–8, 132–3, 168, 170, 171, 198–200, 231–2; resources of ethnic businesses, 11–14, 47–8, 133–9, 194, 197, 237; skills in ethnic businesses, 133–7, 204–5, 232
Butterworth, E., 212

capital accumulation by migrant workers, 12
Caribbean, *see* West Indies
Carter, C.F., 240
Castles, S., 33, 34, 150
Cater, J.C., 40, 50, 165, 191, 195, 199, 204, 205, 213, 214, 215, 216, 217, 219, 220, 232, 234, 246
Cavalli, C., 103
Cayton, H., 240
CBI (Confederation of British Industry), 20, 23, 26, 27
Central Statistical Office, 218, 220
CERC (*Centre d'Etude des Revenus et des Coûts*), 26, 29
Chevannes, M., 135
China, migrant workers from: in United Kingdom, 16, 35; in United States, 16, 44, 45, 46, 47, 48, 49, 51, 149, 193–4
Chinese restaurants, 14, 35
Choy Wong, C., 44
City of Bradford Metropolitan District Council, 214, 219
Clark, D., 123
class (social), 155, 158, 164, 243
clothing manufacturing industry, 35, 51, 83, 108–12, 166–88
Clough, E., 242
Coe, W.E., 65, 66
Cohen, A., 123, 168, 186, 242
Cohen, R., 58
colonialism, 150, 151, 189–90, 233
conditions of work, in ethnic businesses, 18, 48, 109, 112
Conservative Central Office, 105
Conservative Party (UK): policy towards ethnic business, 143–6, 234; policy towards small businesses, 53–4, 105–6, 124, 143–6
Constantinides, P., 34
construction industry, 129
Crawford, W.H., 62, 240
credit, 172–3, 186, 204
criminal business activity, 91–2
Cromer, G., 241
Cross, T., 246
Crotty, R.D., 60
Cuba, migrant workers from, 44
Cullen, L.M., 60

Cullingworth Committee, 218
culture, as a factor promoting business success, 11–12, 36, 45, 47–8, 58, 70–2, 139–40, 166–88, 193, 200–6, 231, 232, 235
culture entrepreneur, the, 90–2
culture suppression in ethnic businesses, 103–4
Curran, J., 134
Cyprus, migrant workers from, 10, 34, 105–24, 126; *see also* Greek Cypriots, Turkish Cypriots

Dahya, B., 12, 190, 212, 217, 219, 245, 246
Daniel, W.W., 218
Davis, J., 57
Davis, W., 104
Dawson, J., 40
Day, C., 31
decline in level of small business activity, 21–6, 39; reasons for, 23–5, 39–43
Department of the Environment, 144, 212
Department of Manpower Services, 240
Dhooge, Y., 117
diamond trade, Jewish involvement in, 78
Dieten, J., 21, 26
discrimination: in access to finance, 13, 19, 48, 137, 237; in access to premises, 137, 209–27; in the labour market, 18, 34, 45, 46–7, 66, 67, 68–9, 93, 114–19, 155; in housing, 46–7, 212–19
distributive trades, 129, 131; *see also* retail trade, wholesale trade
Doherty, J., 246
Douglas, M., 12
Drake, St C., 240
Du Bois, W.E., 142
Dugmore, K., 218
Duncan, S.S., 211, 215, 218

East Africa, Asian migrant workers from, 13, 35, 36, 129, 140, 149–65, 189–210
economic decentralization, 30–3
economic context of small businesses, 7–8, 9, 21–30
economic recession, effect on small businesses, 2, 28–9, 39–43, 105–7, 122–4
Economists' Advisory Group, 7, 133
Eisenstadt, S.N., 241
Elliott, B., 29, 43, 131
Emden, P., 85
Endelman, T.M., 80
entrepreneurial activity, theories of, 44, 89–92, 123, 166–88, 233, 239
Erikson, E., 52
Ernst, K., 207

estate agents, 105, 215–17, 224–7
ethnic business: business opportunities for, 14–19, 45–6, 76–7; business resources of, 11–14, 47–8, 133–9, 194, 197, 237; business skills in, 133–7, 204–5, 232;conditions of work in, 18, 48, 109, 112; cultural attributes underlying, 11–12, 36, 45, 47–8, 139–40, 166–88, 193, 200–6, 231, 232, 235; culture suppression in, 103–4; definitions of, 49, 58–9; in an ethnic enclave, 49–52, 52–4, 171; and an ethnic majority, 57–72, 235–6; and ethnic niches, 8, 14–16, 49–52, 94–8, 132–3, 168, 170, 171, 198–200, 231–2; family labour in, 17–18, 34–5, 48, 113, 168, 194, 196–7, 235; general discussions of, 33–6, 44–6, 166–8, 231–8; hours of work in, 17–18, 34–5, 48, 112, 168; industrial relations in, 51, 117–18, 237–8; and informal social networks, 138, 169, 171, 182–3, 184–5, 235–6; labour costs in, 18, 51, 110–11, 112; labour supply for, 13, 17, 137–8, 194, 235; in the 'open market', 16–19, 77–83, 89–104, 138, 193–4, 198–200, 206–7; research agenda concerning, 234–8, 239–40; and residential patterns, 132–3, 221–3; and social mobility, 81–2, 85–8, 151, 161–4, 190, 191, 233; and structural position of migrants, 12–13, 45, 46–7, 52, 149–57, 158, 164–5, 190, 207–10; theories of, 45–6, 149–50, 166–8, 192–4, 205–10, 231–4; and unemployment, 121–2, 153; variability in performance of, 5–6, 8, 35, 44–5, 77–85, 125–9, 140–1, 175–81, 190–2, 200–5, 219–27
ethnic niche, 8, 14–16, 49–52, 94–8, 132, 168, 170, 198–200, 231
ethnicity: theories of, 50–2, 57–9, 168–70; as an industrial relations strategy, 66–70, 117–18
Europe, small businesses in, 20–38, 41–3
Eurostat, 20, 22, 30

Fair Employment Agency, 70
Fallers, L.A., 244
family labour: in ethnic businesses, 17–18, 34–5, 48, 113, 168, 194, 196–7, 235; in small businesses, 196–7, 235
Farley, N., 96
Farrell, M., 68, 69, 240
Feit, S., 139
Fenton, M., 211, 218, 243
Feuchtwanger, L., 81
finance, sources for ethnic businesses, 13, 47–8, 79, 80–1, 91, 92, 137, 194, 197, 237
Firth, R., 89, 100, 241
Fish, D., 43
Flett, H., 218
Foerster, R., 93, 96
Foner, N., 4, 139
Forester, T., 191
Forrest, R., 218
Franklin, S.H., 20
Frazier, E.F., 47, 139, 142, 245, 246
Freedman, M., 44

Gambling, T., 232
Ganguly, P., 6
Garigue, P., 89, 100, 241
Gee, K.P., 232
Geertz, C.,123, 168
George,V., 242
Gershuny,. J.I., 7, 25, 30
Gibbon, P., 60, 67, 69, 70
Giliomee, H., 240
Gill, C., 240
Giovannini, M.J., 236
Gish, O., 156
Glazer,N., 47, 48, 73, 167
Goffee, R., 29, 105, 235, 239, 245
Gough, R., 240
Gray, F., 218
Greece, migrant workers from, 44, 51
Greek Cypriots, 34, 108, 109, 112, 117, 118
Greenberg, D., 81
Grillo, R.D., 57
Grizzard, N., 85, 86
Gross,N., 74

Hannerz, U., 91, 92, 193
Harbinson, J.F., 69
Hart, K., 95
Hatch, J.C.S., 218
Hechter, M., 57
Henriques, H.S.Q., 76
Herman, H.V., 242
'hidden economy', 6, 8, 235
Hirschman, C., 46
Holzberg, C.S., 236
Home Affairs Committee, 125, 137
homeworking, 26, 28, 35
hours of work: in ethnic businesses, 17–18, 34–5, 48, 112, 168; in small businesses, 18

Ianni, F.J., 92
ILEA Research and Statistics Group, 241
immigration: control of, 155; and small businesses, 33–6; into United Kingdom, 2, 151–65

imperialism, 164, 189–90
India, migrant workers from, 12, 15, 44,74, 126, 127, 128, 129, 130, 134, 135, 136, 138, 149–65, 189–210
Indian restaurants, 14
individualism, 12, 43, 51
industrial relations, 51, 66–70, 117–18, 237–8
informal social networks, 138, 169, 171, 182–3, 184–5, 235–6
Ireland, migrant workers from, 11, 13, 79, 126, 134, 135, 136, 140, 141
Isherwood, B., 12
Italian restaurants, 96–104
Italy, migrant workers from, 34, 36, 89–104, 112

Jacobs, J., 82
Japanese migrants in the United States, 44, 45, 47, 48, 49, 51, 149, 193–4
Jayawardena, C., 243
Jenkins, R., 232, 233
Jews, in business, 13, 44, 52, 73–88, 140, 149, 192
'joking relationships', 173–4
Jones, P.N., 218, 246
Jones, T.P., 40, 50, 165, 190, 191, 195, 199, 204, 205, 206, 213, 215, 219, 220, 246
Juliani, R., 52

Karn, V., 211, 215, 217, 218
Kearsley, G., 246
Kim, D., 44
kinship, 17–18, 34–5, 48, 51, 113, 168–70, 171
Kirby, D., 40
Kohler, D., 241
Korean migrants in the United States, 44, 47, 48, 51
Kosack, G., 33, 34, 150
Kosmin, B.A., 73, 85, 86, 87, 240, 241, 242
Krausz, E., 86, 213, 241

labour costs in ethnic businesses, 18, 110–11, 112
Labour Party (UK): policy towards ethnic businesses, 144–5; policy towards small businesses, 144–5
Ladbury, S., 43, 108, 114, 120, 232, 233, 234, 242
Lambeth, London Borough of, 132, 133, 137, 140, 145
Laurence, D., 192
Layard, P.R.G., 153
Leoni, P., 97
Leuwenberg, J., 108

Levy, C., 86, 87
Lieberson, S., 46
Liebow, E., 245
Light, I., 16, 28, 44, 45, 47, 48, 49, 50, 52, 167, 193, 208, 223
Lipset, S.M., 39
Lorenzoni, G., 31, 33, 239
Lovell-Troy, L., 44, 51
Lyon, M.H., 207, 246
Lyons, F.S.L., 66

McCutcheon, A., 64
McEvoy, D., 40, 50, 165, 191, 195, 199, 204, 205, 213, 215, 219,220, 222, 246
Macfarlane, A., 240
McGee, T.G., 154
Malta, migrant workers from, 10, 126
Manchester Law Centre, 155
Mansergh, N., 70
manufacturing industry, 129, 237; *see also* clothing manufacturing industry, textile manufacturing industry
Marin, U., 89, 94, 95, 97
Mariti, P., 31, 32
market trading, 174–5
Marks and Spencers, 1, 85
Markwalder, D., 44
Marris, P., 36
Mars, G., 6, 8, 12, 233, 235
Marshall, G., 241
Marx, K., 39
Mayer, A., 44
Mayer, A.C., 245
Mendras, H., 20
Mens en Milieuvriendelijk Ondernemen (MeMO), 37–8
'merchant ideology', 11
'middleman minorities', 192–5
migrant workers: labour market position of, 10, 33–4, 133–6; and small businesses, 33–6; structural position of, 12–13, 45, 46–7, 52, 149–57, 158, 164–5, 190, 207–10
Miles, C., 156
Miles, R., 237
Miller, R., 70, 71
Millerson, G., 242
Mills, C.W., 44, 245
Misra, B.B., 152
Modell, J., 44, 45, 46, 48
Moody, T.W., 61
Moore, R., 212, 218, 245
Mordsley, B.I., 29
Mouzelis, N.P., 243
Moynihan, D.P., 47, 48, 73, 167
Mullins, D., 207, 215, 223

multi-national corporations, 60
Murie, A., 218
Murray, R.C., 71

NEDO (National Economic Development
   Office), 31, 32, 33
Newcomer, M., 34
Niehoff, A., 139
Niehoff, J., 139
Nielsen, F., 39
Nikolinakos, M., 156
Northern Ireland, 47–52
Nowikowski, S.E., 232, 233, 234, 242, 243,
   244

Oakley, R., 107, 108, 109, 110, 111, 241
O'Connor, J., 41
O'Dowd, L., 70, 240
OECD (Organization for Economic
   Cooperation and Development), 26
Ofari, E., 139, 142
Osborne, R.D., 70, 71

Pakistan, migrant workers from, 10, 11, 12,
   15, 18, 51, 74, 126, 127, 128, 129, 134,
   135, 136, 166–88, 189–210, 236
Palmer, R., 34, 89, 95, 232
Parker, J., 218
patronage, 240; *see also* informal social
   networks
Patterson, H., 69, 240
Peach, C., 212, 213
peasants, EEC policy towards, 20
peddling, 78–9
Pettenati, P., 27, 30, 31
Phillips, M., 133
Phizacklea, A., 237
Piore, M.J., 42
Pollins, H., 73, 232, 241
political context: of ethnic business activity,
   1, 53–4, 141–6, 234; of small business
   activity, 8, 20–1, 41–3, 53–4, 105–6, 124,
   143–6
Portes, A., 49
Poulantzas, N., 243
Prais, S.J., 85, 86, 87
Prato (Italy), textile industry in, 31–3
premises, access to, 137, 209–27
Price, C., 92, 95
Price, R., 237
professions, as an avenue of social mobility
   for ethnic minorities, 86–8, 114–16,
   159–60
'protestant ethic', 58, 70–2, 169, 231, 241
protestants in Northern Ireland, 47–52

Quarmby, J., 242

Raban, J., 101
racial disadvantage, 190, 191, 209–10
racism, 138, 149
'rag trade', *see* clothing manufacturing
   industry
RCDIW (Royal Commission on the Distribution of Income and Wealth), 21,
   28, 29
recruitment into employment, 66, 69, 111,
   116–17
redundancy, 7, 28
Reeves, F., 7, 10, 15, 17, 48, 128, 135, 137,
   143, 191, 232, 242
Reid, A., 240
Reiss, A., 199
research agenda, concerning ethnic
   businesses, 234–8, 239–40
residential segregation, 132–3, 221–3
restaurants, 14, 34, 35, 44, 50, 96–104, 108,
   112, 171
retail trade, 15, 16, 21, 26, 49–52, 108, 130,
   131, 158, 191, 195–210, 219–27
Reuss-Ianni, E., 92
Rex, J., 150, 189, 212, 218, 245
Robinson, V., 211, 213, 215, 217, 218, 245,
   246
Rogaly, J., 237
Rokkan, S., 39
Rolston, B., 70, 240
Rosentraub, M.S., 52
rotating credit associations, 48, 50, 239
Routh, G., 213
Runnymede Trust, 213
Rushforth, M., 29

Sabel, C.F., 42
Sacks, P.M.,240
Saifullah Khan, V., 26, 28, 222, 242
Scarman, Lord, 1, 125, 144, 233
Scase, R., 29, 105, 235, 239, 245
Schmool, M., 85, 86, 87
Schneider, J., 92
Schneider, P., 92
Schutz, A., 169, 244
Select Committee on Small Businesses, 143
Senior, H., 64
Sephardim (Jewry), 74–6, 78, 80
service sector industries, 29–30, 92–104,
   108–9, 112–13, 129, 130, 237
Shack, W.A., 244
Shah, S., 168, 242, 244
Shapiro, E., 84

Sharma, H.P., 154
Shepherd, M.A., 79
shopkeepers, 15, 21, 42, 50–2, 53, 108, 195–210, 219–27; *see also* Asian shop-keepers, retail trade
Simmel, G., 244
Simmons, L., 218
Singh, K., 223, 242
Sivanandan, A., 155
Skellington, R., 218
skills, in business, 17, 28, 111, 133–6, 151, 197
Skinner, E.P., 244
small businesses: decline in numbers of, 21–6, 39–43; definition of, 241; economic context of, 7–8, 9, 21–30, 39–43, 105–7; economic vulnerability of, 39–43, 105–7, 122–4; in Europe, 20–38; family labour in, 196–7, 235; general discussions of, 5, 6–9, 20–38, 39–43, 131, 195–210, 235; and the 'hidden economy', 6, 8, 235; and life-styles, 8, 36–8; political context of, 8, 20–1, 41–3, 53–4, 105–6, 124, 143–6; recent increase in numbers of, 26–38, 39
Smith, C., 156
Smith, D.J., 125, 129, 157, 162, 200, 218, 237, 243
Smith, D.M., 99
Smith, N.R., 133
social mobility, 81–2, 85–8, 151, 161–4, 190, 191, 233
Somerset, A., 36
Sontz, A.L., 34
South Asia, migrant workers from, 2, 10, 12, 46, 50, 51, 130, 132, 140, 141, 149–228; *see also* Bangladesh, East Africa, India, Pakistan
Sowell, T., 91
Spodek, H., 151
Srivistava, S.R., 246
Stanworth, M.J.K., 133
state policy: and ethnic businesses, 1, 53–4, 141–6, 234; and small businesses, 8, 20–1, 41–3, 105–6
Stewart, A.T.Q., 59
Stokes, E., 53
structural position of migrant workers, 12–13, 45, 46–7, 52, 149–57, 158, 164–5, 190, 207–10

Tabb, W.K., 246
Taebel, D., 52
Tambs-Lyche, H., 11, 167
Tawney, R.H., 241

taxation, 29, 42
Terrell, H., 45
Tesco, 1, 85
textile manufacturing industry: general, 12, 31, 80, 151–65; in Northern Ireland, 62–3, 64, 240; in Prato, Italy, 31–3
theories of ethnic business, 45–6, 149–50, 166–8, 192–4, 205–10, 231–4
Thies, G., 31, 32
Tinker, H., 189, 190, 207, 246
Tomlinson, M., 70
Tomlinson, S., 189, 190, 245
trade unions, 32, 117–18, 237–8
Trainor, B., 240
Tribe, M.A., 246
Trow, M., 44
Turkish Cypriots, 34, 51, 105–24

unemployment, 7, 20, 28, 121–2, 153
Urban Institute, 142

van den Tillaart, H.J.M., 26
variability in the economic performance of ethnic business, 5–6, 8, 35, 44–5, 77–85, 125–9, 140–1, 175–81, 190–2, 200–5, 219–27
Veblen, T., 101
Velleman, P., 50

Waldinger, R., 51
Wallman, S., 35, 57, 242
Ward, G., 237
Ward, R., 7, 10, 12, 15, 17, 48, 128, 137, 141, 143, 191, 201, 214, 218, 232, 233, 242, 243
Washington, B.T., 141, 142
Watson, J.L., 4, 16, 34, 35, 92
Webb, B., 84
Weber, M., 71, 231, 241
Werbner, P., 11, 167, 168, 169, 181, 232, 244, 245
Werbner, R.P., 244, 245
West Indian business activity, 15, 35, 48, 125–46
West Indies, migrant workers from, 2, 10, 15, 35, 48, 125–46
Whyte, W.F., 92
wholesale trade, 16, 138, 158, 172
Williams, B., 79
Wilson, K., 49
Wilson, P., 132, 133, 136, 140
Wilson, T., 71
Winchester, S., 213, 246
Wischnitzer, M., 74
women workers, 18, 108–9, 111, 135, 242

Woodhall, M., 153
Woods, R., 213
world economic system, 40–1, 150–7
Wright, F., 240

Yancey, W., 52
Yogev, G., 78